WOMEN
IN THE BIBLE

WOMEN

IN THE BIBLE

MIRACLE BIRTHS, HEROIC DEEDS, BLOODLUST AND JEALOUSY

John Baldock

Capella

This edition published in 2006 by Arcturus Publishing Limited
26/27 Bickels Yard, 151–153 Bermondsey Street,
London SE1 3HA

In Canada published for Indigo Books
468 King St W, Suite 500,
Toronto, Ontario M5V 1L8

ISBN-13: 978-1-84193-404-4
ISBN-10: 1-84193-404-6

The right of John Baldock to be identified as author of this Work has
been asserted by him in accordance with the Copyright, Designs and
Patent Act 1988

Project Editor: Nigel Matheson
Cover Design: Elizabeth Healey and Maki Ryan
Design: Elizabeth Healey
Layout: Alex Ingr
Picture Research: Anya Martin

Printed in China

Contents

7

Introduction

Apart from a few women such as Eve, Mary (the mother of Jesus) and Mary Magdalene, the women in the Bible are generally eclipsed by their male counterparts. This state of affairs not only mirrors the status assigned to women in Western society over the last 2,000 years, it also reflects the patriarchal nature of both the Jewish and Christian religions. And yet a closer study of the Bible reveals that women were once regarded as the equals of men rather than subject to them. We read of women who were priestesses in the ancient religions of the Near East, who served as judges and prophets to the early Israelites, and who saved the Jewish people on more than one occasion from extinction at the hands of their enemies. Even Wisdom, which is described in the Book of Proverbs as the 'fountain of life', was personified as a woman.

ABOUT THIS BOOK

As its title suggests, *Women in the Bible* retells the stories of the women, both great and humble, who people the pages of the Old and New Testaments. It also includes some of the women encountered in the biblical books known as the Apocrypha (by Protestants) or the Deuterocanon (by Catholics and Orthodox Christians). These stories range from accounts of miraculous births and heroic deeds to tales of trickery, intrigue and murder. There are also stories of true love, and of incest, adultery, polygamy and women's exploitation and abuse by men. Most, but not all, of the women in the Bible are included in these pages. Those who have been omitted appear as little more than names in the lengthy genealogical lists in certain books of the Old Testament.

The order in which the women's stories are presented follows the standard chronology of the books of the Bible rather than the alphabetical order favoured by some other authors. Two underlying stories are thus told at the same time: the unfolding history of a people and their religion, from the arrival of Abraham in Canaan to the emergence of the first Christian churches, and the changing status of women in religion and society over three millennia. As each story is related in its entirety, the book may also be dipped into at random.

The book is divided into two parts and five sections:

Part One: The Old Testament
1. The Pentateuch
2. The Historical Books
3. The Writings, the Prophets and the Apocrypha

Part Two: The New Testament
4. The Gospels
5. The Acts of the Apostles, the Epistles and the Book of Revelation

LEVELS OF MEANING IN THE BIBLE

The women's stories retold in this book are, as far as possible, a faithful retelling of the stories told in the Bible. Additional comments on the characters and suggestions as to the possible underlying meaning of the stories have been kept to a minimum so that you are at liberty to approach them in whichever way you wish. If you are interested in getting at the underlying meaning of a particular story, the following scheme for the interpretation and understanding of scripture may be useful. Advocated in the thirteenth and fourteenth centuries by St Bonaventure, Dante and others, it suggests that we can understand a text according to four principal levels of sense or meaning: the literal, the allegorical, the moral and the anagogical or spiritual. The literal sense always comes first, because it contains the rest. Without it, it would be impossible to understand the others, not even the allegorical. However, as Dorothy L. Sayers pointed out in the introduction to her translation of Dante's *Divine Comedy*, 'the literal meaning is the least important part of it.' Her comments on Dante's masterpiece – itself an allegory of the Way to God – can also be applied to the narratives contained in both the Old and New Testaments, for she says, 'although the literal story … is a true one, and the characters in it are real people, [it] is nevertheless an allegory … the story with its images is only there for the sake of the truth which it

symbolizes, and the real environment within which all the events take place is the human soul.' (*The Divine Comedy*, 14) An example of the use of allegory within the Bible itself is to be found in St Paul's letter to the Galatians (4:22–31), in which he states that Hagar and Sarah – the mothers of Abraham's children – are an allegory for two covenants (*see below*, Hagar, page 23). The four levels of meaning can be summarized as follows:

1. *Literal* – this is the shell, the outer level of meaning, at which the words can be understood at their face value.
2. *Allegorical* – each element of the text is understood as standing for something else.
3. *Moral or personal* – the text is understood in a way that is relevant to our own life.
4. *Anagogical* – this is the kernel, the innermost level, at which conscious understanding is transformed into spiritual insight or direct perception.

Sometimes a woman's name hints at the allegorical significance of her story at the same time as expressing her personality or status: Eve translates as 'Mother of all living' or 'Life'; Hagar (the Egyptian maid who fled from her mistress into the desert) means 'Flight' or 'Fugitive'. A name can also be intentionally ironic: Jezebel (who corrupted a king) means 'Chaste'; Delilah (the woman who discovered the secret of Samson's great strength) means 'Delicate'. In one or two instances, a woman's name is altered to indicate a change in her nature or spiritual standing, as is the case with Abraham's wife, whose name was changed from Sarai ('Argumentative') to Sarah ('Princess') when she gave birth to Isaac and God announced that she would be 'the mother of nations'.

Numbers also have a part to play in conveying the possible underlying meaning of a woman's story. The most common numbers are three, seven, twelve and forty. Whether they are employed to express a quantity (say, of people) or a period of time, these numbers frequently signify a change of nature or a spiritual transformation. For example, when Moses fled from Egypt to Midian he met the seven daughters of Jethro; Queen Vashti refused to obey her drunken husband on the seventh day of feasting; Jacob's wives gave birth to twelve sons who gave their names to the twelve tribes of Israel; Jesus raised Jairus's daughter from the dead when she was twelve years old, and healed a woman who had haemorrhaged for twelve years; both Esau and Isaac were forty years old when they married their wives; the Israelites' journey from Egypt to the Promised Land coincided with forty years in the wilderness; the people of Israel enjoyed forty years of peace after Deborah had led their defeat of the Canaanite army.

BIBLICAL REFERENCES

This book follows the traditional formula for designating chapters and verses: Exodus 2:4 refers to the second chapter of Exodus, verse 4; Numbers 12:1–15 refers to a passage in the twelfth chapter of Numbers, verses 1 to 15 inclusive.

Part 1
The Old Testament

The Hebrew Bible, known to Christians as the Old Testament, opens with the story of God's creation of the world and of the primordial couple, Adam and Eve, who initially lived at ease with their Creator in his garden. But when they failed to follow God's instruction not to eat the fruit of the tree of knowledge, they set in motion a pattern that was to be repeated by subsequent generations. For whenever human beings chose to follow their own will rather than that of their Creator, they were afflicted with one kind of disaster or another.

However, what may appear to be a disaster to human eyes is often presented as a God-given opportunity to begin life anew by attempting to follow the will of God. This was the case with Noah and his family, who were spared from the flood that wiped out the rest of humanity, and with Lot and his daughters, who escaped the destruction of Sodom and Gomorrah. A similar theme recurs throughout the historical books that cover the period from the Israelites' occupation of the land of Canaan to the fall of the kingdoms of Judah and Israel. Whenever the Israelites turned their backs on God they were overcome by their enemies, only for a new leader to emerge – a judge, king or prophet – who would urge them once more to follow the Way of God.

The theme continues in those books of the Old Testament written after the fall of the kingdom of Judah and the exile in Babylon. It is fair to say that women are given a bad press in all this: from Eve to Jezebel and beyond, they are often portrayed as the cause of the misfortunes that befell the people of Israel and their ancestors. In this regard, the role assigned to women in the Old Testament reflects the changing attitude towards women, as both society and religion become increasingly patriarchal. For example, when God created Eve we are told that she was Adam's equal. In the early history of the Israelites, women were the equals of men in that they held important positions as prophets and judges, and occasionally officiated as priests. Certain women – e.g. Deborah, Esther and Judith – also acquired the stature of national heroes. At the other extreme, women were considered to be the property of their 'father's house', a term that embraces the immediate family, the clan and the tribe.

The Christian view of the Old Testament was summarized by St Augustine, who said, 'The Old Testament is nothing but the New covered with a veil, and the New is nothing but the Old unveiled.' From the earliest times, Christians have understood many of the people and events described in the Old Testament as prefiguring prominent figures and events in the New.

The correspondence between events in the Old Testament and events in the New – known as 'typology', from the Greek *tupos*, meaning 'stamp' or 'mould' – had a profound influence on Christian art during the European Middle Ages, leading to the complex decorative schemes to be found in many medieval churches and cathedrals. Indeed, the representation in art of figures and events from the Old Testament is largely confined to Christian art since such representation was generally proscribed by the Jewish religion.

1 **The Pentateuch**
From Eden to the wilderness years

The first women

Also known as the Law (the Torah) or the Five Books of Moses, the Pentateuch attained its definitive form in the fifth century BC, during or shortly after the Jewish exile in Babylon, but it contains material from much older traditions said to predate this by at least another 500 years. Its five books are Genesis, Exodus, Leviticus, Numbers and Deuteronomy. Genesis and Exodus together take us from the creation of the world to the Israelites' escape from Egypt and their journey through the wilderness to the land of Canaan. Leviticus is essentially a book of religious and social law, while Numbers and Deuteronomy combine further accounts of the Israelites' journey with additional religious and social legislation. The Pentateuch concludes with the death of Moses on the threshold of the Promised Land.

EVE

MEANING: MOTHER OF ALL LIVING, OR LIFE

The first woman in the Bible.

† BIBLICAL REFERENCE: Genesis 1:27; 2:21–4:2; 4:25

In weaving together two accounts of the creation of the universe from different traditions, the opening chapters of Genesis offer us contrasting images of the nature of the relationship between man and woman. In the first account, which dates from c.400BC and is the more recent of the two, the relationship is seen as one of equals for we are told that God 'created humankind [adam] in his own image, in the image of God he created them; male and female he created them'. (1:27) For their food, he gave them all the seed-bearing plants and all the trees with seed-bearing fruit. However, in the second account, which is dated to 1000–900BC, we are told that God first created 'the man', then the plants, animals and birds. He then caused the man to fall into a deep sleep, and while he was asleep he removed one of his ribs and made it into a woman. When the man saw her, he said, 'she shall be called Woman [Hebrew ishshah] because she was taken out of Man [ish]'. (2:23) Once he had created them, God told the man and woman that they could freely eat the fruit from every tree in the garden, except for the 'tree of the knowledge of good and evil, for in the day that you eat of it you shall die.' Initially the primordial couple lived in a state of paradisal innocence, for we are told that they 'were both naked,

ABOVE

The creation of Eve: although it is said that Eve was formed from Adam's rib, she was his equal in that she too was made in the image of God

and were not ashamed'. (2:25) But then the serpent appeared on the scene and asked the woman whether God had forbidden them from eating the fruit of any tree in the garden. She replied that God had told them not to eat the fruit of the tree 'in the midst of the garden, neither shall you touch it, lest you die.' The serpent contradicted her, saying that they would not die. Rather, God knew that if they ate the fruit their eyes would be opened and they would be like God, knowing good and evil. At this the woman looked at the tree with fresh eyes, and saw that the fruit was to be desired because it was a source of wisdom. She took the fruit, ate it and gave some to her husband. Their eyes were opened, and becoming aware of their nakedness they covered themselves with garments made by sewing leaves together.

Later, when the man and woman heard God walking in the garden, they hid themselves from his presence. But God called out to the man, 'Where are you?'

'I heard you in the garden, and was afraid, because I was naked, and hid myself,' replied the man.

'Who told you that you were naked? Did you eat the forbidden fruit?'

'The woman gave me the fruit, and I ate it.'

'What have you done,' God asked the woman.

'The serpent beguiled me,

and I ate.'

Then God said to the woman, 'I will give you great pain in childbearing, and yet you will yearn for your husband and he shall have dominion over you.' And to the man he said, 'Because you listened to the voice of your wife and ate the forbidden fruit, the ground is cursed because of

ABOVE
Banished to distant plains: Cain's wife and children were condemned to share Cain's nomadic existence

you. You will labour to produce food from it all the days of your life, until you return to the ground from which you were taken. For you are dust, and to dust you shall return.' God then banished the man and woman from the garden and placed a guard over the tree of life. Following their banishment into the world outside the garden, Eve bore Adam three named sons – Cain, Abel and Seth – as well as other sons and daughters, thus paving the way for the generations

ABOVE

The waters are rising: Noah and his family were to be spared by God
because he was a righteous man

that are described in the subsequent chapters of Genesis and the other books of the Pentateuch.

According to the Jewish Talmud (books of extra-biblical commentary and interpretation), Eve was Adam's second wife. His first wife was Lilith ('Lily'), who demanded to be treated as his equal. When her demand was not met, she flew away into the night rather than submit to his authority. Adam's refusal to treat her as his equal and her subsequent replacement by Eve may be due to Lilith's association with death, whereas the name Eve means 'Life'. The name Lilith, which is derived from the old Semitic word *lel* or *lelath*, meaning 'night' (Knappert, 189), appears in the Jerusalem Bible (Isaiah 34:14), but the same verse in the King James Version employs 'screech-owl' while the Revised Standard Version uses 'night hag'. Lilith may have evolved from the ancient Sumerian goddess or demoness of the same name who is depicted in a Sumerian relief (*c.*2000BC) with wings and clawed feet and accompanied by owls.

The story of Adam and Eve has been retold so many times that it has taken on a surprising degree of reality in our human consciousness. It is also open to many interpretations. For some people, Genesis provides a literal account of the creation of the human race, according to which we are all descended from Adam (the first man) and Eve (the first woman). For others, it is an ancient myth concerning our human predicament and the apparent discord between our human and spiritual natures. Exponents of the latter interpretation have suggested that Eve represents both our spiritual essence, which lies concealed within the individual human being (Adam), and our quest for spiritual wisdom (the 'forbidden fruit'). The relationship between the man and the woman in the story is thus more about the relationship between different aspects of the human psyche than about matters of gender.

Eve in art

Because the Fall of humankind is an essential part of Christian teaching, the story of Adam and Eve has long featured prominently in Christian art. The conventions governing images of the primordial couple were well established in European art by the early twelfth century. The most common scenes featuring Eve include the creation of Eve from Adam's rib; Adam and Eve living harmoniously with God in the Garden of Eden; Eve plucking an apple from the tree and handing it to Adam, the serpent watching on from nearby; and the expulsion of Adam and Eve from the Garden of Eden. The popular perception of Eve has been influ-

enced as much by works of art as by religious teaching. For example, Michelangelo's *Creation of Eve* (from Adam's rib) on the ceiling of the Sistine Chapel is dwarfed by its neighbour, the evocative *Creation of Adam*, thus giving powerful visual expression to the patriarchal teaching that woman is subordinate to man, a theme that seems to be underlined by the fact that Eve is shown being created from Adam's rib. Moreover, artists of the medieval and Renaissance periods perpetuated the idea that Eve was the indirect cause of humankind's fallen state through their depiction of her standing beside the 'tree of the knowledge of good and evil', offering its forbidden fruit to Adam, while the serpent wound itself around the trunk or through its branches. In some instances the serpent was given human facial features bearing a strong resemblance to those of Eve. A 12th-century carving by Gislebertus at Autun Cathedral in Burgundy even depicts Eve weaving her way, serpent-like, through foliage. However, her near-horizontal pose may simply have been the sculptor's solution to the problem of fitting her onto the shallow stone lintel. The couple's emotional anguish portrayed in some versions of the *Expulsion from Paradise* was also perhaps intended to convey something of the suffering experienced by

many as a consequence of the human condition. One of the earliest and most powerful of these emotionally-charged works is *The Expulsion* (1424–5) by Masaccio in the Brancacci Chapel, Santa Maria del Carmine, Florence.

THE WIFE OF CAIN

The woman who married a fugitive.

✝ BIBLICAL REFERENCE: Genesis 4:17

The cultural and social tensions created by the shift from a seminomadic way of life to the more settled existence demanded by farming provide the background to the story of Eve's two sons, Cain and Abel, according to which Cain, 'a tiller of the ground', killed Abel, 'a keeper of sheep'. (4:1–16) Although Cain was himself forced to become a nomad as punishment for his crime – God sentenced him to be 'a fugitive and a wanderer on the earth' – he is, however, credited with building the first city.
The significant transition from a nomadic to an urban way of life is introduced through the figure of Cain's nameless wife. Although she is given only the briefest of mentions in the Bible, she was the mother of Cain's son Enoch ('Consecrated'), and when Cain became the founder of a city he named it after his son.

ADAH AND ZILLAH

MEANING: ADAH, ADORNED OR ORNAMENT; ZILLAH, SHADOW

The wives of the first polygamist.

† BIBLICAL REFERENCE: Genesis 4:19–24

Further cultural advances – music and metalwork – are introduced with Adah and Zillah, the wives of Lamech, the first polygamist and the great-great-great-grandson of Cain. Adah was the mother of Jabal, 'the father of those who dwell in tents and have cattle', and Jubal, 'the father of those who play the lyre and pipe'. Zillah was the mother of Tubal-Cain, the 'forger of all instruments of bronze and iron', and a daughter, Naamah (meaning 'Loveliness'). Lamech was also the father of Noah (5:28–9), but we are not told whether Noah's mother was Adah or Zillah.

The following lament which Lamech sang to his wives gave rise to the legend that when Lamech was out hunting he slew Cain, having mistaken him for a wild animal.

> Adah and Zillah, hear my
>   voice;
> you wives of Lamech, hearken
>   to what I say:
> I have slain a man for
>   wounding me,
> a young man for striking me.

> If Cain is avenged sevenfold,
>   truly Lamech seventy-
>   sevenfold.   (4:23–4, RSV)

As with many legends that have sprung up around biblical figures, however, it is pure legend: genealogically, Cain was Lamech's great-great-great-grandfather, and therefore could not have been the 'young man' referred to by Lamech.

THE DAUGHTERS OF MEN

The women who married the sons of God.

† BIBLICAL REFERENCE: Genesis 6:1–4

As human beings began to multiply upon the face of the earth, the 'sons of God' were attracted to the 'daughters of men' and took some of them to be their wives. The offspring of these mixed divine-human marriages were the Nephilim – 'the mighty men of old, the men of renown'. In later times these superhuman beings were said to have been the aboriginal inhabitants of the Promised Land, for when Moses sent spies ahead of him into Canaan they reported back that they had seen the Nephilim there. (Numbers 13:33) However, the author of Numbers does not explain how the Nephilim survived the Flood that had

wiped out every living thing except for Noah, his wife and children, and the animals that had accompanied them in the ark.

THE WIFE AND DAUGHTERS-IN-LAW OF NOAH

The women who repopulated the earth after the Flood.

† BIBLICAL REFERENCE: Genesis 6:5–10:32

According to *The New Oxford Annotated Bible*, the birth of the Nephilim 'is related to demonstrate the increase of wickedness on the earth'. (NOAB, 8) In Genesis, the birth of the Nephilim is followed by a description of God's regret at having created human beings for they had brought nothing but wickedness into the world. He thus decided to rid the earth of 'humankind and beast and creeping things and birds of the air, for I am sorry that I have made them'. (6:5–7) Noah, who in God's eyes was a righteous man, was spared from the ensuing flood together with his wife, their three sons – Shem, Ham and Japheth – and their wives. (7:13) When the floodwaters eventually subsided, the earth was repopulated by the children of Noah's sons and their wives. (9:18)

The matriarchs

The terms 'patriarch' and 'matriarch' are frequently used to describe the men and women in the Pentateuch who were the founding ancestors of God's people. All too often, however, the role of the matriarchs is eclipsed by that of the patriarchs, primarily because the latter feature so prominently in the biblical accounts and because the priesthood that retells their story has always been predominantly male.

In the Book of Isaiah, God reminds us of the equal role played by men and women in salvation history, saying:

> Listen to me, you who seek
>   salvation,
> you who seek the Lord.
> Consider the rock from which
>   you were hewn,
> and the quarry from which you
>   were dug.
> Consider Abraham your father
>   and Sarah who gave you
>   birth... (ISAIAH 51:1–2)

Through God's repeated promises to the matriarchs that their sons would each become 'a great nation', the stories of the matriarchs provide the genealogical origins of the tribal groups and nations that peopled the Middle East. However, the greatest of the matriarchs – Sarah, Rebekah and Rachel – are all initially described as barren. When they do eventually bear children it is because God had 'opened their womb'. As with the creation of humankind – Adam and Eve – the births of the matriarchs'

children are thus presented as an act of divine rather than human will. But once the nation has been established in the narrative, women are consigned to a less important role in the unfolding history of its people. Socially and legally, they came to be considered the property of 'their father's house' – a term that can signify the immediate family, the clan or the tribe – as is revealed in the story of Rachel and Leah (Jacob's wives), whose father Laban chased after them when Jacob left the land of his father-in-law, taking his wives with him (*see below*, Rachel and Leah).

SARAI/SARAH

MEANING: SARAI, ARGUMENTATIVE OR MY PRINCESS; SARAH, PRINCESS

The woman who married Abraham and became 'the mother of a multitude'.

† BIBLICAL REFERENCE: Genesis 11:29–31; 12:5–13:1; 16:1–6; 17:15–21; 18:6–15; 20:1–21:12; 23:1–2, 19; Hebrews 11:11; 1 Peter 3:6

When we first meet Sarah and Abraham in Genesis they are known by different names: Sarai and Abram. (11:29) The couple accompanied Terah, Abram's father, when he set out from Ur of the Chaldees for the land of Canaan, but they settled at Haran. After Terah's death, God instructed Abram to go 'to the land that I will show you, and I will make of you a great nation'. (11:31–12:2) So Abram travelled to Canaan, where he built an altar to God, after which he continued into the Negeb. When a severe famine struck the land, Abram journeyed to Egypt to escape the famine. But before entering Egypt, he said to Sarai, 'You are a beautiful woman, and when the Egyptians see you they will say, "This is this man's wife," and they will kill me. Tell them that you are my sister, so that my life will be spared because of you.' When Abram and Sarai entered Egypt, the Egyptians were so taken with Sarai's beauty that they sang her praises to Pharaoh, who took her

into his house and made her his wife, and showered gifts of servants and livestock on Abram. When misfortune befell Pharaoh because of his adultery with Sarai, he summoned Abram and asked him why he had not told him that Sarai was his wife, and had instead said that she was his sister. Pharaoh then gave Sarai back to Abram and told him to leave the country. So Abram left Egypt with Sarai and with Lot, his nephew, who was journeying with them. They travelled up through the Negeb to Bethel, where Abram had earlier built an altar, and it was here that Lot and Abram parted company (*see below,* The wife and daughters of Lot). After Lot had left, Abram settled in the land of Canaan, and God told him to walk the length and breadth of the land that would be peopled with his descendants. So Abram moved his encampment to Mamre, an ancient sacred site near Hebron, and there built another altar to God. (13:14–18) God spoke with Abram again after the latter had defeated in battle an alliance of four kings who had captured Lot,

ABOVE

Act of selflessness: the barren Sarah offered her Egyptian maid Hagar to Abraham so that he could continue his bloodline

Abram's nephew, and after he had been blessed by Melchizedek, the priest-king of Salem. (14:1–21) When Abram lamented that he remained childless and without an heir, God instructed him to make a sacrifice and he then made a covenant with Abram regarding the promised land. (15:2–21) Because Sarai remained barren, she offered her Egyptian maid, Hagar, to Abram that he might father a child by her, and in due course Hagar bore him a son, Ishmael. (*See below,* Hagar.)

When Abram was ninety-nine, God appeared to him once more and again made a covenant with him concerning the land of Canaan, telling Abram that he would be the father of 'a multitude of nations'. In recognition of this, his name would no longer be 'Abram'. From thenceforth, his name would be 'Abraham',

meaning 'father of a multitude'. As for Abraham's side of the covenant, he was to be circumcised, and all his male descendants were to be circumcised when they were eight days old. God then told Abraham that his wife's name was to be changed from Sarai to Sarah. Moreover, God promised Abraham that she would bear him a son; she would be the mother of nations, and her descendants would be kings of peoples. When he heard this, Abraham fell to the ground laughing at the thought of a 100-year-old man and a 90-year-old woman bringing a son into the world. But God repeated that Sarah would bear him a son the following year, and that he was to be called Isaac. (17:1–21) God later appeared to Abraham again, saying that he would return in the spring, when

Sarah would give birth to a son. Sarah, who was listening from the entrance to the tent, heard this and laughed to herself for she had long since passed through the menopause. And God heard her, and asked Abraham, 'Why did Sarah laugh, and say, "Will I really have a child in my old age?" Is there anything that the Lord cannot do?' Because Sarah was afraid, she denied having laughed, but God contradicted her, saying, 'Yes, you did laugh!' (18:6–15) According to Carlo Suarès, the change of name from Sarai to Sarah and Abram to Abraham – which coincides with the birth of Isaac – signifies the attainment of perfection: for a woman, this is represented symbolically as the age of 90; for a man, the age of 100. This attainment of perfection is also expressed as the establishment of the covenant between God and Abraham. (Suarès, 153)

After the destruction of Sodom and Gomorrah (*see below,* The wife and daughters of Lot), Abraham moved his encampment to the land of Gerar. In a scenario that recalls his earlier stay in Egypt, Abraham once again passed Sarah off as his sister and she was taken from him by the local ruler, King Abimelech. But God appeared to Abimelech in a dream, and told him that he would be punished with death because he had taken another

ABOVE
Forced to flee: Sarai treated the pregnant Hagar so harshly that she fled but later an angel appeared and told her to go back to her mistress

man's wife. Abimelech protested his innocence, saying that he had not laid hands on her. Moreover, Abraham had told him that Sarah was his sister, and she had told him that Abraham was her brother. Abimelech asked Abraham what he had done to cause him to treat him like this. Abraham offered the same explanation that he had given Sarah when they entered Egypt: he would be killed if it were thought she was his wife. And he told Abimelech that she was indeed his sister – or rather, his half-sister – saying, 'She is indeed my sister, the daughter of my father, but not the daughter of my mother. And when God caused me to travel away from my father's house, I said to her, "At every place we come to, say of me, 'He is my brother.'"'

Abimelech then told Abraham that he was welcome to live in his land, and he gave him gifts of silver, livestock and servants, and he gave Sarah back to him. Then Abraham prayed to God, and God healed Abimelech, and his wife and female slaves whom he had made barren because of Sarah. And God visited Sarah and fulfilled his promise to her, and she conceived and gave birth to a son, Isaac. Earlier, Sarah had laughed at the thought of bearing a child in her old age, and she laughed again now that she had given birth to Isaac (whose name means 'He laughs'), and she said, 'God has given me good reason to laugh, and everyone who hears of this will laugh with me.' One day, after Isaac had been weaned, Sarah saw him playing with Ishmael, Abraham's son by Hagar, and she told Abraham to banish Hagar and Ishmael for she did not want him to have the same rights of inheritance as her own son, Isaac. (20:1–21:12)

Sarah died at Hebron in the land of Canaan when she was 127 years old. Because he was a foreigner, Abraham asked the Hittites – the inhabitants of Canaan at the time – for a piece of land in which he could bury Sarah.

For 400 shekels he bought the field of Machpelah from a Hittite by the name of Ephron, and in the field was a cave in which he buried Sarah. (23:1–19) Although Abraham was about 137 years old when Sarah died, he 'took another wife, whose name was Keturah' (*see below*, Keturah).

The author of the Letter to the Hebrews draws on the example set by Sarah, saying that it was her faith in God that enabled her to conceive a child when she was past child-bearing age. (Hebrews 11:11) Peter likewise holds Sarah up as a model for Christian wives to follow, telling them that they are now her children if they lead righteous lives, free from fear and worry. (1 Peter 3:6)

Sarah in art

Although Sarah is the first of the matriarchs, images of her are relatively uncommon because of the greater importance placed on her husband Abraham in his seminal role as founder of the three monotheistic 'Abrahamic' religions (Judaism, Christianity and Islam), and on her son Isaac. Sarah occasionally features in scenes showing Abraham and his family on their journey from Ur to Canaan; but she appears more frequently in scenes from the story of her maid Hagar, in particular scenes connected with the sending of Hagar out into the wilderness (*see below*).

HAGAR

MEANING: FLIGHT OR FUGITIVE

The Egyptian slave who became a surrogate mother.

† BIBLICAL REFERENCE: Genesis 16; 21:9–17; 25:12; Galatians 4:24

Hagar was the Egyptian maid or slave girl of Sarah, Abraham's wife. The meaning of her name – 'Flight' or 'Fugitive' – is appropriate since her flight from her mistress is an important element in her story. Hagar is introduced into the story of Sarah and Abraham at the point at which we are told that Sarah – or Sarai, as she was still called – was barren. Sarah was then between sixty and seventy, and thus beyond the age at which she

ABOVE
Marching orders: Abraham gave Hagar some bread and a skin of water
and bade farewell to her and their son Ishmael

could reasonably be expected to give her husband a son, and so she suggested to Abraham that Hagar become her surrogate and bear him a child. Abraham accepted Sarah's advice, and Sarah gave Hagar to him as his wife. When Hagar knew she had conceived she began to treat her mistress with contempt, and so Sarah complained about her behaviour to Abraham, saying, 'Her insulting behaviour is your fault. It was I who gave the slave girl to you, but now she has conceived she despises me. May the Lord judge between me and you!' Abraham replied, 'Your slave girl is yours to do with as you wish.' And Sarah treated Hagar so harshly that she fled. An angel found her by a spring of water in the desert, and he said to Hagar, 'Where have you come from, and where are you going?' Hagar replied, 'I am fleeing from my mistress Sarai.' And the angel told her to go back to her mistress and submit to her. He also told her that her descendants would be beyond number, and that she was to name her son Ishmael (meaning 'God hears'), 'because God has heard your distress'. Because she had been spoken to by God, Hagar named him 'God of seeing', meaning that she had seen God and remained alive after seeing him. So the spring in the desert by which the angel found her was called Beer-lahai-roi ('The well of

one who sees and lives'). And Hagar bore Abraham a son, whom he named Ishmael, when Abraham was eighty-six years old. (16:1–16)

Some time after the birth of Isaac, Sarah saw Abraham's two sons playing together and was afraid that they would be treated as equal heirs, so she told Abraham to send Hagar and Ishmael away. This displeased Abraham, but God spoke with him and told him to do as Sarah had said. He also told him not to be anxious about Ishmael and Hagar, for his lineage would be perpetuated through his son Isaac, while Ishmael would become the father of a great nation, for he too was Abraham's son. Early the next morning, Abraham gave Hagar some bread and a skin of water, lifted Ishmael up onto her shoulders, and sent her on her way. She wandered off into the desert of Beersheba. When the water skin was empty, she placed her child under a bush and went and sat about a bowshot away because she could not bear to see him die. God heard the crying of the abandoned child, and a voice from heaven told Hagar to pick up the boy and keep him safe for he was to become a great nation. Then God opened Hagar's eyes, and she saw a well of water from which she filled the water skin and gave the child a drink. God watched over the boy as he grew

up and became an archer. Ishmael settled in the desert of Paran; and when he was of an age to marry, his mother got him a wife from Egypt. (21:9–21) Ishmael had twelve sons, who became the heads of twelve tribes. (25:12–16)

While explaining to his Galatian followers that it was preferable to seek spiritual freedom rather than remain a slave to religious law, Paul cites the example presented by Hagar and Sarah to illustrate two covenants, saying, 'Scripture tells us that Abraham had two sons, one by a slave girl and one by a freewoman. The son of the slave girl was born according to the ways of human nature; but the son of the freewoman was born according to [God's] promise. This is an allegory: these women embody two covenants. One was given on Mount Sinai – this is Hagar,

whose children are born in slavery – and Sinai is a mountain in Arabia that corresponds to the present earthly Jerusalem, for she is in slavery together with her children. But the heavenly Jerusalem is free, and she is our mother. ... And we are like Isaac, children of the promise. Just as in those days, when the son who was born according to the ways of human nature persecuted the child born according to the ways of the Spirit, so it is now. ... But we are not children of the slave girl but of the freewoman.' (Galatians 4:22–31)

Surrogate parenthood was a subject of some controversy in the closing decades of the twentieth century, when the practice received widespread publicity. Yet it was not uncommon in ancient Mesopotamia, Abraham and Sarah's birthplace: ancient legal codes from Babylon and Assyria

ABOVE
Salvation in the desert: an angel appeared to Hagar and saved her and Ishmael from dying of thirst

allowed a barren wife to give a maid or slave girl to her husband in order to continue the bloodline.

Hagar and Ishmael have a special place in the Islamic tradition (as indeed does Abraham). Not only is Ishmael regarded as the ancestor of the Arabs, but according to the Qur'an he helped Abraham build the Kaaba in Mecca – a square-shaped shrine toward which Muslims turn when praying, and around which they circle during the annual pilgrimage (the *Hajj*). Hagar and Ishmael's sojourn in the desert is also commemorated during the pilgrimage. The 'hastening', which entails passing seven times at a fast walk or run between the two hills of Safa and Marwa, emulates Hagar's increasingly frantic search for water in the desert. Pilgrims may also drink from the Well of Zamzam, the spring of water that God caused to emerge from the ground to prevent Hagar and Ishmael from dying of thirst: it now flows beneath the Great Mosque in Mecca. The spring takes its name from the Arabic word *zam* – meaning 'stop' – because the water gushed out of the ground so fast that Hagar shouted, '*Zam! Zam!*' – 'Stop! Stop!'

Hagar in art

The majority of images of Hagar depict her at either the beginning or the end of her ordeal. In the former, the principal figures are Hagar, Abraham (who is shown sending her away), and a tearful Ishmael, sometimes with Sarah in the background. The theme of the angel saving Hagar and Ishmael from dying of thirst and starvation in the wilderness offered artists a potentially more dramatic subject, as evidenced in paintings that show the angel alighting, wings still outspread, next to Hagar. Both scenes were fairly common in seventeenth-century European art.

KETURAH

MEANING: INCENSE

The second wife of Abraham, and mother of six of his sons.

† BIBLICAL REFERENCE: 25:1–4

Sarah had died when Abraham was about one hundred and thirty-seven years old, after which he 'took another wife, whose name was Keturah'. The six sons of Keturah and Abraham were Zimran, Jokshan, Medan, Midian, Ishbak and Shuah. When Abraham died at the age of one hundred and seventy-five, he left everything to Isaac, his son by Sarah his first wife. He gave gifts to his other sons, but while he was still alive he sent them eastwards, away from Isaac. Keturah's sons are said to be the ancestors of six Arabic tribes of southern and eastern Palestine. (Deen, 276) The descendants of her son Midian frequently feature in the unfolding history of the Israelites.

THE WIFE AND DAUGHTERS OF LOT

The woman who was turned into a pillar of salt and whose daughters committed incest with their father.

† BIBLICAL REFERENCE: Genesis 19:15–17, 26, 30–8; Luke 17:32

Lot's unnamed wife is remembered for having been transformed into a pillar of salt when she turned around and looked back at the fire and brimstone pouring down on the cities of Sodom and Gomorrah, but the retelling of her story usually omits to say how she and her husband came to be in Sodom in the first place. When Terah had left Ur with his son Abram (before his name was changed to Abraham) and daughter-in-law Sarai (Sarah), he took with him his grandson Lot (the son of Abram's deceased brother Haran, and thus Abram's nephew). After the death of Terah, Lot remained with Abram during his sojourns in Canaan and Egypt. By the time they reached the Negeb, the two men had acquired large herds of livestock, so large that the land was unable to support both men's herds. Friction between their herdsmen prompted Abram to suggest it was time for the two men and their families to go their

separate ways. Lot chose to move into the fertile valley of the Jordan, pitching his tents near the city of Sodom, while Abram remained in Canaan. (11:31–13:13)

Some years later, two angelic messengers came to Abraham. After they had told him that Sarah, his 90-year-old wife, would bear him a son, the two angels left Canaan for the city of Sodom. At the city gate they encountered Lot, who offered the strangers hospitality for the night. Later that night the entire male population of Sodom surrounded Lot's house and demanded that he bring out his visitors so that they could have sex with them. Aware of the traditional obligation of a host to protect his visitors from harm, Lot offered his two unmarried daughters in their place. But the men of Sodom rejected his offer and threatened to break into Lot's house, at which the angels blinded them. They then told Lot that they were about to destroy Sodom because God had heard of the great outcry against its inhabitants. Lot went out to warn his future sons-in-law – the men who were betrothed to marry his daughters – but they thought he was merely joking. As dawn broke the next morning the angels urged Lot to take his wife and daughters and leave the city of Sodom. But Lot was slow to leave, so the angels took hold of him, his wife and his two daughters and led them out of the city. 'Now flee for your life,' said the

ABOVE
No looking back: angels led Lot and and his daughters away from Sodom.
Behind them is Lot's wife who had been turned into a pillar of salt

and fire and brimstone began to rain down on Sodom and Gomorrah, destroying the cities and the entire valley, along with all their inhabitants and everything that grew there. But Lot's wife, who was walking behind him, looked back, and she became a pillar of salt. Lot was afraid to stay in Zoar and soon moved into the hills where he lived in a cave with his two daughters. Believing their father to be the only man left alive after the destruction of the cities of the plain, Lot's elder daughter suggested to the younger that they get him drunk and seduce him so 'that we may preserve offspring through our father'. They each got him drunk on successive nights, and seduced him while he was oblivious to what was going on. In due course Noah's daughters each bore a son: the elder daughter's son was named Moab, the younger's Ben-ammi. The descendants of Moab were the Moabites; those of Ben-ammi were the Ammonites. (19:1–38)

The story of Lot, his wife and his daughters, and the destruction of Sodom and Gomorrah is open to many interpretations, many of which focus on the punishment meted out by God on Lot's wife for disobeying the angels' instruction not to look back at the cities of the plain, and on the men of Sodom for practising homosexuality (to which we owe the term 'sodomy'). A more benign

interpretation suggests that the reactions of Lot and his wife to the angels' instruction to leave the city and not look back mirror our own potential response to the divine will – either we ignore it, like Lot's wife, or we respond to it reluctantly, like Lot, who prefers to go a little distance rather than travel right up into the hills. Like mountains, hills are 'high places' and traditional metaphors for the meeting-place of the human and divine realms, or the ascent to a higher level of spiritual evolution. By contrast, the 'cities of the plain' and those who dwell in them represent a level of existence in which we are governed by the whims and desires of our lower self, our self-centred will. In this context, the drunken Lot's seduction by his daughters may be seen as a metaphor for spiritual blindness, for we are told that Lot was totally unaware of what was happening. A very different type of interpretation suggests that the story of Lot's wife and the destruction of Sodom and Gomorrah explains the origin of certain topographic features – i.e. the pillar of salt and the desolation of the area around the Dead Sea – while the incest of Lot's daughters explains the common ethnic origins of the Moabites, Ammonites and Israelites at the same time as asserting the superiority of the latter. (*Oxford Companion to the Bible*, 467)

angels, 'Do not look back or stop in the plain. Flee to the hills or you will be destroyed.' Lot protested that although the strangers had saved his life he was afraid of fleeing to the hills in case disaster overtook him on the way and he died. Instead, he asked the angels if he could go to a town that was closer – only a little town at that – and thus be saved. This is how the town came to be known as Zoar, meaning 'Little'. By the time Lot reached Zoar the sun was high in the sky,

Whatever interpretation we apply to the story of Lot and his daughters, it seems ironic that Lot was considered to be the only person righteous enough to be saved from the destruction that befell Sodom and Gomorrah, and yet one of the first things he did afterwards was to commit incest, albeit unknowingly, with his daughters.

The example set by Lot's wife is cited by Jesus when the Pharisees questioned him about the coming of the kingdom of God, 'On that day, let him who is on the roof, with his goods in the house, not come down and take them away; likewise, let him who is in the field not turn back. Remember Lot's wife.' (Luke 17:32)

Lot's wife and daughters in art

The subject of Lot's seduction by his daughters had particular appeal to post-Renaissance artists, including Lucas van Leyden, Albrecht Altdorfer and Orazio Gentileschi. Sometimes both daughters are shown lying beside the drunken Lot; at others, one daughter is with Lot while

ABOVE
Incestuous love: believing their father to be the last man on earth, Lot's daughters set about seducing him

the other is seated or lying in the background. All three figures are in various stages of undress.

MILCAH

MEANING: COUNSEL

The girl who married her uncle.

† BIBLICAL REFERENCE: Genesis 11:29; 22:20–3

Milcah was Abraham's niece, the daughter of his brother Haran. She married another of Abraham's brothers – her uncle Nahor – for whom she bore eight children, the youngest of whom was Bethuel, father of Rebekah (*see below*) and Laban.

REUMAH

MEANING: EXALTED OR RAISED UP

The young woman who became a concubine.

† BIBLICAL REFERENCE: Genesis 22:24

Reumah was Nahor's concubine, and the first woman in the Bible to be described as such. She bore Nahor four children, making him the father of twelve in total. It is worth noting that the status of a concubine within the polygamous societies of early biblical times was that of a second or secondary wife. She therefore had certain legal rights.

REBEKAH

MEANING: CAPTIVATING, ENSNARER OR NOOSE

The story of the young woman from Nahor who married Abraham's son Isaac and gave birth to his twin sons Esau and Jacob, and how she tricked Esau out of his birthright.

† BIBLICAL REFERENCE: Genesis 24:1–67; 25:19–28; 26:1–11; 26:35; 27:5–17, 42–6; 49:31

The intertwined relationships of Abraham's descendants are perpetuated with Rebekah, the daughter of his nephew Bethuel and grand-daughter of his niece Milcah. Rebekah became the wife of Abraham's son Isaac, for whom she bore the twins Esau and Jacob. The various meanings of her name – 'Captivating', 'Ensnarer' and 'Noose' – seem appropriate for she not only captivated Isaac's heart, she also devised a plot that ensnared Isaac into giving the special blessing reserved for her elder son Esau to her favourite, her younger son

Jacob. And yet, as Rebekah's story reveals, the plot she devised brought about the change in status of her two sons that God had foretold while they were still in her womb.

When Abraham was well advanced in years, he summoned Eliezer, his oldest and most loyal servant, and instructed him to go to Abraham's homeland and there find a wife for Isaac, because he did not want his son to marry a Canaanite woman. Eliezer asked, 'What if the woman refuses to return with me? Should I then take your son back to the land from which you came?' Abraham replied, 'Whatever you do, do not take my son back there. The Lord God who took me from the land of my birth and who swore to me, "To your descendants I will give this land," will send his angel ahead of you, so that you

 ABOVE
Rebekah at the well: Abraham sent his servant Eliezer to find a wife for his son Isaac as God had decreed

can find a wife there for my son.' Eliezer set off for Nahor in Mesopotamia, taking all kinds of gifts from Abraham and ten of his master's camels. When he arrived at Nahor, he stopped outside the city and made his camels kneel down by the well. It was the time of evening when the women came to draw water, and Eliezer prayed to God, saying, 'Grant me success, and show enduring love to my master Abraham. While I am standing by the well, I shall say to one of the young women, "Please, lower your pitcher into the well and give me a drink," and if she says, "Drink, while I water your camels," let her be the one you have ordained for Isaac. By this I shall know that you have shown enduring love to my master.' While he was still speaking, out of the city came Rebekah, a beautiful young virgin, the daughter of Bethuel who was the son of Milcah, wife of Abraham's brother Nahor. Rebekah made her way to the well, a water pitcher on her shoulder. She lowered it into the water and filled it, and was walking back when Eliezer ran over to her. He asked her to give him a drink, which she did. And when he had finished drinking, she said, 'I will draw water for your camels too, until they have drunk enough.' So saying, she emptied her pitcher into the trough and then ran back and forth to the well

until she had drawn water for all the camels. While she was doing this, Eliezer looked on in silence, wondering whether God had granted his mission success or not. When the camels had finished drinking, he took out a gold ring and two gold bracelets, gave them to her, and said, 'Please tell me, whose daughter are you? Is there room at your father's house for us to spend the night?' Rebekah replied that she was the daughter of Bethuel, the son that Milcah delivered to Nahor, and that they had plenty of straw and fodder, and a room for the night. When he heard this, Eliezer praised God for having shown his enduring love for Abraham, and for leading him to the house of his master's brother. Rebekah ran home to tell what had happened. When her brother Laban had heard what she had to say, and had seen the gold ring and bracelets she was wearing, he ran out to the well and invited the man to their house. Having unloaded the camels and given them their fodder, he gave Eliezer and his companions water to wash their feet. A meal was set before Eliezer, but he refused to eat until he had explained the purpose of his journey. He began by telling them that he was Abraham's servant, and that God had blessed his master and made him a very wealthy man, granting him numerous flocks and herds, gold

and silver, and male and female slaves; and how Sarah, Abraham's wife, had borne him a son in his old age, and Abraham had made over everything he owned to him. Eliezer then told them why Abraham had sent him to Nahor, how he had prayed to God by the well, of his meeting with Rebekah, and how he had praised God for guiding him to choose the daughter of his master's brother as a bride for his

son. After he had finished speaking, Laban and Bethuel told Eliezer that it was not for them to contradict what God had ordained, and charged him to take Rebekah with him so that she could become Isaac's wife, as God had decreed. And when they asked Rebekah whether she was willing to go with Eliezer, she replied, 'Yes, I will go.' The next morning, before she set off with Eliezer on the return journey to Canaan, her parents and brother blessed her, saying, 'May you be the mother of thousands, and tens of thousands, and may your descendants overcome their enemies.' Meanwhile, Isaac had settled in the Negeb, and as he was walking in the fields one evening he looked up and saw some camels approaching. Rebekah also looked up, and when she saw Isaac she got down from her camel and asked Eliezer who the man was who was walking in the fields. He replied, 'My master.' So she covered herself with her veil. When Eliezer had told Isaac everything that had happened, Isaac took her into his tent, and Rebekah became his wife. (24:1–67)

Isaac was forty when he married Rebekah, but because she was barren he prayed to God to grant them a child. God answered his prayer, and

ABOVE

Sibling rivalry: watched by his wife Rebekah, Isaac mistakenly gave his blessing to Jacob as Esau hunted deer in the fields

Rebekah conceived, but the children inside her struggled so much that she said, 'If this is what it is going to be like, why go on living?' And she consulted God, who said to her, 'There are two nations in your womb, two rival peoples; one will be stronger than the other, and the elder will serve the younger.' In due course, Rebekah gave birth to twins. The first-born was red and had a hairy body, so they named him Esau. (The Hebrew word for 'hairy' sounds like Seir, the region of the Edomites, Esau's descendants.) Then his brother was born, and because he was grasping Esau's heel with his hand he was called Jacob. (His name is a wordplay on the Hebrew word for 'heel', and is taken to mean 'He takes by the heel', or 'He supplants'.) Isaac was sixty when

his sons were born. Esau grew up to be a hunter, a man who loved roaming in the open country, whereas Jacob was a peaceful man who stayed within the encampment of tents. Esau was Isaac's favourite, because he liked eating the game he brought him, but Rebekah preferred Jacob. On one occasion, Esau returned from the open country. He was hungry, and Jacob was cooking a lentil stew, so he said to Jacob, 'Give me some of that red stuff, for I am famished!' – he was thus given the name 'Edom'. (This is another play on words, as 'Edom' sounds like the Hebrew word for 'red'.) Jacob answered that he would give him some stew in exchange for the birthright Esau inherited because he was Isaac's first-born son. 'What use is a birthright to me

when I'm at death's door?' retorted Esau. Jacob said, 'Give me your word first.' So Esau gave him his word, and sold his birthright to Jacob in exchange for some bread and lentil stew. When he had eaten, he got up and went on his way. That was how little Esau thought of his birthright. (25:19–34)

When the country was hit by famine, Isaac went to Gerar, the land of King Abimelech, king of the Philistines. And God appeared to Isaac and told him not to go down to Egypt; he should stay in the country that God would show him. God then reaffirmed the promise he had made to Abraham, Isaac's father. In fulfilment of that promise, God would give the land to Isaac's descendants who would multiply and become as numerous as the stars in heaven. So Isaac stayed in Gerar, and when the inhabitants asked him about Rebekah, he replied that she was his sister, for he was afraid they would kill him if he told them that this beautiful woman was his wife. One day, when Isaac had been in Gerar for a while, Abimelech looked out of his window and saw Isaac fondling Rebekah. He summoned him, and said, 'Surely, this woman is your wife! How could you say, "She is my sister"?' Isaac replied, 'I thought I might be killed because of her.' Abimelech said, 'How could you do this to us? One of the people might

ABOVE
The reconciliation of brothers: Jacob supplanted his brother twice but in the end Esau forgave him

easily have slept with your wife, and we would have been guilty because of you.' So Abimelech warned his people that whosoever laid a hand on Isaac or Rebekah would be put to death. (26:1–11)

When Isaac was old and blind and unsure how much longer he would be of this world, he summoned his first-born son Esau and told him to go hunting. With the game Esau killed he was to make a tasty dish of the kind his father was fond of eating; and, when Isaac had eaten it, he would give him his blessing. Rebekah overheard this, and when Esau had left to go hunting she told Jacob what Isaac had said to Esau. She then told him to kill a couple of kids from the flock so that she could make the kind of savoury dish Isaac liked to eat, and he was to take this to his father so that he might bless him. Jacob – who had already obtained his elder brother's birthright in exchange for some lentil stew – protested, saying that Esau was hairy whereas he was smooth-skinned. If his father realized that he was being cheated, he would curse him rather than bless him. But Rebekah replied, 'Let the curse be on my head, my son. Just do as I tell you, and bring me the kids.' So Jacob went and fetched them, and gave them to his mother, and she prepared a dish of the kind Isaac loved to eat. She

then took her elder son Esau's best clothes, dressed her younger son Jacob in them, and covered his arms and the smooth part of his neck with the skins of the kids. She handed him the special dish she had prepared, and Jacob took it to his father. 'Father,' he said. 'Yes,' answered Isaac, 'which of my sons are you?' Jacob replied, 'Esau, your first-born. I have done as you told me. Sit up and eat some of the game I have brought you, and then give me your blessing.' Isaac asked him to come closer so that he could make sure that the son in front of him really was Esau. His suspicions were aroused, however, for he remarked that the voice was Jacob's but the hairy arms were Esau's. So he asked him, 'Are you really my son Esau?' And Jacob answered, 'I am'. After Isaac had eaten the meal, he told his son to kiss him, and as his son kissed him he sniffed at his clothes and recognized Esau's smell, and he blessed him thinking that he was Esau. When Esau returned from hunting and went to receive his father's blessing, Rebekah and Jacob's subterfuge was discovered. Esau asked his father to bless him too, but the special blessing reserved for the eldest son could only be given once, and the blessing given to Jacob could not be undone. Esau exclaimed, 'He was rightly named Jacob, for he has now supplanted me

twice. First he took my birthright, and now he has taken my blessing!' And Esau vowed that when his father died he would kill Jacob. His words were repeated to Rebekah, who warned Jacob of his brother's threat and told him to seek refuge with her brother Laban in Haran. When Esau's anger had waned, she would send someone to bring him back, and she added, 'I do not want to lose both my sons on the same day!' She then went to Isaac to express her loathing for the local Hittite women, saying, 'If Jacob were to marry one of them, there would be nothing left to me to live for.' And Isaac sent him away to Paddan-Aram, to Rebekah's brother Laban, that he might marry one of his daughters. (27:1–28:5) This is the last we hear of Rebekah while she was alive, and nothing is said about how or when she died. However, we learn later that she had been buried in the cave in the field of Machpelah, together with her husband Isaac and his parents, Abraham and Sarah, for when Jacob was on his deathbed he charged his son Joseph to bury him there among his ancestors. (49:29–31)

Rebekah in art

By far the most popular scene from the story of Rebekah in Christian art is her meeting with Eliezer at the well outside the town of Haran, for their meeting is interpreted by Christians as prefiguring the Annunciation. In most representations of the scene, the bearded Eliezer holds out a gift or gifts to the young Rebekah who is standing beside the well, a water pitcher in her hands. Other scenes from Rebekah's story are associated with her plot to obtain the special blessing of her elderly husband Isaac for her favourite son Jacob. Some scenes show the almost blind Isaac giving his blessing to Jacob; others show him refusing to repeat the special blessing for his elder son Esau, the rightful recipient. Rebekah is frequently present in both scenes, either as a support for Jacob or as the observer of Esau's rejection.

DEBORAH

MEANING: BEE

Rebekah's nurse.

† BIBLICAL REFERENCE: Genesis 24:59; 35:8

Deborah accompanied Rebekah when she left her family home to marry Isaac. When she died, she was buried under an oak tree at Bethel.

JUDITH, BASEMATH AND MAHALATH

MEANING: JUDITH, PRAISED; BASEMATH, FRAGRANT; MAHALATH, SICKNESS OR LYRE

The three women who became the wives of Esau.

† BIBLICAL REFERENCE: Genesis 26:34–5; 28:9; 36:2–5

Judith and Basemath were two Hittite women whom Esau took as his wives when he was forty. They are said to have 'made life bitter' for Esau's parents, Isaac and Rebekah. (26:34–5) Mahalath was the daughter of Abraham's son Ishmael, whom Esau took as his third wife when he realized that his father was not pleased that he had married two local women. (28:9) When the three women are mentioned again in the genealogical list of Esau's descendants (the Edomites) in Genesis 36, there is some confusion, for their names are not the same: Basemath is given the name Adah ('Adorned'), while Ishmael's daughter Mahalath is given the name Basemath. As for the other wife, she is named as Oholibamah ('Tent of the high places'; Lockyer, 29) instead of Judith, and the name of her father also differs from that given in 26:34. It has been suggested that this confusion stems from the wives having both a personal name and a second name. (*ibid.,* 29) Between them Esau's wives bore him five sons: Adah was the mother of Eliphaz; Basemath of Reuel; Oholibamah of Jeush, Jalam and Korah.

RACHEL AND LEAH

MEANING: RACHEL, EWE; LEAH, TIRED OR COW
(OXFORD COMPANION TO THE BIBLE, 428)

How Laban tricked Jacob into marrying his two daughters, one of whom was fertile and the other who remained barren for many years.

† BIBLICAL REFERENCE: Genesis 29

After Rebekah had told Isaac that she did not want her son

RIGHT
A match made in heaven: Jacob kissed Rachel and wept openly in gratitude after rolling away the stone that covered the well

Jacob to marry a Hittite woman, as his brother Esau had done, Isaac summoned Jacob, and said, 'You are not to marry a Canaanite woman. Go to Padaan-Aram in Haran, to the house of Bethuel your mother's father, and take as a wife one of the daughters of Laban, your mother's brother.' (28:1–2) One night while on his way east, Jacob had a dream in which he saw a ladder set between heaven and earth, with angels descending and ascending it. And God appeared to him and reiterated the promise that he had made to Abraham and to Isaac, that the land where he was would be given to his descendants, and that his descendants would multiply and be as numerous as the dust on the earth. God also promised him that he would not desert him until the promise had been fulfilled. When Jacob awoke the next morning, he named the place Bethel, meaning 'The house of God'. (28:11–19) When Jacob arrived in Haran, he came across a well with three flocks of sheep lying beside it. The mouth of the well was covered with a large stone, which was too big for one man to move on his own, so the well remained sealed until all the flocks had gathered to drink from it. Jacob asked the shepherds where they were from, and

ABOVE
The price of a wife: Jacob struck a deal with Laban –
seven years' labour for one of his daughters

when they replied that they were from Haran, he asked if they knew Laban, the grandson of Nahor. They said that they knew him, and then told him that the woman approaching with a flock of sheep was Laban's daughter Rachel. Jacob remarked that the sun was still high in the sky and suggested the shepherds water their sheep and then take them back to graze. They replied, 'We can't do that until all the shepherds are here to roll the stone away; only then can we water the sheep.' While they were still talking, Rachel – who was a shepherd – arrived with her father's sheep. And when Jacob saw Rachel, the daughter of Laban his mother's brother, with Laban's sheep, he went up to the well, rolled the stone away on his own, and watered his uncle's flock. He then kissed Rachel and wept openly, and told her that he was her father's relative, Rebekah's son, and Rachel ran and told her father. As soon as Laban heard the news about Jacob his sister's son, he ran to greet him, and embraced him, and welcomed him into his home. Jacob had been there a month when Laban told him it was not right that, just because he was his relative, he should work for him for nothing. And he said, 'Tell me what you want in the way of wages.' Now Laban had two daughters: Leah, the elder, who is said to have been

'weak-eyed', and the beautiful Rachel, with whom Jacob had fallen in love. So Jacob said, 'I will work seven years for you in exchange for your daughter Rachel.' Laban accepted, saying, 'It is better that I give her to you than to a stranger. Stay and work for me.' And Jacob worked seven years for Rachel, but to him it seemed only a few days because he loved her so much. When the seven years were up, Jacob asked Laban for Rachel, and Laban brought everyone together for a great banquet. But when night came, he took his daughter Leah and brought her to Jacob, and Jacob slept with her. (Laban gave his slave girl Zilpah to Leah to serve as her maid.) And when Jacob awoke in the morning to find Leah beside him, he said to Laban, 'What have you done to me? Did I not work for you for Rachel? Why have you cheated me?' Laban, who was Aramean, replied, 'In our land it is not customary to marry off the younger daughter before the first-born. See out this week of wedding festivities, and I will give you my other daughter in exchange for another seven years working for me.' Jacob accepted, and when the week's festivities for his marriage to Leah were over Laban gave him Rachel to be his wife. (Laban gave his slave girl Bilhah to Rachel to serve as her maid.) And Jacob slept also with Rachel, whom he loved more than

Leah, and he worked for Laban for another seven years. God saw that Leah was unloved, and she conceived and gave birth to a son while Rachel remained barren. Leah named her son Reuben (meaning 'See, a son') because God had seen her sorrow. And she said, 'Surely my husband will love me now.' She gave birth to another son, whom she named Simeon (Hebrew *shama*, meaning 'Heard'), saying, 'Because God has heard that I am unloved, he has given me this son too.' She conceived again and gave birth to a third son, whom she called Levi (Hebrew *lawah*, 'Joined'), because she believed that the birth of three sons would join Jacob to her. When she conceived again and gave birth to her fourth son, she said, 'This time I will praise the Lord,' and so she called him Judah (Hebrew *hodah*, 'Praise'). After this Leah had no more children. (29:1–35)

Rachel became jealous of her sister, because she herself had borne no children for Jacob, and she said to him, 'Give me children, or I shall die!' This made Jacob angry with Rachel, and he riposted, 'Am I in the place of God, who has withheld motherhood from you?' Then Rachel gave him her maid Bilhah, so that she might have children through her, and Jacob slept with her and she conceived. When Bilhah gave birth to a son for Jacob, Rachel proclaimed, 'God

has been my judge, and has heard my prayer and given me a son.' She called him Dan (meaning, 'He judged'). Bilhah conceived again, and when she gave birth to a second son for Jacob, Rachel said, 'I have wrestled against my sister, and have won!' This son she named Naphtali ('Wrestler'). (30:1–8) Then Leah, who had stopped bearing children, gave her maid Zilpah to Jacob. When Zilpah gave birth to a son, Leah exclaimed, 'What good fortune!' and gave him the name Gad ('Fortune'). And when Zilpah gave birth to a second son, Leah said, 'How blessed I am!' and named him Asher ('Blessed'). (30:1–13)

One day at wheat-harvest time, Reuben found some mandrakes in the field and brought them to his mother Leah. (The mandrake is a Mediterranean plant with a fleshy root, formerly used widely in medicine and magic, and considered by the ancients to be an aphrodisiac. The Hebrew words for 'mandrake' and 'love' are similar. NJB, 29.) Rachel asked Leah to give her some of her son's mandrakes, but Leah replied, 'Is it not enough for you to have taken my husband? Would you take my son's mandrakes as well?' So Rachel made a deal with her, saying, 'He can spend the night with you in exchange for your son's mandrakes.' When Jacob came home that evening, Leah went out to

meet him and told him that she had hired him for the night in exchange for her son's mandrakes, and Jacob spent that night with her. God heard Leah and she conceived, and when she gave birth to a fifth son for Jacob, she said, 'God has rewarded me for giving my maid to my husband. So she named him Issachar (a name that combines the Hebrew words for 'man' and 'wages'; *Oxford Companion to the Bible*, 336). And Leah conceived again, and bore a sixth son for Jacob, and said, 'God has given a fine dowry; now my husband will honour (Hebrew *zabal*) me because I have given him six sons, and she named her son Zebulun. She then bore Jacob a daughter, whom she called Dinah (meaning, 'Justice' or 'One who judges'; Lockyer, 45). Then God remembered Rachel, and he opened her womb and she conceived. When she gave birth to a son, she felt that God had taken away her shame, and she named him Joseph ('He adds'), saying, 'May God add another son for me!' (30:14–25)

Meanwhile, Jacob was still working for Laban. But after the birth of Joseph he asked Laban if he would let him leave and return to his own country. In the event, however, Jacob struck a deal with him whereby he would stay on condition that he could build up his own flock while continuing to

tend Laban's. Through a combination of good husbandry and trickery, he became so prosperous at Laban's expense that Laban's sons grew jealous. Jacob also noticed that his relationship with Laban was deteriorating. It was then that God appeared to Jacob and commanded him to return to the land of his fathers. Jacob called Rachel and Leah to him and told them of the change in their father's attitude towards him, and of how Laban had tricked him many times over his wages. When he told them that God had commanded him to leave and return to the land of his birth, they answered that they were unlikely to inherit anything from their father since he now looked on them as outsiders. Not only had he sold them, but he had used up all the money he had received for them. They added that whatever wealth God had reclaimed from Laban belonged to them and their children, and they concluded by telling Jacob to do whatever God had told him to do. Without telling Laban that he was leaving, Jacob promptly mounted his family on camels,

ABOVE
The journey into Canaan: while Jacob and his wives were travelling between Bethel and Ephrath, Rachel died giving birth to a son, Benjamin

and together with his herds and flocks set out for the land of Canaan to go to his father Isaac. But before they left, Rachel stole her father's household idols. It was three days before Laban learned that Jacob had fled, perhaps because Laban had moved his encampment three days' journey away from Jacob's. Taking his kinsmen with him, Laban set off in pursuit. When he caught up with Jacob in the land of Gilead seven days later, he chided him for having carried off his daughters like hostages, and for leaving without letting him know so that he could have joyfully sent him on his way with music and singing. Laban complained that he had not even let him kiss his daughters goodbye, and said, 'It is within my power to do you harm, but the God of your father came to me last night and said, "On no account say anything to Jacob." Perhaps you really left because you longed for your father's house, but why did you steal my gods?' Jacob replied, 'I was afraid that you would take your daughters from me by force. But whoever is found to have your gods shall not stay alive. In the presence of my kinsmen, go through what I have, and take it.' Jacob did not know that Rachel had stolen them. Laban searched Jacob's tent, then Leah's, then the tent of the two maids, but found nothing, so he went into Rachel's tent. Now Rachel had hidden the household gods in a saddlebag, and was sitting on them. As Laban searched her tent, she apologized for not standing in his presence but 'the way of women' was upon her. Although he searched thoroughly, Laban found nothing. Then Jacob vented his anger at Laban, asking him what he had done to cause him to hound him. He then complained lengthily about all the injustices he felt Laban had done him during the twenty years he had spent working for him. In reply, Laban said, 'These daughters are my daughters, these children are my children, this livestock is my livestock; everything here belongs to me. But what can I now do about my daughters or the children they have borne?' So saying, Laban suggested that the two men make a pact, which they commemorated with a cairn that was to serve as a boundary marker between them. The next morning Laban rose early, embraced his daughters and grandchildren, and set off on the journey home. (30:25–31:55)

After Laban had left, Jacob sent messengers to Seir, in the land of Edom, to seek a reconciliation with his brother Esau. Jacob followed, but sent his wives, his children and all his possessions ahead of him across the ford over the river Jabbok. During the night, while Jacob was alone, a man wrestled with him.

At daybreak the man told him that from thenceforth he would no longer be called Jacob, but Israel (meaning 'He has striven with God') for he had striven with God and men, and had prevailed. The next day he met Esau, and the two brothers became reconciled. They then parted, and Jacob and his family continued their journey to the land of his birth. When they arrived at Shechem in the land of Canaan, Jacob made camp outside the city and purchased the land on which he pitched his tents from the sons of Hamor, the ruling clan of the city, and there erected an altar. (32:3–33:20) It was while they were at Shechem that Leah's daughter Dinah was raped (*see below* Dinah).

From Shechem, Jacob and his wives journeyed further into the land of Canaan. While they were travelling between Bethel and Ephrath (Bethlehem), Rachel went into labour and died while giving birth to another son. As she was dying, she named her son Ben-Oni ('Son of my sorrow'), but his father named him Benjamin ('Son of the right hand' or 'Son of the South'). Rachel was buried on the road to Ephrath. (35:16–20) Leah was buried at Machpelah, in the cave where Abraham and Sarah, and Isaac and Rebekah, had been buried (49:31), but no mention is given of when or where Leah died.

Between them, Rachel, Leah,

Bilhah and Zilpah were the mothers of Jacob's twelve sons, who gave their names to the twelve tribes of Israel (the name by which Jacob became known after he wrestled with the angel by the ford over the river Jabbok). Leah was the mother of Reuben, Simeon, Levi, Judah, Issachar and Zebulun (and Dinah); Rachel was the mother of Joseph and Benjamin; Bilhah, of Dan and Naphtali; Zilpah, of Gad and Asher.

Rachel and Leah in art

Images of Jacob and his two wives are widespread in Christian art and range from intimate scenes of the meeting between Jacob and Rachel at the well to large-scale family groups of Jacob, his two wives and their two maids, together with their twelve children. Other large-scale scenes depict Rachel sitting on her father's idols, and the reconciliation between Jacob and Esau.

ZILPAH

MEANING: DROOPING

A maid who became the surrogate mother of two of Jacob's twelve sons.

† BIBLICAL REFERENCE: Genesis 29:24; 30:9–10

Leah's maid. Mother of Jacob's sons Gad and Asher.

(*See above,* Rachel and Leah.)

BILHAH

MEANING: FALTERING, BASHFUL

A maid who became the surrogate mother of two of Jacob's twelve sons.

† BIBLICAL REFERENCE: Genesis 29:29; 30:3–7; 35:22

Rachel's maid. Mother of Jacob's sons Dan and Naphtali. While Jacob's caravan made camp en route from Ephrath to Mamre, Leah's son Reuben (Jacob's firstborn) entered Bilhah's tent and slept with her. (35:22)

DINAH

MEANING: AVENGED OR JUDGED

The girl whose rape was cunningly and brutally avenged by her brothers.

† BIBLICAL REFERENCE: Genesis 34:1–19, 31

Dinah was the daughter of Leah and Jacob. While Jacob's family were camped outside the city of Shechem, Dinah went out to visit the local women. She caught the eye of Shechem, the son of Hamor the Hivite, the local ruler, and he took her by force and raped her. He fell in love with her and said to his father Hamor, 'Get me this girl. I want her to be my wife.' Meanwhile, Jacob had heard how his daughter had been violated, but said nothing because his sons were out in the country tending his livestock. Hamor duly went to discuss the matter with Jacob, and while he was visiting him Jacob's sons returned. They were outraged at the dishonour brought on the tribe by Shechem's rape of Jacob's daughter, but deceived Hamor into believing that they were willing to accept the proposed marriage on condition that all the

 ABOVE
The bloodbath of Shechem: Simeon and Levi avenged the rape of Dinah, their sister, by killing all the male inhabitants of the city

Shechemites were circumcised. While the Shechemites were still sore from their circumcision, two of Dinah's brothers – Simeon and Levi – avenged themselves by killing Hamor and his son and all the male inhabitants of the city. When Jacob's other sons discovered the massacre, they too avenged themselves for the violation of their sister, plundering the city and taking captive the women, children and livestock. When Jacob reprimanded Simeon and Levi for creating a situation whereby the Canaanites might take up arms against him, they replied, 'Should Shechem be allowed to treat our sister like a whore?' (34:1–31)

THE DAUGHTER OF SHUA

The woman who married Jacob's son Judah.

† BIBLICAL REFERENCE: Genesis 38:1–2; 12

This young woman, the daughter of a Canaanite man named Shua, married Leah's son Judah and bore him three sons: Er, Onan and Shelah. Judah met her while he was staying with Hirah, an Adullamite (a resident of Adullam, near Bethlehem; NOAB, 48). Some time later, after his wife had died, Judah went with Hirah the Adullamite to his sheep-shearers at Timnah. While on the road to Timnah, he met his daughter-in-law Tamar, who

by then was the widow of his sons Er and Onan (*see below*).

TAMAR

MEANING: PALM TREE

The story of how a young woman married two brothers, both of whom died, and then played a clever trick on her father-in-law to expose his poor treatment of her.

† BIBLICAL REFERENCE: Genesis 38:6–30

Tamar was chosen by Judah as a wife for Er, his first-born son. When Er was killed by God for having offended him, Judah told his second son Onan to take his brother's wife and do 'the duty of a brother-in-law'. (This duty refers to the ancient custom by which a brother married his deceased brother's widow in order to provide male offspring that would maintain their father's name and patrimony. *See below,* Women and the law.) Knowing that any sons would not legally be his and that his anticipated share of his father's inheritance would thus be diminished accordingly, whenever Onan made love to Tamar he spilled his semen on the ground. (This is the origin of 'onanism', an alternative word for both masturbation and *coitus interruptus*.) What he did displeased God, who killed him too. After the death of this second son, Judah was afraid that a similar fate awaited his third son Shelah if he married

Tamar, and so he told her to go back to her father's house until Shelah had grown up. Tamar returned home and had been living with her father for some time when news reached her that her father-in-law was en route to Timnah. Knowing that Shelah was by then of an age to marry and yet Judah had not given her to him to be his wife, she changed out of her widow's clothes, put on a veil to cover her face, and went and sat at the entrance to Enaim, which was on the road to Timnah. When Judah saw his daughter-in-law Tamar at the roadside, he did not recognize her and took her to be a harlot (or cult prostitute) because her face was veiled, and he went over to her and asked her to sleep with him. She said, 'What will you give me for sleeping with you?' He answered, 'I will send you a kid from my flock.' Tamar then asked him to give her something to serve as his pledge until he sent the kid, and he said, 'What shall I give you as a pledge?' She replied, 'Your seal and cord and the staff in your hand.' So Judah gave them to her and slept with her, and Tamar conceived. Then she left, and exchanged her veil for her widow's clothes. When Judah sent his friend Hirah the Adullamite with a kid from his flock to recover the items he had left as a pledge, he could not find the woman. He asked the local

men where the prostitute was who had been sitting at the roadside, but they replied that no prostitute had been there. So he went back to Judah and told him he could not find her; moreover, according to the locals, no prostitute had been there. 'Then let her keep the things,' said Judah, 'lest we be laughed at. I at least sent the kid, but you could not find her.' Some three months later, Judah was informed that his daughter-in-law had played the harlot, and that her misconduct had left her pregnant. Judah cried out, 'Bring her out, and let her be burned alive!' As Tamar was being led out, she sent a message to her father-in-law, 'It was the man to whom these belong who made me pregnant. Please establish who owns this seal, this cord and this staff.' Judah recognized them, and said, 'She is in the right and I am not, for I did not give her to my son Shelah.' And he did not sleep with her again. When her pregnancy reached full term, Tamar gave birth to twins. As they emerged from her womb, one of them put his hand out, and the

ABOVE
Sins of the father: Judah mistook his daughter-in-law Tamar for a prostitute and struck a bargain that would rebound on him

midwife caught hold of it and tied a scarlet thread around it, marking him as the first to be born. But he drew his hand back, and out came his brother. She exclaimed, 'What a breach you have opened for yourself!' He was therefore called Perez ('A breach'). Then his brother came out with the scarlet thread round his hand, and he was named Zerah.

ABOVE
All in the family: Tamar was married to Er and Onan
and then became pregnant by their father Judah

Women from the time of Egypt and the Exodus

In Genesis 39 the setting for the narrative moves from Canaan to Egypt, with the sale of Joseph by his brothers to some passing traders. Joseph's father Jacob/Israel and his household followed him later to escape the famine in their own land. The increasingly harsh treatment of the Israelites by the Egyptians led to their massed exodus under the leadership of Moses.

THE WIFE OF POTIPHAR

The Egyptian woman who tried to seduce Jacob's son Joseph, and when she failed had him put into prison.

† BIBLICAL REFERENCE: Genesis 39:7–19

Rachel's son Joseph was Jacob's favourite, and his brothers grew so jealous that they plotted to get rid of him. At first they thought of killing him, but Leah's son Reuben persuaded them not to harm him. Instead, they sold him to some traders in a passing caravan. He was taken to Egypt, where he was sold to Potiphar, the captain of Pharaoh's guard, who took him into his house. (37:1–38) When Potiphar saw how capable and trustworthy Joseph was, he put him in charge of running his household and looking after his possessions. Now Joseph was so good-looking that after a while Potiphar's wife was attracted to him and sought to seduce him. The first time she asked him to sleep with her, he rebuffed her, saying, 'My master has put me in charge of his house and entrusted me with everything that he owns. Nothing is withheld from me except you, because you are his wife. How then could I do anything so wicked, and sin against God?' Potiphar's wife spoke to him every day, but he refused to sleep with her or spend any time with her. One day when Joseph went into the house to work, the servants were all outside, and Potiphar's wife caught hold of him by his robe and said, 'Sleep with me.' But Joseph fled out of the house, leaving his robe behind. When she realized he had run off but that she still had his robe in her hands, she called out to the servants, 'Look at this! My husband has brought a Hebrew

▲ ABOVE
A woman scorned: Potiphar's wife showed her husband Joseph's robe and claimed he had tried to rape her

ABOVE

Unrequited love: when the servants were away, Potiphar's wife
caught hold of Joseph and tried to seduce him

into our house to humiliate us! He tried to rape me, but when I screamed he ran out of the house leaving his robe behind.' She kept Joseph's robe with her until his master came home, and then she told him the same story. When his wife said, 'See! This is how your servant has treated me,' he became incandescent with rage and had Joseph put into Pharaoh's prison.

In the Islamic tradition Potiphar's wife is known by the name Zuleykha, and the story of Joseph and Zuleykha has become one of the great love stories of Persian and Arab literature.

The wife of Potiphar in art

Images of Potiphar's wife's attempted seduction of Joseph are fairly widespread, but artists have represented the scene in a variety of ways. For example, Rembrandt's *Joseph Accused by Potiphar's Wife* in the National Gallery, Washington DC, shows Potiphar's wife seated on the side of her bed. She is gesturing towards a disconsolate Joseph, who stands on the other side of the bed, while beside her stands her husband, listening intently to her accusation. On the other hand, Tintoretto's *Joseph and Potiphar's Wife* in the Prado, Madrid, is dominated by the naked figure of Potiphar's wife posed wantonly on her bed. Other artists depict Joseph flee-ing from his master's wife who has a hold on the outer garment he is about to leave behind as he makes his escape.

ASENATH

MEANING: GIFT OF THE SUN-GOD (EGYPTIAN)

The Egyptian girl who married Joseph.

† BIBLICAL REFERENCE: Genesis 41:45, 50; 46:20

Asenath, daughter of Potiphera, priest of On, became Joseph's wife after Pharaoh had released Joseph from prison for having wisely interpreted his dreams, and promoted him to the status of governor of all Egypt. (The city of On, also known as Heliopolis, was the centre of worship to the sun-god Re.) Asenath bore Joseph two sons, who were given Hebrew rather than Egyptian names. He named their first-born son Manasseh ('Making to forget'), saying 'For God has made me forget my hardships and my father's house'. He named their second son Ephraim ('Fruit'), because 'God has made me fruitful in the land of my affliction'. The death of Joseph some years later brings the Book of Genesis to a close.

The ploy that Rachel used to ensure her younger son Jacob received his father Isaac's blessing in place of Esau, his elder brother, is mirrored when Joseph's and Asenath's sons go to receive Jacob's blessing. As Jacob placed his hands on their heads, he crossed them over at the last minute so that Ephraim, the younger son, received the blessing from Jacob's right hand. He was thus given precedence over his elder brother, as Jacob had been given precedence over Esau before him. After the Israelite's occupation of Canaan, Ephraim's descendants – the Ephraimites – were to become the dominant tribe of the northern kingdom of Israel.

Asenath in art

Asenath is sometimes present in scenes of Jacob blessing Joseph's sons, Manasseh and Ephraim. According to James Hall, the Middle Ages saw Manasseh as representing the Jews and Ephraim the Gentiles, and interpreted Jacob giving his special blessing to his younger son as symbolizing the Christian Church superseding Judaism. (Hall, 177)

SHIPRAH AND PUAH

MEANING: SHIPRAH, PROCREATE OR BEAUTY; PUAH, CHILD-BEARING OR SPLENDID

The two Hebrew midwives who disobeyed the Pharaoh.

† BIBLICAL REFERENCE: Exodus 1:15–21

Shiprah and Puah were serving as midwives in Egypt some time after Joseph's death, when the country was ruled by a Pharaoh who had not heard of the Hebrew who had once been governor of Egypt. Concerned that the greatly increased population of Hebrews posed a threat to his own people, Pharaoh began to deal harshly with them; but the more he oppressed them, the more the Hebrews increased in number. So Pharaoh told Shiprah and Puah that when they attended Hebrew women in childbirth they were to kill all the male children and allow the female children to live. But the two midwives were God-fearing women, and so they disobeyed Pharaoh's order and allowed the boys to live. Pharaoh summoned them to him and asked them why they were letting the male children stay alive. The midwives replied, 'Hebrew women are not like Egyptian women. They are sturdy women and give birth before the midwife arrives.' And God dealt kindly with the midwives, and because they were God-fearing women gave them families of their own. Meanwhile, the Hebrews continued to increase in number, and so Pharaoh issued an order to all his people, saying, 'Throw every new-born male Hebrew child into the Nile, but let the girls live.' In view of their profession as midwives, the alternative meanings of the names Shiprah ('Procreate') and Puah ('Child-bearing') are extremely appropriate.

JOCHEBED

MEANING: GLORY OF GOD

The woman who saved her baby son's life by placing him in a basket and floating it on the Nile.

✝ BIBLICAL REFERENCE: Exodus 2:1–11; 6:20

A 'daughter of the house of Levi', Jochebed married her nephew Amram. (6:20) She gave birth to a son after Pharaoh had announced that all male Hebrew children were to be killed at birth by being thrown into the Nile. Seeing that he was a healthy baby, she hid him for three months. But when she was no longer able to keep him hidden, she acquired a basket made from papyrus plants and coated it with bitumen and pitch. Having put her child in the basket, she placed it among the reeds that bordered the river. The boy's sister positioned herself a short distance away so that she was able to see what happened to him. It was then that Pharaoh's daughter came down to the river to bathe, and noticing the basket among the reeds she sent one of her maids to fetch it. On opening the basket, Pharaoh's daughter discovered the baby, which was crying, and she took pity on it, saying, 'This is a Hebrew child.' The child's sister now approached and said to Pharaoh's daughter, 'Shall I go and find you a Hebrew woman to nurse the child for you?'

'Yes,' she replied, and the girl went and fetched the child's own mother. When they returned to the river bank, Pharaoh's daughter said to the woman, 'Take this child away and nurse him for me, and I will pay you for doing so.' So the woman took the child away and nursed him, and when he had grown up she returned him to Pharaoh's daughter, who brought him up as her son (*see below*, the daughter of Pharaoh).

Apart from being mentioned in genealogical lists, nothing more is said about Jochebed. However, as the story related in Exodus continues to unfold we learn that she was the mother of three children – Aaron, Miriam and Moses – who were each to play a significant role during the Israelites' escape from bondage in Egypt and their journey towards the Promised Land.

Jochebed in art

Because of her limited mention in the Bible, images of Jochebed are largely confined to scenes that depict her placing the infant Moses on the Nile. One of the best known examples is *Moses Being Placed on the Waters*, by the seventeenth-century French painter Nicholas Poussin, in the Ashmolean Museum, Oxford, in which the distraught Jochebed, who has just placed Moses on the river, turns to look at her disconsolate husband Amram who is walking away. The painting also features Moses' elder brother Aaron and his sister Miriam.

THE DAUGHTER OF PHARAOH

The Egyptian princess who saved the life of a Hebrew baby boy.

✝ BIBLICAL REFERENCE: Exodus 2:5–11

This otherwise unidentified

ABOVE
Escape from the Pharaoh: the infant Moses was placed in a basket of papyrus and left among the reeds by the side of the Nile

young Egyptian woman discovered the infant Moses hidden in a reed bed while she was bathing, and she raised him as her son. She named him Moses (Hebrew *moshe*, meaning 'to draw out'), 'because I drew him out of the water'. (*See* Jochebed *above* for the rest of her story.) The name Moses is also said to derive from an Egyptian word meaning 'to beget a child'. (NOAB, 68)

The daughter of Pharaoh in art

The discovery of the infant Moses on the Nile is a fairly common subject in Christian art for it was seen as prefiguring the flight to Egypt of Jesus' parents and their newly-born child. The scene is usually dominated by Pharaoh's daughter, who is often sumptuously dressed, and her maidservants who are showing her the infant they have just

recovered from the river. Moses' sister Miriam, who watched over her baby brother, is sometimes seen in the background.

ZIPPORAH

MEANING: BEAUTY OR BIRD

The priest's daughter who married Moses and circumcised their son herself.

✝ BIBLICAL REFERENCE: Exodus 2:16–22; 4:20–6; 18:2–7

Zipporah was one of seven daughters of a Midianite priest called Jethro, who was also known as Reuel ('Friend of God', from the Hebrew words *reu*, meaning 'friend' and *el*, meaning 'God'). When Moses was a young adult, he killed an Egyptian who was beating a Hebrew. Fearing that news of this would reach Pharaoh's ears, Moses fled to the land of Midian. Moses was sitting by a well when

Zipporah and her sisters came to draw water for their father's flock. Some shepherds tried to drive the girls away, but Moses came to the girls' aid and helped them water their sheep. When the girls returned home, their father asked them why they were back so soon, and they replied that an Egyptian had protected them from some shepherds. He had even drawn water for them and watered their flock. On hearing this, their father told them to fetch the man and invite him to eat with them. Moses stayed on in Jethro's house, and the priest gave him his daughter Zipporah for a wife. She bore him a son, whom he named Gershom 'because I am a stranger [Hebrew *ger*] in a foreign land.' (2:16–22) She also bore him a second son who was called Eliezer (from the Hebrew *Eli*, meaning 'my God' and *ezer*, meaning 'help'), for Moses said 'The God of my father is my help and has delivered me from Pharaoh's sword.' (18:4)

While Moses was looking after Jethro's flock, God spoke to him from out of a burning bush and commanded him to return to Egypt to rescue the people of Israel and lead them to 'a land flowing with milk and honey.' (3:1–10) When God had finished speaking with him, Moses went to Jethro and having requested his permission to go back to Egypt he set off with his wife and two sons. At one of the places

ABOVE
Plucked from the waters: Pharaoh's daughter discovered Moses and raised him as her own son

ABOVE
To the rescue: Moses protected the daughters of Jethro
from a group of belligerent shepherds

they stopped at along the way, God met Moses and tried to kill him. Zipporah seized a flint knife, cut off her son's foreskin, and touching Moses' feet with it, said, 'You are my bridegroom in blood!' And God let go of Moses, for she had said 'bridegroom in blood' because of the circumcision. (4:18–26) (In ancient times, blood was used to seal a covenant or bond, especially between God and his people. *See* Exodus 24:8.) What happened to Zipporah immediately after this incident and during the Israelites' exodus from Egypt is omitted from the biblical account, and we do not hear of her again until her father Jethro took her with her two sons to rejoin Moses at the Israelites' encampment on the way to Mount Sinai. There Jethro advised his son-in-law to delegate some of the responsibilities he had taken upon himself to a carefully selected group of lay leaders or judges. Moses gratefully followed his father-in-law's advice. Meanwhile, Jethro returned to his home, presumably with his daughter and grandsons, for we hear no more about them.

With regard to God's attempt to kill Moses while on his way to Egypt, some authorities suggest that he incurred God's displeasure because he had neglected to circumcise his son according to the earlier covenant made between God and Abraham. (Genesis 17:9–14) Perhaps this

was because Moses had married into a non-Hebrew family, and his wife may not have wished her child to be circumcised. In which case, Zipporah's prompt circumcision of her son and her declaration that Moses was her 'bridegroom in blood' could indicate her acceptance of the Hebrew covenant with God. Whether this is the case or not, Zipporah has the distinction of being one of only three women in the Bible who are recorded as having performed a circumcision – a ritual that was traditionally performed only by men. (For the other two women, *see* Women Martyrs, page 159.)

Zipporah in art

Zipporah is usually depicted together with her six sisters at the well from which they went to draw water for their father Jethro's flocks. However, the scene is generally dominated by the figure of Moses driving away the shepherds who were harassing the seven girls. The girls are normally placed behind Moses, but one of them – presumably Zipporah – tends to be visually more important than the others. Some artists turned the incident into a visually dramatic scene. For example, in *Moses and the Daughters of Jethro*, by the sixteenth-century Italian Mannerist painter Rosso Fiorentino, the foreground is dominated by the fight between

Moses and the shepherds. The drama of the combatants' violently contorted bodies is heightened by the fact that they are naked or semi-naked. Jethro's daughters look on with consternation from the background.

MIRIAM

MEANING: BITTERNESS, OR POSSIBLY BELOVED (FROM EGYPTIAN MARYÏ)

The story of the girl who saved her baby brother Moses and became a prophetess and leader of the Israelite women, and yet ended her days in disgrace.

† BIBLICAL REFERENCE: Exodus 2:4, 7–8; 15:20–1; Numbers 12:1–15; 20:1

Miriam was the daughter of Jochebed and Amram, and sister to Aaron and Moses. When Moses was born and hidden in the reeds, she watched over him until he was found by Pharaoh's daughter (*see above*, Jochebed). Miriam was with the Israelites some years later when they escaped from Egypt, by which time she had earned the title of prophetess. After the momentous crossing of the sea, when the waters rolled back to allow the Israelites to cross and then flooded back to drown the pursuing Egyptians, Moses and all the people sang a great song in praise of God for their victory. Then Miriam took up a tambourine, and the women of Israel did likewise, and she led them in a

celebratory dance while chanting the refrain of the victory song. (15:20–1) Later still, while the Israelites were encamped at Hazeroth in the wilderness, Miriam and her brother Aaron criticized Moses for having married a Cushite woman (*see below*). They then questioned the uniqueness of Moses' role as spiritual leader to the Israelites, saying, 'Is Moses the only one through whom God speaks? Has he not spoken through us also?'

And God heard them, and called them together with their brother Moses to the tent of meeting, where he took on the form of a pillar of cloud and told them that he appeared to prophets in visions and spoke to them through dreams. Not so Moses, with whom he spoke face to face and to whom he revealed himself in his true form. How, then, did they dare to criticize his servant Moses? As the cloud of God's presence left them, Miriam was

afflicted with a terrible skin disease that turned her as white as snow. Aaron turned to his sister, saw her erupting skin, and then turned to plead with Moses that she should not be punished for their folly. And Moses prayed to God, begging him to heal her. God replied, 'If her father had done no more than spit in her face, would she not remain unclean for seven days? Have her excluded from the encampment for seven days, and then have her

ABOVE
Prophetess and sister of Moses: Miriam led the women of Israel in a celebratory dance after crossing the Red Sea

brought back in.' So Miriam was excluded from the camp for seven days, and the Israelites did not move on from Hazeroth until she had returned. (Numbers 12:2–15) Miriam died while the people of Israel were encamped at Kadesh, in the wilderness of Zin, and there she was buried. (Numbers 20:1)

Miriam in art

Miriam is sometimes portrayed in scenes showing her baby brother Moses being placed on the Nile by their mother Jochebed or in scenes of his discovery by the daughter of Pharaoh and her maidservants. She is also some-times identifiable in scenes of the crossing of the Red Sea, as one of the crowd of Israelites looking back from the shore as the pursuing Egyptians are drowned beneath the returning waters.

ELISHEBA

MEANING: GOD IS MY OATH
The wife of Aaron, and sister-in-law to Moses and Miriam.

✝ BIBLICAL REFERENCE: Exodus 6:23

Elisheba was the daughter of Amminadab, and sister of Nahshon, a prince of the tribe of Judah. By becoming the wife of Aaron the priest, she connected the royal and priestly tribes together. Elisheba was the mother of Aaron's four sons: Nadab, Abihu, Eleazar and Ithamar.

THE CUSHITE WOMAN

The non-Israelite woman who became Moses' wife.

✝ BIBLICAL REFERENCE: Numbers 12:1

While the Israelites were encamped at Hazeroth, Moses' sister and brother (Miriam and Aaron) criticized him for marrying a Cushite woman. Some authorities suggest they were referring to Zipporah, a non-Hebrew, and that the term 'Cushite' refers to Midianites and other Arabic peoples. Other authorities suggest that the Cushite woman was Moses' second wife, an Ethiopian, who, along with many others of her race, followed the Israelites out of Egypt.

COZBI

MEANING: DECEIVER OR DECEPTION

The non-Israelite woman whose marriage to an Israelite caused a plague, and caused her death.

✝ BIBLICAL REFERENCE: Numbers 25:6–16

Chapter 25 of the Book of Numbers relates that when the Israelites were camped at Shittim, they began to 'play the harlot with the daughters of Moab' (the local Moabite women), who seduced them into worshipping their own gods. That the Israelites had turned their back on him aroused God's anger. He spoke to Moses, and Moses

instructed the Israelite leaders to kill any of their people who had embraced the religion of Baal. At the precise moment that non-Hebrew women were being denounced as a threat to Israel because of their potential to lure the men away from their own religion to worship foreign idols, an Israelite named Zimri, son of Salu who was head of a family in the Simeonite tribe, brought a Midianite woman into the camp. This woman was called Cozbi, daughter of Zur, the chief of a Midianite clan. The couple entered the camp while the people were still weeping at the tent of meeting for having incurred God's anger. They were seen by Phinehas, grandson of Aaron the priest, who entered Zimri's tent and killed them both by driving a spear through their bellies. His action stemmed the plague that had suddenly afflicted the Israelites, killing 24,000 of them. For Phinehas's act of atonement and his defence of the Hebrews' religion, God granted him and his descendants (the Levites) the priesthood in perpetuity. God then instructed Moses to harass the Midianites because they had seduced his people into worshipping Baal, and because of the trouble Cozbi had caused them the day they were struck down with a plague. (25:1–17) When the Israelites went to war against the Midianites, they killed all the

Midianite men and took the women and children captive. But Moses was furious with them when they returned to the encampment with their captives and booty, and said, 'Why have you spared these women's lives? They are the same women who caused the people of Israel to turn away from God and caused the plague to descend on his people. You are to kill every male child, and every woman who has ever slept with a man. Spare the lives of the maidens who have never slept with a man, and keep them for yourselves.' (31:1–18)

MAHLAH, NOAH, HOGLAH, MILCAH AND TIRZAH

MEANING: MAHLAH, DISEASE; NOAH, REST; HOGLAH, PARTRIDGE; MILCAH, COUNSEL; TIRZAH, DELIGHTFUL

Five feisty young women who challenged the laws of inheritance.

† BIBLICAL REFERENCE: Numbers 26:33; 27:1–7; 36:10–12

We first encounter these five young women – the daughters of a certain Zelophehad, a member of the tribe of Manasseh – in a census that God instructed Moses to take of the whole Israelite community. (26:33) The census – conducted on the Plains of Moab, near the River Jordan on the opposite bank to the city of

Jericho – counted those aged twenty or over, and was intended to ascertain the size of each of the twelve tribes so that when they entered Canaan its territory could be divided up and allocated appropriately among them. At the time of the census, a family inheritance had to remain within the family. Women were consequently excluded from inheriting the property of their fathers, because when they married it would pass into the hands of their husband's family. After the census had been taken, Zelophehad's daughters appeared before Moses and the whole community to plead their case, saying, 'Our father died in the wilderness, and he had no sons. Why should his name be erased because of this? Since he had no sons to inherit from him, treat us like our father's kinsmen and give us some property.' Moses took their case before God, who said, 'The daughters of Zelophehad are right. You will give them a property to inherit with their father's kinsmen, and you will see that their father's inheritance is passed on to them. And you will say to the people of Israel, "If a man dies and has no sons, his inheritance will pass to his daughter."' (27:1–8) Afterwards, the heads of the Manasseh tribe went to Moses, saying, 'God has commanded you to give the inheritance of our brother Zelophehad to his daughters. But if they marry

someone from another Israelite tribe, their inheritance will pass out of our tribe. The inheritance of the other tribe will be increased, and ours will diminish. And when the jubilee for the people of Israel comes, their inheritance will pass permanently out of our tribal heritage.' Moses then addressed the people, saying, 'What you say is right. This is what God has commanded for the daughters of Zelophehad, "They may marry whoever they wish, on condition that they marry within their father's tribe, for the inheritance of the Israelite people is not to pass from one tribe to another."' The daughters of Zelophehad duly married sons of their father's fellow tribesmen, and since they married into families descended from Manasseh the son of Joseph, their inheritance remained within the tribe of their father. (36:1–12)

SHELOMITH

MEANING: PEACEFUL

The Israelite woman whose son was stoned for blasphemy.

† BIBLICAL REFERENCE: Leviticus 24:10–23

Shelomith, daughter of Dibri of the tribe of Dan, was the wife of an Egyptian for whom she bore a son. During the exodus from Egypt her son quarrelled with an Israelite, and blasphemed the name of God. He was taken before Moses, who sentenced him to be stoned to death.

Women and the law

The laws relating to women are many and complex, but the following examples should give a taste of the status of women at the time of the Exodus.

We have already seen instances where a man had more than one wife. The situation of the second and subsequent wives was governed by a law stipulating that the husband was to treat her as equal to his first wife with regard to food, clothing and marital rights. If he failed to fulfil any of these legal obligations, she was free to leave her husband. (Exodus 21:10–11) If a man seduced a virgin, he was obliged to make her his wife and pay her father the marriage present. If her father refused to permit the marriage, the seducer had to pay the father the marriage present for virgins. (*ibid.*, 22:16–17) At her time of menstruation and following the birth of a male child, a woman was deemed ritually 'unclean' for a period of seven days, and for two weeks after the birth of a female child. Births were followed by a period of 'purification' of thirty-three days for a boy child and sixty-six for a girl, after which the woman would make a sacrifice. (Leviticus 12:1–8) However, the translation of the Hebrew words *tāhôr* and *tāmē* as 'clean' and 'unclean' gives them a negative sense that is not present in the original text. Rather, ritual 'impurity' was associated with 'power rather than pollution' and 'moments … linked to the nature and power of the divine, a power that contains death and destruction as well as life and creation.' Ritual impurity was 'the result of contact with the sacred' arising from acts of procreation and care for the dead. (*Oxford Companion to the Bible*, 633) A woman was expected to be a virgin when she married for the first time. If she was found not to be, she was to be stoned to death for bringing disgrace upon her father's house. (Deuteronomy 22:20–1) If a virgin betrothed to a man was seduced or raped by another man and the incident happened in a town, both the man and woman were to be stoned to death: the woman for not crying out for help; the man for having intercourse with another man's wife. If the incident happened in the country-side, only the man was stoned because there would have been no one to come to the woman's aid. (*ibid.*, 22:23–7) One of the most significant laws was the levirate marriage law, which we encountered above in the case of Tamar and the sons of Judah (*see* Tamar). If a husband died childless, his widow could not remarry outside the family. One of his brothers had to marry her, and their first-born son was given her dead husband's name so that 'his name will not be obliterated from Israel'. If the brother refused to make her his wife, she could take him before the elders of the town and publicly humiliate him by taking off his sandal and spitting in his face, saying, 'This is what is done to a man who refuses to restore his brother's house.' (*ibid.*, 25:5–10, NJB).

2 The Historical Books
The Land of Canaan

The events related in the Pentateuch conclude with the death of Moses within sight of Canaan, but God did not allow him to enter the land because he had disobeyed him in the desert of Zin. Before Moses died, God appointed Joshua son of Nun as his successor who would lead the Israelites into Canaan. The first of the historical books, which recounts the conquest and the subsequent occupation of Canaan, bears his name. The second book – Judges – covers the period between the settlement of Canaan and the establishment of a monarchy, during which the leaders of the Israelites were known as judges. The Book of Ruth provides a quiet, idyllic interlude. The two Books of Samuel recount the early years of the monarchy, during which Saul was anointed as the first king of Israel and David united the kingdoms of Israel and Judah. The two Books of Kings recount the continuation of the monarchy under King Solomon, the latter part of whose reign saw the division of Israel into the two kingdoms of Israel and Judah. The reigns of Solomon's successors brought further decline which culminated in the conquest of the two kingdoms by the Assyrians and the Persians and the deportation of Jews to Babylon and Susa. The two Books of Chronicles, which repeat much of the material in the books already mentioned, have been omitted from this section which concludes with the story of Esther, the eponymous heroine of the Book of Esther.

RAHAB

MEANING: PROUD

The prostitute from Jericho who sheltered two Israelite spies and whose life was spared by Joshua when his army captured the city.

† BIBLICAL REFERENCE: Joshua 2; 6:16–17, 22–5; Matthew 1:5; Hebrews 11:31; James 2:25

Since Moses was not permitted to enter the Promised Land, it was left to Joshua – the young man whom God had appointed as his successor – to lead the Israelites across the Jordan after Moses had died. From his camp at Shittim, to the east of the Jordan, Joshua sent two spies to reconnoitre the land of Canaan, especially the city of Jericho. When the spies came to Jericho they found lodging in the house of Rahab, a prostitute. But news reached the king's ears that some Israelite men had entered the city to spy out the land, and so he sent word to Rahab ordering her to hand the men over, because they were spies. Rahab, who had meanwhile hidden the men under a pile of flax stalks on her roof, replied that the men had indeed been with her, but she had no idea where they came from nor where they were going. She told the king's men that they had left her so as to pass through the city gates before they were closed at nightfall; and she added that, if they hurried after them, they would overtake them. The king's men left the city as the gates were closing, and went in pursuit of the spies as far as the fords across the Jordan. When the moment of danger had passed, Rahab returned to the spies hidden on her roof and told them that the Canaanites' courage had evaporated before the reputation of the God of the Israelites. So she

struck a bargain with them, asking the spies to guarantee the safety of her and her family in return for the kindness she had shown towards them. Rahab then helped the men to escape down a rope hung from her window, for her house was built into the walls of the city. She told them to hide in the hills for three days, long enough to give those who had gone in pursuit of them time to return to the city. In return for her help, the spies gave Rahab a scarlet cord, telling her to hang it from her window and to gather all her relatives into her house so that they would not be harmed when the Israelites took the city.

After spending three days in hiding, the spies reported back to Joshua and told him what Rahab had said about the weakened morale of the Canaanites. The next morning Joshua moved the Israelites forward to the banks of the Jordan. The first to enter the water were the priests carrying the ark of the covenant: as their feet touched the river, its waters parted, allowing the people to cross over on dry land. And when all the people had crossed, the priests came out of the Jordan and its waters returned to their previous level. Before the Israelites began their siege of Jericho, all the males were circumcised and given time to heal, and the people

ABOVE
Quid pro quo: Joshua spared Rahab and members of her family
in return for helping the Israelite spies

celebrated the Passover. The siege of the city lasted seven days. On each of the first six days, seven priests blowing trumpets of rams' horns led the ark and the soldiers of Israel in a procession that passed once around the walls of the city. On the seventh day, the procession passed seven times around the city. At the end of the seventh circuit the people let out a great shout, the walls of the city fell down and the Israelites put all of its inhabitants to the sword – except for Rahab and her family, whom Joshua had ordered to be spared and who were led to the safety of the Israelite camp by the young men to whom she had given shelter during the attack.

Rahab and her family lived on in the land of Israel, and she continued to have a role in the nation's unfolding history for the genealogy of Jesus that opens the Gospel of Matthew names this former prostitute as the mother of Boaz (*see* Ruth, page 79). She was thus the great-grandmother of Jesse (father of King David) and a distant ancestor of Jesus (Matthew 1:5–6). The story of Rahab was clearly well enough known for her to be referred to by name in two of the New Testament letters. The author of the Letter to the Hebrews includes Rahab in his list of the great heroes and heroines of the past who had demonstrated a profound faith in God: Noah, Abraham, Sarah, Jacob, Moses, Rahab, Gideon, Samson, David … (Hebrews 11:31). The Letter of James pairs together the two extreme examples of Rahab and Abraham – the prostitute and the 'friend of God' – to illustrate the proposition that 'faith without works is dead' (James 2:25–6). In Psalms 87 and 89, the name Rahab (meaning 'Proud') is employed as a poetical name for Egypt.

Women from the time of the judges

The Book of Judges relates how the Israelites repeatedly 'played the harlot', or 'did evil in the sight of God'. That is, they turned away from God to worship the indigenous Canaanite gods.

As their punishment for this, they were placed in the hands of their enemies where they remained until their suffering prompted them to turn to God for help. It was at such times that a leader or 'judge' arose from within the community of Israel to deliver the people from their oppressors and return them to the Way of the Lord. When a judge died, the people returned to their former ways until another judge emerged from among them. The judges of Israel include one woman, Deborah (*see below*).

ACHSAH

MEANING: ADORNED

The young woman who was offered as a prize to the man who captured a town.

† BIBLICAL REFERENCE: Joshua 15:16–19 (repeated in Judges 1:12–15); 1 Chronicles 2:49

Achsah was the daughter of Caleb, a member of the tribe of Judah. Following the death of Joshua, Caleb was one of the leaders in the campaign against the Canaanites. After a succession of victories, he marched on the town of Debir, formerly known as Kiriath-Sepher. He promised his daughter Achsah in marriage to whoever captured the town, and it was captured by Othniel, younger son of Caleb's brother Kenaz. Either she or her husband asked Caleb to give her some arable land as a dowry, but then Achsah went back to her father and asked him for more, saying, 'Since you have given me some land in the Negeb, give me some springs of water too.' Caleb granted her request and gave her the upper and lower springs. (Joshua, 15:15–19) Achsah's husband Othniel was the first to be appointed a 'judge of Israel'. The fourth judge was Deborah.

DEBORAH

MEANING: BEE

A prophetess and the only woman to become a judge of Israel, Deborah inspired a famous victory over the Canaanite army.

† BIBLICAL REFERENCE: Judges 4:4–10, 14; 5:1–15

Deborah holds a unique place among Israelite women and in the annals of Israel's history: she was not only a prophetess and the only woman judge (or ruler) of Israel, she was also a military leader. Deborah became judge at a time when the Israelites had been oppressed by Jabin, Canaanite ruler of Hazor, for twenty years, and she delivered justice from her seat beneath a palm tree known as Deborah's Palm between Ramah and Bethel

in the hill country of Ephraim. She sent for the Israelite general Barak, son of Abinoam from Kedesh in Naphtali, and encouraged him to send his forces against those of Sisera, commander of the Canaanite army, saying to him, 'God has commanded, "Go! March to Mount Tabor, and there gather ten thousand men from the tribes of Naphtali and Zebulun. I will lure Sisera, commander of Jabin's army, into an encounter with you by the river Kishon, and I will deliver him into your hands."' Barak replied, 'If you come with me, I will go; if you do not come with me, I will not go, for I do not know how to prophesy the day when the Lord will grant me success.' Deborah agreed to go

ABOVE
Woman of many talents: Deborah was a prophetess, a judge and a military leader. She is remembered in the Song of Deborah

Mount Tabor, he mustered his entire army and nine hundred chariots. It was then that Deborah said to Barak, 'Arise! For today is the day that the Lord has delivered Sisera into your hands. Is God himself not leading you into battle?' As Barak charged down from Mount Tabor with ten thousand men behind him, God put to rout Sisera's entire army and his chariots. Sisera himself jumped down from his chariot and fled on foot. Meanwhile Barak pursued the retreating chariots and foot soldiers, and the Israelites put Sisera's entire army to the sword. Not a man was spared. The victory over Sisera and Jabin, ruler of Hazor, is celebrated in the so-called 'Song of Deborah' (5:1–31) – a song *about* her, not by her – one of the oldest remaining examples of Hebrew poetry. As well as praising Deborah and proclaiming her a 'mother of Israel', the song chastises those Israelite tribes that did not send men to join Barak's army. The song also sings the praises of another woman – Jael – for her part in Sisera's demise. It concludes with the information that the country enjoyed forty years of peace following the victory over Sisera and Jabin's army – that is to say, forty years before the Israelites again 'did what was evil in the eyes of God', as a result of which they were again handed over to their enemies.

with Barak, but she forewarned him, 'This road will not lead you to glory, for God will deliver Sisera into a woman's hands.' So saying, she arose and went with Barak to Kedesh, from where he summoned the ten thousand men from Naphtali and Zebulun. (4:1–10)

When Sisera was informed that Barak had encamped on

JAEL

MEANING: GOAT

The woman who used a tent-peg to murder Sisera, the defeated Canaanite general.

† BIBLICAL REFERENCE: Judges 4:17–22; 5:24–7

Jael was married to Heber, a member of the nomadic Kenites, who had left his tribe and pitched his tents near Kedesh. After his defeat at the battle of Kedesh, Sisera fled on foot and sought refuge at Heber's encampment because the Kenites were at peace with Sisera's overlord, Jabin the ruler of Hazor. Jael came out to meet Sisera and, telling him there was nothing to fear, offered him shelter in her tent, and covered him with a rug. When he asked her for a little water to drink because he was thirsty, she gave him some milk and covered him up again. Sisera then told Jael to stand at the entrance to the tent, and instructed her that if anyone came and asked her if a man was in the tent she was to say 'No'. But Jael picked up a tent-peg and mallet, and crept silently back to Sisera, who had fallen asleep from exhaustion. Placing the tent-peg on the sleeping man's temple, she drove it right through his skull into the ground. When Barak arrived in pursuit of Sisera, Jael went out to meet him, and said to him, 'Come with me, and I will show you the man you are looking for.' Barak followed her

ABOVE
A treacherous hostess: Jael offered Sisera shelter in her tent
and then drove a tent peg through his skull

into her tent, and there saw Sisera lying dead with the tent-peg through his temple. (4:17–22) As Deborah had prophesied, God had delivered Sisera into a woman's hands. The Song of Deborah praises Jael for her act in a terse language that emphasizes the ignominious end of this general who had led an army of thousands of men. (5:26–7) And yet Jael broke the ancient rule of hospitality, according to which a host became responsible for the safety of his or her guest(s). It was also considered the height of ignominy for a soldier to be killed by a woman (*see below, The woman of Thebez*).

THE MOTHER OF SISERA

The mother who waited in vain for her son to return from war.

† BIBLICAL REFERENCE: Judges 5:28–30

From the brutal murder of Sisera, the Song of Deborah moves to a poignant portrayal of Sisera's mother waiting at home for her son to return. Evoking the heart-felt concern that a mother of any age might feel for her child, the Song describes her at her window, watching out for her son and listening out for the sound of his chariot and horses, asking herself aloud, 'Why is he so long in coming home? What can be holding him up?' A wise maid gives her an answer that the mother gladly picks up and

repeats, 'They are collecting up the spoils of war and sharing them out: a girl or two for each man; dyed and embroidered stuff for Sisera, an embroidered scarf for me.'

The Song of Deborah concludes with the words 'and the country had peace for forty years.' But at the end of this time the Israelites once again 'did what was evil in God's eyes', and the cycle of punishment and salvation recommenced.

THE WIVES AND CONCUBINE OF GIDEON

The mothers of Gideon's seventy-one sons.

† BIBLICAL REFERENCE: Judges 8:30–1

The degree to which it was considered humiliating for a soldier to be killed by a woman is illustrated by the story of Gideon's son Abimelech. Gideon,

who was another of the military leaders to rescue the Israelites from the hands of their enemies and be appointed judge of Israel, is said to have had many wives. Between them they gave him seventy sons, but he also had a son by an unnamed concubine from Shechem. He named the concubine's son Abimelech. (8:30–2) When Gideon died, the people of Israel turned away from God and worshipped Baal. (8:33–34)

THE WOMAN OF THEBEZ

How Abimelech avoided the shame of being killed by a woman.

† BIBLICAL REFERENCE: Judges 9:53

After Gideon's death, Abimelech confronted his seventy half-brothers in his father's house at Ophrah and killed them all, except for one who escaped. Abimelech was then appointed

ABOVE

Gruesome death: as Deborah had prophesied, God had delivered Sisera into a woman's hands

ruler of Israel, but after three years the people rebelled against him. A sequence of bloody battles ensued in the course of which Abimelech gained the upper hand and destroyed the cities of his enemies. (9:5–50) When he captured the city of Thebez, the inhabitants took refuge in a fortified tower within the city walls. Having barricaded themselves in, they went up onto the roof. Abimelech approached the door of the tower and was about to set fire to it when a woman threw down a millstone that hit him on the head, cracking open his skull. Abimelech instantly called his armour-bearer to his side, and said, 'Draw your sword and kill me, so that it can not be said of me, "A woman killed him."' When the Israelites saw what had happened, they all returned to their homes. (9:50–5)

THE DAUGHTER OF JEPHTHAH

How a rash promise cost Jephthah the life of his beloved daughter.

† BIBLICAL REFERENCE: Judges 11:30–40

The story of Jephthah's daughter is set in a time when the Israelites had once again provoked God's anger by worshipping pagan gods. God punished them by handing them over to the Ammonites, who 'crushed and oppressed … all the people of

Israel who were beyond the Jordan in Gilead, the land of the Amorites.' The Ammonites also crossed the Jordan and fought against the tribes of Judah, Benjamin and Ephraim (10:8–9). The punishment meted out to them caused the Israelites to repent, put away their pagan idols, and pray to God to deliver them from their oppressor. But to ensure their deliverance they

needed a competent military leader, so the elders of Gilead approached a certain Jephthah who lived in the land of Tob. Now Jephthah was the son of a prostitute, but his father's wife had given birth to other sons who, when they were grown up, had turned Jephthah out and denied him any rights of inheritance. He fled to the land of Tob, where he led a gang of raiders,

 ABOVE
The last dance: before she was sacrificed by her father, Jephthah's daughter withdrew into the mountains with her companions

and it was here that the elders of Gilead came to him and asked him to lead them against the Ammonites. Before he engaged the Ammonites in battle, Jephthah made a vow to God, saying, 'If you deliver the Ammonites into my hands, then whoever comes out of my house to greet me on my victorious return will be dedicated to you, and I will offer them up as a burnt offering.' Jephthah duly defeated the Ammonites, but when he returned home the first person to come out of his house to greet him was his daughter, his only child. On seeing her, he tore at his garments because of the vow he had made to God. When Jephthah explained to his daughter the cause of his grief, she willingly accepted her fate, but on one condition: he first allow her to go into the mountains for two months with her companions to mourn the fact that she would die unmarried and childless. It later became the custom for the daughters of Israel to go into the mountains annually for four days to lament the fate of Jephthah's daughter. Her father judged Israel for six years.

Opinions differ as to whether Jephthah actually sacrificed his daughter or not, since human sacrifice was anathema to the Hebrew people. Some scholars insist the text clearly indicates that he did so, while others suggest that he made a burnt offering of an animal and that he 'sacrificed' his daughter by dedicating her to God, meaning that she spent the rest of her life as a virgin in the service of the temple. (Lockyer, 184) Yet others suggest the story of Jephthah's daughter was devised to explain the annual custom, referred to at the end of chapter 11 in Judges, whereby the daughters of Israel withdrew into the mountains for four days. It has even been suggested that 'there was a pagan cult … which was adopted by the Israelite women [and] when the origins of these rites had been forgotten, the story was invented to

ABOVE
A rash promise: Jephthah's daughter greeted her father, unaware of his vow to sacrifice the first person who emerged from his house

explain them.' (*Literary Guide to the Bible*, 17)

THE WIFE OF MANOAH

The barren woman who became the mother of Samson.

† BIBLICAL REFERENCE: Judges 13:2–24; 14:2–4, 9

When the people of Israel again 'did what was evil in God's eyes', God handed them over to the Philistines. At this time an angel appeared to the wife of a certain Manoah of Zorah, of the Danite tribe, and told her that although she had remained barren for many years she would conceive and give birth to a son. 'From now on,' said the angel, 'you are to drink no wine or strong drink, and eat nothing unclean. No razor is to shave your son's head, for he is to be a Nazirite [one who is consecrated to God] from birth, and he will begin to deliver the Israelites out of the hands of the Philistines.' The woman repeated to her husband what the angel had said, and her husband pleaded with God to instruct them in how to bring up their child. The angel appeared again, and gave instructions to both the woman and her husband. When her son was born she named him Samson. (13:2–24) The few remaining references to Manoah's wife are to be found in the story of Samson's first wife, the woman of Timnah.

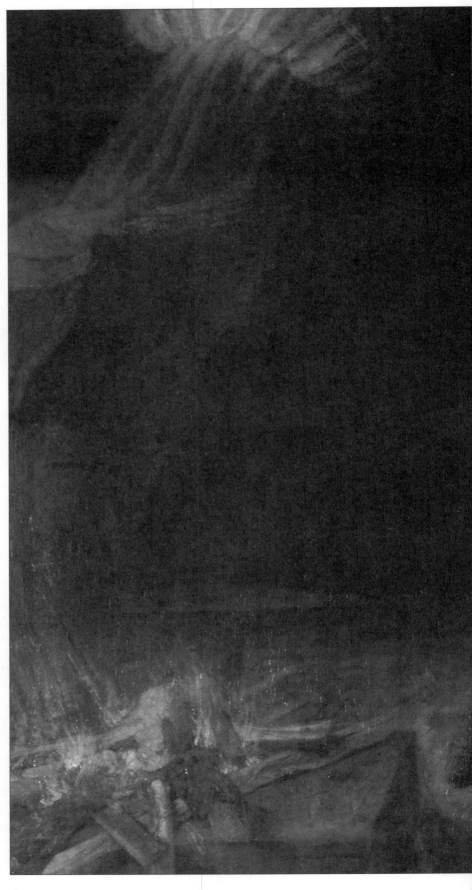

ABOVE
Divine guidance: Manoah and his wife prayed to God for instructions on how to bring up Samson

THE WOMAN OF TIMNAH

The Philistine girl who married Samson and tricked him into telling her the answer to a riddle.

† BIBLICAL REFERENCE: Judges 14:1–15:6

When Samson had grown up he went into Timnah, where he saw a Philistine girl who attracted him. He went home and told his mother and father about her, saying that he wanted her to be his wife, but they said, 'Why do you have to take a wife from among these uncircumcised Philistines? Is there not a woman among our own people?' Samson insisted, 'Get this woman for me; she is the one I want.' His mother and father were unaware that all this came from God, who was seeking to promote a dispute with the Philistines, since at that time they had Israel in their power. Samson went back to Timnah, and as he approached the vineyards a young lion came roaring at him. The Spirit of God filled Samson and he tore the lion to pieces with his bare hands, but he did not tell his mother or father what he had done. He continued to Timnah and talked with the woman, and he grew fond of her. A few days later, he went back to Timnah to make the woman his wife, and on the way he made a small detour to see the carcass of the lion he had killed. To his surprise the lion's body had become home to

a swarm of bees, and was filled with honey. He scraped out the honey with his hands and ate it as he went on his way. When he came back to his mother and father, he gave them some of the honey to eat but did not tell them about the lion's carcass. Samson's father went down to the woman of Timnah and, according to the custom for young men, Samson gave a feast to celebrate his marriage. The Philistines brought him thirty companions, whom Samson challenged with a riddle. If they were able to answer it during the seven days of the wedding feast, he would give them thirty linen robes and thirty festal robes; if they could not, then they had to give the same number of robes to him. The men accepted the challenge, and Samson gave them the riddle to solve, 'Out of the eater came something that is eaten; out of the strong came something sweet.' Three days passed during which they were unable to solve the riddle. On the fourth day they said to Samson's wife, 'Were we invited here to be robbed? Persuade your husband to explain the riddle, or we shall burn you alive with all your father's house.' She went to Samson and burst into tears, saying, 'You must hate me and not really love me at all, because you have set my compatriots a riddle and not told me the answer.' He replied, 'I have not told even my father or mother, so

why would I tell you?' She cried on his shoulder for the remaining days of the seven-day-long feast. She was so persistent that on the seventh day he told her the answer, and she told her compatriots. Before the sun set on the seventh day, the Philistine men went to Samson and said, 'What is sweeter than honey? What is stronger than a lion?' Samson riposted, 'If you had not ploughed with my heifer, you would not have solved my riddle!' The Spirit of God then took hold of Samson, and he went down to the Philistine city of Ashkelon where he killed thirty men, took their garments, and gave the festal garments to the men who had solved his riddle. He was in such a rage that he then went back to his father's house, and his wife of a few days was given to the companion who had served as Samson's best man. Shortly afterwards at wheat-harvest time, Samson visited his wife and would have slept with her but her father would not let him enter her bedroom. 'I thought you hated her,' said her father, 'so I gave her to your companion. Her younger sister is even better looking than her. Have her instead.' Samson now determined to vent his anger on the Philistines, so he caught three hundred foxes, set fire to their tails and then turned them loose in the Philistines' wheat fields where they set on fire both the sheaves and the standing wheat, and the vines and olive groves as well. The Philistines asked who had done this, and were told, 'Samson, the Timnite's son-in-law, because the Timnite took his wife and gave her to his companion instead.' On hearing this, the Philistines went and burned alive the woman of Timnah, her father and her father's house. And Samson swore to them that he would not rest until he had had his revenge. He wreaked havoc among the Philistines, killing a thousand of them single-handedly with the jawbone of an ass, and then made his way to Gaza. (14:1–16:1)

The woman of Timnah in art

Images of the woman of Timnah are rare, but one example of note is Rembrandt's *Samson Telling His Wedding Guests a Riddle* (1638) in the Gemäldegalerie, Dresden. The wedding feast is dominated by the sumptuously dressed central figure of Samson's new bride, who seems to be ignored by her husband as he leans to one side to tell his guests the riddle whose answer she will eventually squeeze out of him.

THE PROSTITUTE FROM GAZA

The prostitute who was visited by Samson.

† BIBLICAL REFERENCE: Judges 16:1–3

While Samson was in Gaza he saw a prostitute, and he went into her house and slept with her. When the Gazites learned that Samson was in their midst, they set a trap for him and lay in wait all night at the city's gate, saying, 'Wait until daybreak, then we will kill him.' But Samson stayed in bed with the woman only until midnight, then he arose, took hold of the city gates and gateposts, tore them out of the ground and, putting them over his shoulder, carried them off.

DELILAH

MEANING: DESIRED, DELICATE OR LANGUISHING

The lover who tricked Samson into revealing the secret source of his strength.

† BIBLICAL REFERENCE: Judges 16:4–21

Delilah was the woman with whom Samson fell in love after his escapade with the prostitute in Gaza. 'Desired' is an appropriate name for her, since Samson's desire for her proved to be his undoing, whereas the alternative meanings of her name – 'Feeble' or 'Delicate' – bring a touch of irony to her story, for her notoriety is solely due to her having brought about the downfall of the strong man of Israel. After Delilah had become Samson's lover, the Philistine leaders went to her and asked her to persuade him to reveal the secret of his great strength, and how they could overpower him, so that they might bind him and

make him their prisoner. In return they would each give her 1,100 silver shekels. So Delilah asked Samson to tell her where his great strength came from, and what was needed to tie him up and render him powerless. The first few times she asked him, Samson gave her false answers, and he easily broke his bonds before the Philistine men whom Delilah had hidden in an antechamber could emerge from their hiding-place. Then Delilah said to him, 'How can you say you love me, when I am clearly not in your heart. Three times now you have had your fun with me and avoided telling me the source of your great strength.' And she continued to pester him day after day until, grown sick and tired of her nagging, he finally told her the truth, saying, 'A razor has not touched my head since the day I was born, for I became a Nazirite dedicated to God while still in my mother's womb. If my head were to be shaved, my strength would leave me and I would become as weak as any other man.' Aware that Samson had now told her the truth, Delilah sent for the Philistines. Having lulled Samson to sleep, his head in her lap, she called out to one of the hidden Philistines who emerged and shaved Samson's head, and the sleeping man's strength left him. Then Delilah cried out, 'The Philistines are upon you,

 ABOVE
A lover's treachery: Delilah betrayed the slumbering Samson to the Philistines.
When they cut off his hair, his strength left him

Samson!' He awoke from his sleep, thinking to himself, 'I shall break free of these bonds as before, and shake myself free.' But he did not know that God had left him, and the Philistines seized him, gouged out his eyes, and took him to Gaza. There they shackled him in chains and put him in prison. To celebrate his capture, the Philistines offered a great sacrifice to their god Dagon, and the people called for Samson to be brought out so that he could amuse them. Now the building they were in was crowded with people, including all the leaders of the Philistines. Samson told the small boy who was serving as his guide to lead him to the building's two central pillars, and when he had taken hold of the pillars Samson called out to God, begging God to remember him and to give him his strength one last time. Then Samson shouted, 'Let me die with the Philistines!' And he heaved on the pillars and the building collapsed, killing all the Philistines and Samson with them. (16:4–30) He had judged Israel for twenty years when he died.

Delilah in art

Although some images exist of Delilah on her own, she is more usually depicted with Samson lying beside her in a drunken stupor. The Philistines that Delilah hid in her room are shown either still in hiding or, having emerged from their hiding-place, they are cutting off his hair. The popularity of the story of Samson and Delilah has been captured in other art forms too – for example, Saint-Saëns' opera *Samson et Dalila,* Handel's oratorio *Samson* and Milton's *Samson Agonistes.*

THE MOTHER OF MICAH

The simple woman who worshipped God and yet broke his commandments.

† BIBLICAL REFERENCE: Judges 17:1–7

The story of Micah the Ephraimite and his mother is full of irony and contradiction. When Micah's mother had 1,100 silver shekels stolen from her, she cursed the thief in front of her son; but her son later confessed to her that he was the thief, and she blessed him. When Micah returned the money to her, she announced that she was dedicating the money to God on her son's behalf and promptly gave 200 shekels to a silversmith who made her two idols – one carved, the other cast – which were placed in Micah's house. (Micah and his mother had thus broken two of the Ten Commandments: 'Thou shalt not steal' and 'Thou shalt not make any graven image.') Micah had a shrine in his house and had made himself some priestly garments and idols. He had also installed one of his sons as his priest. The story of Micah and his mother concludes with the words, 'Thus it was in the days before Israel had a king, when everyone did as they thought best.'

THE LEVITE'S CONCUBINE

The woman who died from severe sexual abuse and whose husband found a gruesome way to avenge her death.

† BIBLICAL REFERENCE: Judges 19:1–20:6

The story of the Levite's concubine is prefaced with a reminder that 'in those days … there was no king in Israel,' and the extreme physical abuse to which the woman is subjected unleashes a sequence of brutal events that fills the concluding chapters of the Book of Judges, thus bringing to a violent close the pre-monarchical phase of Israelite history. Because of its length, parts of the following story have been abridged.

A certain Levite from the hill country of Ephraim took as a concubine (or second wife) a young woman from Bethlehem in Judah. However, the woman left him in a fit of pique and went back to her father's house. She had been there for four months when her husband came after her with a servant and two donkeys, hoping to persuade her to come back with him. When he arrived

ABOVE
A rude awakening: in the morning the Levite found the badly abused body of his dead concubine lying across the threshold

in Bethlehem, the Levite was greeted warmly by his father-in-law, who made him stay for three days. On the morning of the fourth day, the Levite and his concubine got up early and were preparing to leave when the girl's father invited them to have something to eat to fortify themselves for their journey. So they sat down and ate and drank, and then the girl's father said to his son-in-law, 'Spend the night here and enjoy yourself.' When he got up to leave, his father-in-law persisted until the young man agreed to stay another night. The same thing happened on the morning of the fifth day. The young man again rose early with the intention of setting out for Ephraim, but his father-in-law once again urged him to fortify himself for the journey, and to postpone his departure until the heat of the day had passed. So the couple stayed until the sun began to go down. The two men then ate a meal together, and when the Levite got up to leave his father-in-law said to him, 'Look, it is almost evening. Stay the night, and you can set off for home early in the morning.' But he refused to spend the night, and taking his concubine, his two asses and his servant, he went on his way. By the time they reached Jebus (Jerusalem), the daylight was fading fast. The servant said to his master, 'Let us turn off here and spend the night in this Jebusite town.' But his master replied, 'We will not turn off into a foreign town, whose inhabitants are not Israelites. We will go on to Gibeah.' The sun was setting as they approached Gibeah in the land of the tribe of Benjamin, and so they turned off the road to spend the night there. Once he was in the town, the Levite sat in the central square, but no one offered them accommodation for the night. Eventually an old man came by, on his way home from working in the fields. Like the Levite, he was from the hill country of Ephraim. He asked the young man where he was from and where he was going, to which the Levite replied that they were on their way from Bethlehem to his home in the hill country of Ephraim. 'Well,' said the old man, 'you cannot spend the night in the square.' And he took them into his house. Later that evening, some local ruffians besieged the old man's house, beating on the door, and shouting out to the old man to bring out the man who had gone into his house so that they might have intercourse with him. The old man went out to them, saying, 'No, my brothers, you cannot do such a wicked thing. Since this man is my guest, do not do this to him. Take my daughter instead. She is still a virgin. I will bring her out, and you can do with her as you wish, but do not commit such an act against this man.' But the men would not listen to him. So the Levite took hold of his concubine, and gave her to the men. They raped her and sexually abused her all night long, and did not let her go until dawn was breaking. The woman dragged herself back to the old man's house, where she collapsed on the threshold and lay until it was fully light. When her husband got up and opened the door to continue his journey, he found her lying on the threshold. 'Come on! Get up!' he said, 'We must be on our way.' When she didn't answer, he loaded her on to his donkey and left Gibeah to continue his journey to Ephraim. (19:1–28)

On arriving home the Levite took a knife, cut up his concubine's abused body into twelve pieces and sent them throughout Israel. Those to whom they were sent said, 'Nothing like this has ever happened or been seen from the day the Israelites came out of Egypt until today.' Then the whole community of Israel and their tribal leaders gathered at Mizpah in the presence of God, and among them were 400,000 trained foot soldiers. (News of the Israelites' assembly reached the ears of the Benjaminites.) The people asked the Levite to tell them how the crime had been committed, and when he had finished his account of what the men of Gibeah had done to his concubine, he said, 'I sent her throughout the entire country inherited by Israel because these men committed a shameful and depraved crime in Israel. Now, people of Israel, it is for you to discuss what is to be done.' The people were unanimous: they would not go home until they had dealt with the people of Gibeah in a manner that befitted their crime. Having planned their military campaign against the town of Gibeah, the tribes of Israel then sent messengers to the tribe of Benjamin, asking them to surrender the men who had committed the crime so that they could be put to death. The evil that had arisen within Israel would thus be eradicated. But the Benjaminites refused to listen to their fellow Israelites. Instead, they left their towns and gathered at Gibeah to do battle with the people of Israel. On the

 ABOVE
Heavy burden: the Levite loaded his wife upon a donkey and left Gibeah for Ephraim

first day, the Benjaminites defeated the Israelites and massacred 22,000 of them. On the second day, the Benjaminites defeated the Israelites again, killing 18,000 of them. On the third day, the Israelites set an ambush for the Benjaminite forces. In the ensuing rout, 25,000 Benjaminites were killed. But six hundred men escaped into the desert, to the rock of Rimmon, and remained there for four months. Meanwhile, the Israelites put the remaining Benjaminites to the sword – people, livestock and everything that moved – and set fire to all their towns. (19:29–20:48)

THE DAUGHTERS OF JABESH

The young women of Jabesh who were captured and given as wives to the men of the tribe of Benjamin.

† BIBLICAL REFERENCE: Judges 21:12–14

While they were assembled at Mizpah, the Israelites had sworn an oath that none of them would give their daughters in marriage into the tribe of Benjamin. After they had defeated the Benjaminites at Gibeah the Israelites went to Bethel, where they wept bitterly and lamented to God, saying, 'How is it that today one of the tribes of Israel is missing?' They began to feel sorry for the tribe of Benjamin, which had been cut off from Israel, and wondered how they might obtain wives for the few remaining Benjaminites since they had sworn an oath not to give them any of their own daughters in marriage. So they asked among themselves, 'Which of the tribes of Israel did not come to the assembly at Mizpah?' When they had ascertained that no one from Jabesh in the land of Gilead had been present, they sent 12,000 soldiers to Jabesh with the order to slaughter all its inhabitants – men, women and children – but to spare the lives of any virgins. This the soldiers did, and they found four hundred virgins and brought them to the encampment at Shiloh in the land of

 ABOVE
Forced into marriage: the 400 virgins who survived the slaughter at Jabesh were given to the Benjaminites as wives

Canaan. The Israelites then sent word to the six hundred Benjaminites who were at the rock of Rimmon, offering to make peace with them. The Benjaminites returned home and were given the daughters of Jabesh whose lives had been spared, but there were not enough of them for each man to have a wife. (21:1–14)

THE DAUGHTERS OF SHILOH

The young women of Shiloh who were captured and given as wives to the men of the tribe of Benjamin.

† BIBLICAL REFERENCE: Judges 21:21–3

The people again felt sorry for Benjamin, because God had made a gap in the twelve tribes of Israel. The elders of the community wondered what they could do to provide wives for those who were left, since the Benjaminite women had been slaughtered. And they said, 'We must ensure the survival of Benjamin so that a tribe of Israel is not lost. Yet we cannot give them our own daughters to be their wives. However, there is the annual feast of God at Shiloh.' So they told the Benjaminites to go to Shiloh and lie in wait in the vineyards. When the daughters of Shiloh came out to dance, they were to emerge from their hiding-place, seize a woman each and carry them off to Benjaminite territory. And the Benjaminites did this, and took wives for themselves from among the dancers they carried off.

They returned to the land they had inherited, and rebuilt the towns and settled in them. The people of Israel then went their separate ways, each returning to their tribe and clan, and to the land they had inherited.

This episode concludes with the same words that brought the story of Micah's mother (*see above*) to an end: 'Thus it was in the days when there was no king in Israel: everyone did what seemed right in his own eyes.' (21:15–25)

NAOMI, RUTH AND ORPAH

MEANING: NAOMI, PLEASANT; RUTH, FRIEND; ORPAH, FAWN OR STUBBORN

How Ruth, a young widow, went to Bethlehem with her mother-in-law and won the heart of the wealthy Boaz.

† BIBLICAL REFERENCE: Ruth

Although the story of Ruth is set in the same pre-monarchical period as the Book of Judges, its idyllic, romantic mood is in stark contrast to the bloodthirsty events that bring the Book of Judges to a close. Moreover, whereas Judges displays an open hostility to non-Israelites, the Book of Ruth displays a certain sympathy towards them, especially those who – like Ruth – place themselves under the protection of God.

A famine struck the land in the days when Israel was governed by judges, and so Elimelech, an Ephrathite from Bethlehem in Judah, went to stay in the land of Moab, taking with him his wife Naomi and his two sons, Mahlon and Chilion. They made their home in Moab, but Elimelech

ABOVE
On the road to Bethlehem: when Naomi tried to persuade her daughters-in-law
to return to their own homes, Ruth insisted on travelling on with her

died, leaving Naomi alone with her two sons. These took as their wives two Moabite women – Ruth and Orpah – but after about ten years Mahlon and Chilion also died. Bereft of her husband and sons, Naomi decided to return to her homeland with her daughters-in-law for she had heard that the famine was at an end. The three women set off for Judah, but along the way Naomi told her daughters-in-law to return to their family homes. At first they refused, but Naomi was so insistent that eventually Orpah kissed her mother-in-law and returned to her own people. However, Ruth stayed with her, saying, 'Do not beg me to leave you or to stop following you; for wherever you go, I will go; wherever you dwell, I will dwell. Your people will be my people, and your God will be my God. Where you die, I will die and there I will be buried. May God punish me should anything other than death part me from you.' Naomi saw how determined Ruth was to go with her, and so she said no more. The two women travelled on to Bethlehem, and when they arrived there the townswomen said, 'Is this Naomi?' And she replied, 'Do not call me Naomi ('My joy'), call me Mara ('Bitter'), for the Almighty has dealt bitterly with me. I went away full, and God has returned me empty.' (1:1–21)

Naomi and Ruth arrived in Bethlehem as the barley harvest was beginning, and Ruth said to Naomi, 'Let me go into the fields and glean ears of barley in the wake of a man who may look favourably upon me.' And Ruth went to the field to glean behind the reapers, and she was led to a part of the field that belonged to a certain Boaz, a wealthy relative of Naomi's husband. It so happened that Boaz came out to the field, and when he saw Ruth he asked the servant in charge of the reapers, 'Who does that young woman belong to?' The servant replied, 'She is the Moabite girl who came back with Naomi from the land of Moab. She asked me if she could follow the reapers and pick up the grain that fell from the sheaves, and she has been gleaning here since early this morning with hardly a rest.' Then Boaz turned to Ruth, and said, 'Listen, my daughter, do not leave this field or go gleaning in any other, and stay close to my young women. Work in whichever part of the field they are working in. I have instructed my men not to hinder you. And when you are thirsty, drink from the pitchers my servants have filled.' Ruth prostrated herself at Boaz's feet, and said, 'How have I found favour in your eyes, for I am a foreigner?' Boaz replied, 'I have heard about everything you have done for your mother-in-law

since the death of your husband, and how you left your mother and father and the country of your birth to come and live among a people about whom you knew nothing. May God repay you for what you have done, and may you be richly rewarded by God under whose wings you have come to take refuge!' And Ruth said, 'My lord, you are most generous. You have given me comfort, even though I am not one of your servants.' When the workers stopped to eat, Ruth sat with the reapers and Boaz offered her food and drink. After she had gone back to her gleaning, Boaz instructed his reapers not to interfere with her, and to let her glean amongst the sheaves. They were also to let full ears of grain fall on the ground for her to pick up. By evening, Ruth had gleaned a full bushel of barley. She returned to Bethlehem and showed Naomi what she had gleaned, and also gave her the food she had saved. Her mother-in-law asked her where she had been working, and blessed the man who had shown her such kindness. When Ruth told her the man's name was Boaz, Naomi informed her that he was one of their closest relatives. Ruth continued, and told Naomi that Boaz had instructed her to stay close to his servants until the harvest was over. And Ruth kept close to Boaz's women servants, and gleaned until the barley and

ABOVE
Virtue rewarded: Boaz ordered his men t
to let her glean among the sheaves of bar

uth alone,

wheat harvests were at an end. (1:1–2:23)

Meanwhile, Ruth continued to live with her mother-in-law. One day Naomi said to her, 'Daughter, should I not endeavour to seek a home for you and see you happily settled? Now is it not true that Boaz, the man with whose women you were working, is our relation? Tonight he is winnowing barley on the threshing-floor. So wash and perfume yourself, and put on your best robe, and go there. Don't let him see you while he is having his meal. But when he lies down, make a note of where he lies, remove the cover from his feet, and then lie down. He will tell you what to do.' Ruth went to the threshing-floor and did exactly as her mother-in-law had told her. When Boaz awoke in the middle of the night, he was shocked to find a woman lying at his feet. 'Who are you?' he asked. She replied, 'I am Ruth, your maidservant. Spread your cloak over me and redeem me, for I am your next of kin.' (In asking Boaz to spread his cloak over her, Ruth was effectively asking him to take her as his wife and thus redeem her according to the levirate marriage law by ensuring the continuation of her deceased husband's name and family line (*see* Women and the law, page 58). Boaz said, 'May God bless you, daughter, for this act of devotion and loyalty is more generous than your first in that you have not

sought to marry a younger man. But although it is true that I am your close relative, you have a closer relative than me. Stay here for the rest of tonight. In the morning we will see if he wishes to exercise his right of redemption over you. If he does, then so be it. If he doesn't, then I swear by God that I shall. Now lie down until morning.' So Ruth lay at Boaz's feet until morning, but got up before it was sufficiently light for her to be recognized. Before she left, Boaz asked her to spread out her cloak, and he poured six measures of barley into it. He then helped her up with it, and she went back to the town. When Ruth came home, her mother-in-law asked her how she had got on. Ruth told her what Boaz had done, then she handed over to her the six measures of barley, saying, 'The man said, "You must not go back to your mother-in-law empty-handed."' Naomi said, 'You must now wait, my daughter, until you see how this matter is resolved, and I am sure he will not rest until he settles this matter today.' Meanwhile, Boaz went to the gates of the town and sat down. When the relative of whom he had spoken came by, Boaz called him over and invited him to sit down. Then he called over ten of the town's elders, and invited them to sit down also. Turning to the relative, Boaz told him that Naomi was selling the piece of land that belonged to Elimelech,

their relative. He then asked the man if he wanted to use his right of redemption to buy the land in front of witnesses. If he did not wish to exercise this right, he was to say so. The man declared that he wished to redeem the land. 'If you buy the land,' said Boaz, 'you should know that you also take possession of Ruth, the Moabitess, wife of the deceased man, so that his name is continued through his inheritance.' When he heard this, the man replied, 'I cannot redeem the land for myself without jeopardizing my own inheritance. Take the right of redemption and exercise it for yourself.' Boaz then asked the ten elders to bear witness that he had acquired everything that had previously belonged to Elimelech, and to Elimelech's sons Mahlon and Chilion, and that he also acquired Mahlon's widow, Ruth the Moabitess, so as to perpetuate the dead man's name through his inheritance. The elders offered their blessing, and asked that God might make Ruth like Rachel and Leah, who together had built up the house of Israel, and that their family might be like the family of Perez, the son Tamar bore Judah. Ruth became Boaz's wife, and she conceived and gave birth to a son who was nursed by his grandmother Naomi. The local women named him Obed (meaning 'Encourages'), and Obed became the father of Jesse, who was the father of David. (3:1–4:17)

Ruth in art

Since Ruth was the great-grandmother of David, she is considered to have been an ancestor of Jesus and so is often represented in Christian art. Sometimes she is depicted with her mother-in-law Naomi, but more usually she is shown gleaning in Boaz's fields with the figure of Boaz nearby. A loosely related theme is the *Tree of Jesse*, which was particularly popular in the European Middle Ages and is often found in stained-glass windows or decorating the walls of medieval churches. This image derives from a prophecy made by Isaiah concerning Ruth's grandson Jesse, 'There shall come forth a shoot out of the stem of Jesse, and a new stem shall grow from his roots. And the Spirit of the Lord shall rest upon him.' (Isaiah 11:1) For Christians, the 'new stem' referred to here is Ruth's distant descendant, Jesus the Messiah.

PENINNAH

Meaning: Coral or Pearl

The mother who taunted her barren rival.

† BIBLICAL REFERENCE: 1 Samuel 1:2–4

Peninnah was one of the two wives of Elkanah, an Ephraimite from Ramah. She was also the mother of his children, whereas his other wife – Hannah – remained barren. Every year, Elkanah went with his children and two wives to the shrine at Shiloh to make a sacrifice. Afterwards, when he shared the sacrifice out among his family, he would give portions to Peninnah and her sons and daughters; but to Hannah he gave only one portion – even though he loved her more than his other wife – because she had no children. And every year when they went up to Shiloh, Peninnah taunted Hannah because she remained barren. This is the biblical author's last reference to Peninnah, for the focus of his story now shifts to Hannah.

HANNAH

Meaning: Grace

The barren woman who vowed that if God graced her with a son she would give her son back to him, and who named her God-given son Samuel

† BIBLICAL REFERENCE: 1 Samuel 1:2–2:10; 2:21

Like Peninnah, Hannah was a wife of Elkanah, an Ephraimite from Ramah. Every year when Elkanah took his family to the shrine at Shiloh, Peninnah – the mother of Elkanah's children – would taunt his other wife Hannah because she remained childless. But one year, on the day that Elkanah made his sacrifice, Hannah burst into tears and refused to eat anything. Elkanah, who loved Hannah very much, asked her, 'Why are you crying? Why won't you eat anything? Why are you so sad? Am I not more to you than ten sons?' After the family had finished eating, Hannah got up and went to the temple where Eli the high priest was sitting by the door. Weeping bitterly, Hannah made a vow to the Lord, saying, 'Lord of hosts! If you condescend to notice the shame of your servant instead of disregarding her, and are mindful of her and give her a son, then I will give his life to God, and no razor shall ever touch his head.' As Hannah carried on praying silently in her heart, Eli was watching her mouth. He could see that her lips were moving, but as no sound came out he assumed she was drunk and he reprimanded her. Hannah replied, 'No, my lord, I haven't been drinking at all. I've been pouring out my soul to the Lord. Don't think me an unworthy woman, for all the while I have been praying from the depths of my grief and bitterness.' Then Eli told her to go in peace, and said, 'May the God of Israel grant what you have asked of him.' And Hannah replied, 'May you look favourably on your servant.' So saying, Hannah went on her way. And because she was no longer sad, she ate some food. The next morning they got up early and, having worshipped the Lord, set off on the journey home to Ramah. Elkanah slept with Hannah, and God remembered her, and she conceived. In due

ABOVE
Window of opportunity: Michal, daughter of King Saul, helped
David escape in the night from her father – *see* page 89

course Hannah gave birth to a son, and she called him Samuel ('Name of God'), because she had asked God for him. When Elkanah took his family to Shiloh for the annual sacrifice, Hannah stayed at home in Ramah having told Elkanah that she would bring the child once he had been weaned. She would then leave him to spend the rest of his life there. When Samuel had been weaned, Hannah took him up to the temple at Shiloh. She also took a three-year-old bull, an *ephah* of flour and a skin of wine. After the bull had been sacrificed, the child was taken before Eli the high priest. Hannah reminded Eli that she had once stood near him when she was praying to God to give her a son. 'The Lord granted me what I asked, and this is the child for which I was praying. I now hand him back to the Lord. For as long as he lives, he belongs to the Lord.' They then both worshipped God. (1:1–28) This part of Hannah's story concludes with a poem known as the 'Song of Hannah'. As the NOAB explains, 'It was the custom of Biblical editors to insert poems into prose books to increase artistic and religious appeal. The poems may be older or later than the contexts into which they are inserted. In this case the poem seems to be considerably later … but perhaps its greatest claim to fame is that it became the model

for Mary's song of thanksgiving (the Magnificat) in the New Testament (Luke 1:46–55).' (NOAB, 332) Having left Samuel to serve God in the temple with Eli, Hannah and Elkanah returned to their home in Ramah. In the years that followed, when Elkanah went to Shiloh for the annual sacrifice Hannah would take with her a small robe that she had made for Samuel. Before they left on the return journey to Ramah, Eli would bless them, saying, 'May the Lord grant you a child in exchange for the child she has handed over to the Lord.' And over the following years Hannah gave birth to three sons and two daughters. Meanwhile, Samuel grew up in God's presence. (1:1–2:21) Samuel grew up to become a prophet and judge of Israel. (3:19–21, 7:15) When Samuel was old, the people came to him, asking him to appoint a king to govern them, and he anointed Saul, son of Kish, as the first king of Israel. (8:1–5, 10:1)

THE WIFE OF PHINEHAS

The woman whose husband, brother-in-law and father-in-law all died on the same day, and who herself died shortly afterwards in childbirth.

† BIBLICAL REFERENCE: 1 Samuel 4:19–22

Eli, the high priest at Shiloh, had two sons – Hophni and Phinehas. They were also priests, and

assisted their father in the temple; but whereas Samuel grew in both stature and favour in the service of God, Eli's sons used their position to exploit those who came to the sanctuary. When news of this abuse reached Eli's ears, he reprimanded his sons and tried to make them change their ways, but they would not listen to him. God therefore decided to punish them by killing them. (1:3; 2:12–17; 22–5) Some years later the Philistines went to war against the Israelites. When the latter were routed at Aphek, they sent to Shiloh for the ark of the covenant in the belief that God would then make them victorious. Eli's sons accompanied the ark and were both killed when it was captured in battle by the Philistines. A messenger ran back to Shiloh and told Eli of the death of his sons and the capture of the ark. Devastated by this news, Eli fell off his seat and broke his neck and died. His daughter-in-law, the wife of Phinehas, was pregnant and soon to give birth, but when she heard about the capture of the ark and the death of her husband and father-in-law she went into labour and gave birth to her child prematurely. She died very shortly afterwards. As she lay dying, she named her son Ichabod ('No glory'), saying, 'The glory has departed from Israel, for the ark of the Lord has been captured.' (4:22, RSV)

Women from the time of the kings

When Saul failed to comply fully with God's commandment to annihilate the Amalekites (1 Samuel 15:7–10), God sent Samuel to Bethlehem where he had chosen David, one of the seven sons of Jesse, to be king. (16:1)

The author of 1 Samuel relates that while David became filled with the Spirit of the Lord, Saul was emptied of it. (16:13–14) To soothe his troubled soul, Saul asked his servants to find him a skilled lyre player, and so David entered the service of the king. But Saul became jealous of David's military successes and his popularity with the people, and sought to kill him. David fled from Saul, and after some years was anointed king of the southern kingdom of Judah and led his people in a war against the northern kingdom of Israel. After the murder of Saul's son and successor Ishbosheth ('Ishvi' in 1 Samuel 14:49), David became king of the united kingdoms of Judah and Israel. Like Saul before him, David's power declined as he grew older and he experienced a reversal of fortune. The reign of David's son Solomon began magnificently: he was renowned for his wisdom; he built the great Temple of Solomon; and he rebuilt the towns and cities of Israel. Yet towards the end of his reign, Solomon turned away from the Lord and began to worship foreign gods and idols. Under Solomon's successors the kingdom that had been united by David became divided once again into the kingdoms of Judah and Israel.

AHINOAM

MEANING: BROTHER OF PLEASANTNESS or PLEASANT

The wife of Saul, the first king of Israel.

† BIBLICAL REFERENCE: 1 Samuel 14:49–50

Ahinoam was the mother of Saul's three sons – Jonathan, Ishvi (also referred to as Ishbosheth) and Malchishua – and his two daughters – Merab and Michal. Saul also had a concubine named Rizpah, but she is not mentioned until the Second Book of Samuel (*see below*, Rizpah).

MERAB

MEANING: INCREASE

The daughter of King Saul who almost married David.

† BIBLICAL REFERENCE: 1 Samuel 18:17–19

Merab was the elder daughter of King Saul by his wife Ahinoam. When Saul grew jealous of David's popularity, he began to think of ways of getting rid of him and said to himself, 'Rather than me kill him, let the Philistines do it.' And so he offered to give him Merab as his wife on condition that David served him in his fight against the Philistines. In response, David said, 'Who am I, that I should become the king's son-in-law?' But when the time came for them to be married, Saul gave his daughter to another man, Adriel of Meholah.

MICHAL

MEANING: WHO IS LIKE GOD?

The daughter of King Saul who fell in love with David and became his wife, but was then given in marriage by her father to another man.

† BIBLICAL REFERENCE: 1 Samuel 18:20–8; 19:11–17; 25:44; 2 Samuel 3:13–16; 6:16–23

Michal was the younger daughter of King Saul by his wife Ahinoam. She fell in love with David, and when Saul heard of this he thought he could use her to ensnare David and thus put into effect his plan of bringing about David's death at the hands of the Philistines. Rather than speak with David directly, Saul used his servants as intermediaries to suggest that he became the king's son-in-law. When David told them that he had neither sufficient wealth nor rank to become the king's son-in-law, Saul let it be known that the only bride-price he desired was the foreskins of one hundred Philistines. Unfortunately for Saul, David not only passed the test, he returned with the foreskins of two hundred Philistines. Saul grudgingly gave Michal to David as a wife, but he continued to devise ways of killing him. (1 Samuel 18:20–8) On one occasion Saul even threw a spear at David while he was playing the lyre for him, but he missed and David escaped. That same night Saul sent messengers to keep a watch on David's house, for he was intent on killing him in the morning. Michal warned David that unless he escaped during the night, Saul would kill him the next day. Having lowered David down from a window, she lay a statue of one of the household gods in the bed, placed a mop of goat's hair at its head, and then

put a cover over it. When Saul discovered what she had done, he asked her why she had tricked him and let his enemy escape. Michal replied, 'He said, "Let me go, or I will kill you!"' (1 Samuel 19:11–17) Following his narrow escape from Saul, David rejoined Samuel at Ramah. The two men then went to Naioth, from where David fled and went into hiding, living the life of a fugitive until Saul had died. In the meantime, David had taken two more wives – Abigail and Ahinoam (*see below*) – and Saul had given his daughter (David's first wife, Michal) as a wife to a certain Palti ('God liberates') the son of Laish, who was from Gallim. (1 Samuel 25:44) When David became king of Judah, he demanded that Saul's son Ishbosheth return Michal to him. (This was probably to strengthen his claim, as Saul's son-in-law, to

the throne of the deceased king.) She was taken from her husband Palti, who followed her as far as Bahurim, weeping all the way. While they were at Bahurim Abner sent Palti home. (2 Samuel 3:13–16) Later still, after David had united Judah and Israel into a single kingdom, he brought the ark of the covenant back to Jerusalem. The return of the ark was heralded with great rejoicing: it was accompanied on its journey by the shouting of war cries and the sound of horns, while David, wearing only a linen loincloth, danced energetically around it. Michal, the daughter of the late king Saul, happened to look out as the ark was brought into the city and the sight of King David dancing and cavorting around the ark filled her with contempt. When David returned to bless his household, Michal went out to meet him. 'The king

ABOVE
Music to soothe the savage breast: David plucked his harp
as Michal tried to calm her father Saul

of Israel has done himself a great honour today,' she said, 'exposing himself to his serving-maids and making a vulgar exhibition of himself.' And David retorted, 'I was dancing for the Lord, who preferred me above your father or any of his family when he made me leader of his people. And I shall dance for the Lord, and abase myself even further than this. I may appear vulgar to you, but I shall be held in honour by the maids of whom you speak.' And until the day she died, Michal bore no children. (2 Samuel 6:14–23)

ABIGAIL

MEANING: FATHER OF JOY

The quick-witted woman who saved her husband from ruin and became David's second wife.

✝ BIBLICAL REFERENCE: 1 Samuel 25:2–42; 27:3; 30:5, 18; 2 Samuel 3:3

After the death of Samuel and his burial at Ramah, David went into the desert of Maon where there lived a very rich man by the name of Nabal, who had 3,000 sheep and 1,000 goats. Nabal (meaning 'Fool') is described as 'miserly and churlish', whereas his wife Abigail was both beautiful and intelligent. Nabal was away at Carmel overseeing the shearing of his sheep, and David (who was still living the life of an outlaw at this time) sent ten of his men to ask Nabal for provisions in return for the

 ABOVE
Timely intervention: Abigail brought provisions to David and thus saved her foolish husband and his household from certain death

protection he had given earlier to Nabal's shepherds. But Nabal dismissed their request, saying, 'Who is David? Who is this son of Jesse? Shall I give food and drink to men who come from I know not where?' And he sent them away empty-handed. When they returned to David's camp and recounted how Nabal had treated them, David ordered all his men to take up their swords, and he set off for Carmel with four hundred armed men. Meanwhile, one of Nabal's young men went to Abigail and explained to her how David's men had protected her husband's shepherds and flocks, yet Nabal had not taken kindly to their request for provisions and had ranted at them. 'Now,' continued the young man, 'you must decide what you are going to do, for our master and his entire household face being ruined, and he is such an ill-natured brute that no one can say anything to him.' Abigail immediately gathered together a large quantity of provisions, loaded them onto donkeys, and without saying a word to her husband set off towards David's camp. When she saw David and his men marching towards her, she quickly dismounted from her donkey and prostrated herself at his feet. She then spoke at length with him and, having apologized for her husband's behaviour ('Fool by name, fool by nature'), she offered him and his men the provisions she had brought with her, told him that God would protect him and make him ruler of Israel, and asked him to remember her when God had rewarded him. When she finished speaking, David blessed Abigail for her wisdom and her timely intervention, without which he would have slain Nabal and all his men, and he told her to go in peace. Abigail returned home to find Nabal in a drunken stupor, so she postponed telling him what she had done until the next morning. In the morning Nabal was sober, but after Abigail had spoken with him he collapsed, and ten days later he died. When David heard of Nabal's death, he sent word to Abigail asking her to become his wife. Her reply was immediate: she hastily mounted a donkey and, accompanied by five of her maids, she followed the messengers back to David and became his second wife (after Michal). (1 Samuel 25:1–42) David took her with him to Gath, and rescued her when she was captured by the Amalekites (*see below*, Ahinoam). When she was with David at Hebron she gave birth to his second son, whose name is given as both Chileab (2 Samuel 3:3) and Daniel (1 Chronicles 3:1).

Abigail in art

Images of Abigail are generally restricted to her meeting with David. She is often depicted kneeling before him, with her maids and servants bearing provisions behind her, while behind David are men in soldiers' uniforms.

AHINOAM

MEANING: BROTHER OF PLEASANTNESS OR PLEASANT

The woman who became David's third wife.

† BIBLICAL REFERENCE: 1 Samuel 25:43; 27:3; 30:5, 18; 2 Samuel 2:2; 3:2

David took Ahinoam of Jezreel and Abigail with him and his men when he fled to Gath to avoid being killed by Saul. (27:1–3) His two wives were taken captive by the Amalekites, but David caught up with their captors, slew them and regained possession of his wives. (30:5, 18) While Ahinoam was with David in Hebron, where he had been anointed king of Judah, she gave birth to Amnon, David's first-born son.

THE MEDIUM OF ENDOR

The woman who summoned the spirit of Samuel and foretold the death of King Saul and his sons.

† BIBLICAL REFERENCE: 1 Samuel 28:7–25

After the death of Samuel, Saul banished all the mediums and wizards from the land. Meanwhile the Philistines had assembled their army at Shunem ready to do battle with Saul.

When Saul saw the forces amassed against him, he was overcome with fear and asked God for guidance; but no guidance was forthcoming. In desperation Saul asked his servants to find him a medium to consult, and they told him that there was one such medium at Endor. Having disguised himself and changed his clothes, Saul set out for Endor accompanied by two of his men. They visited the medium at night, under the cover of darkness. Saul asked her to foretell what the future held for him by summoning up the spirit of the person whose name he would give her. The medium replied, 'Surely you know that Saul has banished mediums and wizards from the country. So why are you setting a trap for me that will cost me my life?' But Saul tried to reassure her, saying, 'As the Lord lives, you will not be punished for this.' The medium then asked him who she should summon up for him, and he replied, 'Samuel.' But when she made Samuel appear, she shrieked at Saul, 'Why have you deceived me? You are Saul!' The

ABOVE
Under cover of darkness: at Saul's request, the medium of Endor summoned the spirit of Samuel, who foretold that Saul and his sons would be killed in battle

king told her not to be afraid, and asked her to describe the ghostly spirit. From her description, Saul knew that it was Samuel, and he prostrated himself before him. Then Samuel spoke to Saul, saying, 'Why have you summoned me from my rest?' In the ensuing conversation, Saul explained that the Philistines' forces were ranged against him and that God had abandoned him, to which Samuel replied that Saul's predicament was of his own making because he had not obeyed the voice of God. Moreover, on the morrow God would hand the army of Israel over to the Philistines, and Saul and his three sons would be killed in the battle. When Samuel had finished speaking, Saul collapsed to the ground, terrified by what he had been told. He was also weak from hunger, having eaten nothing the previous day. The medium offered him some bread, encouraging him to eat to regain his strength, but he refused. Saul's men joined her in urging him to take some food. When they had eventually persuaded him to eat, the woman killed a fatted calf and made some unleavened bread which she served to Saul and his men. After they had eaten they departed under cover of darkness. (1 Samuel 28:3–25)

The medium of Endor in art
Also described as a necromancer or witch, the woman is usually depicted with Saul and the ghostly spirit of Samuel after she has summoned the latter. Some of Saul's retinue may also be present.

MAACAH

MEANING: OPPRESSION

The woman who became David's fourth wife.

† BIBLICAL REFERENCE: 2 Samuel 3:3

Maacah was the daughter of Talmai, king of Geshur. She gave birth at Hebron to David's son Absalom and his daughter Tamar (*see below*).

HAGGITH

MEANING: FESTIVE OR DANCER

The woman who became David's fifth wife.

† BIBLICAL REFERENCE: 2 Samuel 3:4

Haggith gave birth to David's fourth son Adonijah at Hebron. No further details are given about her.

ABITAL

MEANING: MY FATHER IS DEW

The woman who became David's sixth wife.

† BIBLICAL REFERENCE: 2 Samuel 3:4

Abital gave birth to David's fifth son Shephatiah at Hebron. No further details are given about her.

EGLAH

MEANING: HEIFER

The woman who became David's seventh wife.

† BIBLICAL REFERENCE: 2 Samuel 3:5

Another of David's eight wives. Eglah gave birth to his sixth son Ithream at Hebron. No further details are given about her.

RIZPAH

MEANING: A HOT STONE

The concubine of King Saul who sat and watched over her murdered sons' bodies for a whole summer until they received a proper burial.

† BIBLICAL REFERENCE: 2 Samuel 3:7; 21:8–14

Daughter of Aiah, Rizpah was Saul's concubine. She is first mentioned when Ishbosheth (Saul's son by Ahinoam) accused Abner (commander of Saul's army) of sleeping with her. Since at that time a king's concubines were considered to be royal property, such an act was not only regarded as treasonable, it was also interpreted as a claim to kingship. (NOAB, 378) The accusation was all the more pointed because Abner had risen to a powerful position in Saul's household during the continuing war between Saul and David. Profoundly angered by Ishbosheth's insinuation, Abner vehemently defended his loyalty to Saul's household and then

informed Ishbosheth that from thereon he would do all in his power to transfer the kingdom from the house of Saul to David. (1 Samuel 3:6–10) Later, after David had united the two kingdoms of Judah and Israel, the country was subjected to a famine for three years. David sought guidance from God, who told him that the house of Saul had incurred bloodguilt when it had sought to exterminate the Gibeonites, a non-Israelite people. So David summoned the Gibeonites and asked how he might make amends. They demanded that he hand over Saul's offspring so that they might avenge themselves, and when they were handed over the Gibeonites killed them and left their bodies out in the open. The dead included Rizpah's sons, Armoni and Mephibosheth, and she came and watched over their bodies day and night from the beginning of the barley harvest in May until the rains came in the autumn, driving away the birds and beasts that lived off carrion. When David heard of her long vigil, he gathered up the bones of Saul and his offspring and gave them a proper burial in the family tomb at Zela. (2 Samuel 21:1–14)

BATHSHEBA

MEANING: DAUGHTER OF THE OATH

The beautiful wife of Uriah, a captain in David's army, who was seduced by David and whose husband was sent away to be killed in battle.

† BIBLICAL REFERENCE: 2 Samuel 11:2–11; 26–7; 12:9–14; 24–5; 1 Kings 1:11–31; 2:13–22; 1 Chronicles 3:5

One evening as David was taking the air on the roof of his palace in Jerusalem, he caught sight of a beautiful woman bathing. On enquiring who she was, he learned that she was Bathsheba, the wife of Uriah the Hittite. David sent for her, and she came to him, and after they had slept together she returned home. When Bathsheba realized she had become pregnant she sent word to David, who then sent for her husband Uriah with the intention of concealing his adultery. Having asked Uriah how the war was going, David told him to go home to his wife. But Uriah did not go home: he slept with David's bodyguard at the palace gate instead. When David was told of this, he summoned Uriah again and asked him why he had not gone home. Uriah replied, 'Am I expected to go home and eat and drink and sleep with my wife while the rest of your soldiers are camping out in the open? I will do no such thing.' So David told him to remain at the palace for the next two days, and invited Uriah to eat and drink with him until he had made him drunk. But Uriah again slept with the bodyguard, thus thwarting David's plan. David now adopted another tactic, and in the morning

---

ABOVE
A devoted mother: Rizpah sat and watched over her sons' bodies all summer until David allowed her to give them a proper burial

ABOVE
Vision of beauty: David had caught sight of Bathsheba bathing
from the roof of his palace

wrote a letter to his nephew Joab, commander-in-chief of his army and Uriah's superior officer. The letter, which was to be delivered by Uriah himself, asked Joab to send Uriah into the thick of battle and then withdraw his troops so that Uriah was certain to be killed. David's plan succeeded. On learning that her husband was dead, Bathsheba went into mourning, and when her period of mourning was over David sent for her and made her his wife, and she gave birth to his son. God now sent the prophet Nathan to rebuke David for many things, not least for having sent Uriah to his death so that he could take Bathsheba as his wife. For this, their child would die; and the child died seven days after it was born. David consoled Bathsheba, and she conceived again, and gave birth to a son whom she named Solomon. (2 Samuel 11:2–12:25)

When David was old, his son Adonijah (son by Haggith) began to promote himself, saying, 'I shall be king!' News reached the ears of the prophet Nathan that Adonijah was holding a great banquet to which he had invited everyone, except for Solomon and his supporters, and the guests were chanting 'Long live King Adonijah!' Nathan went to Bathsheba and advised her to go to David to ensure that the elderly king fulfilled the promise he had made that Solomon would

succeed him to the throne. Bathsheba followed Nathan's advice and went to David to plead on her son's behalf. Nathan also spoke in support of Solomon. And David sent for Zadok the priest to anoint Solomon king. The sound of rejoicing that greeted the anointing of Solomon as king interrupted Adonijah's banquet, and caused his guests to fear for their lives. When King Solomon heard of this, he sent for Adonijah who came and prostrated himself at Solomon's feet. (1 Kings 1:5–40) After David had died, Adonijah went to Bathsheba and petitioned her to go to Solomon on his behalf and ask that Abishag the Shunammite

be given to him as his wife. (Abishag was the young girl who nursed David in his old age. *See below*.) So Bathsheba went to Solomon, and asked him not to refuse the small request she was about to make. 'Mother,' he replied, 'make your request. I shall not refuse you.' And she said, 'Let Abishag the Shunammite be given to your brother Adonijah as his wife.' Solomon sensed that this was an attempt to usurp the throne, and said to his mother, 'Why ask for Abishag to be given to Adonijah? Why not ask for the kingdom as well, for he is my elder brother?' Then Solomon swore that Adonijah would die that very same day, and he sent one of his

men to kill him. (2 Samuel 2:10–25) Bathsheba is mentioned in the list of David's wives and sons given in 1 Chronicles, where she is named as Bath-Shua, daughter of Ammiel. She gave

ABOVE
Lasting impression: David had been transfixed by the image of Bathsheba bathing and was prepared to go to any lengths to make her his wife

ABOVE
God's punishment: the baby of David and Bathsheba survived for only seven days

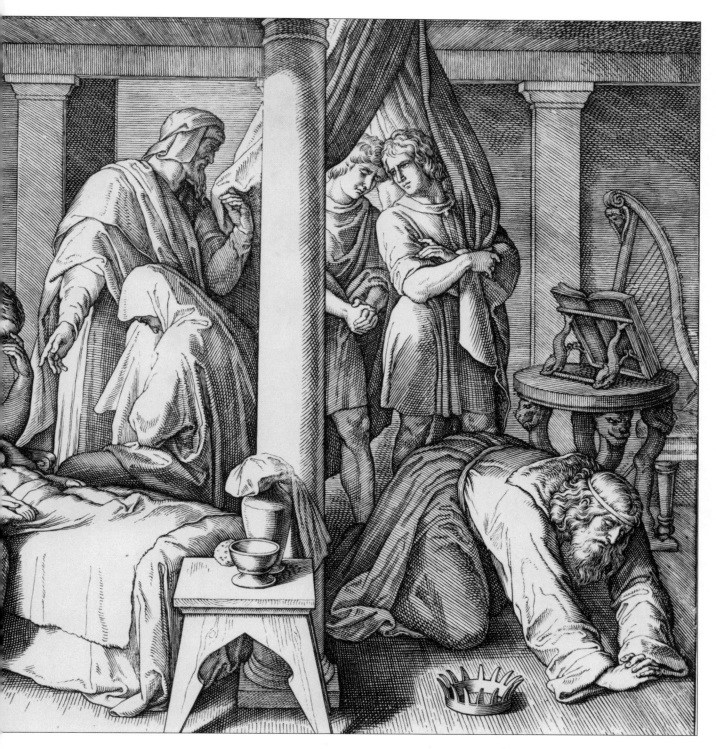

birth to four sons in Jerusalem: Shimea, Shohab, Nathan and Solomon. (1 Chronicles 3:5)

Bathsheba in art

Of David's eight wives Bathsheba is the one most frequently depicted by artists, especially in scenes of her bathing. The latter offered painters the opportunity to place a nude in an outdoor architectural setting; a theme that was particularly appealing to artists working in fifteenth-century Italy because of the early Renaissance interest in both mathematical perspective and the female nude. These exterior scenes

often include David, usually as a small-scale figure discreetly placed in the background.

TAMAR

MEANING: PALM TREE

The beautiful daughter of Maacah and David, who was raped by her half-brother Amnon and avenged by her brother Absalom.

† BIBLICAL REFERENCE: 2 Samuel 13:1–20

Tamar's half-brothers included Amnon, David's eldest son by his wife Ahinoam. Amnon fell in love with the beautiful Tamar, and his love for her developed into an obsession that made him ill. However, because his half-sister was a virgin, he felt unable to do anything to her. Now

Amnon had a friend, Jonadab (son of Shimeah, David's brother), who was very cunning. One morning Jonadab asked Amnon why he looked so haggard day after day, and Amnon told him it was because of his love for Tamar, Absalom's sister. Jonadab suggested that Amnon took to his bed and feigned illness, and when his

ABOVE
The rape of Tamar: filled with lust for his half-sister, Amnon feigned illness so that he could get her on her own. He then seized her

father came to see him he should ask that Tamar come and cook him something and serve it to him. The plan was put into action, and David told Tamar to go to Amnon's house and prepare some food for him, but he refused to eat it. Amnon then sent everyone out of the room, and asked Tamar to bring the food into the inner room. They went into the inner room, but as Tamar was serving Amnon, he took hold of her and said, 'Sister, get into bed with me!' Tamar replied, 'No, brother. Do not force me, for such a thing is not done in Israel. Think of the shame it would bring on me. Where could I go? As for you, you would be vilified throughout Israel. Why don't you go and speak to the king, for he would surely give me to you.' But Amnon would not listen to her pleas, and he took her by force and raped her. Afterwards he was seized with a deep loathing for Tamar, a loathing that was stronger than the love he had previously felt for her. And he said to her, 'Get up, and get out!' Tamar pleaded with him, saying, 'No, brother! The wrong you would do to me by sending me away would be far greater than the wrong you have already done!' But Amnon would not listen to her. Instead, he called his servant and told him to throw her out and bolt the door behind her. Now Tamar was wearing a beautiful long dress, of the kind worn by the king's virgin daughters in earlier times, and when she had been cast out of Amnon's house she tore at her dress, covered her head with ashes and, weeping loudly, made her way home. Her brother Absalom guessed what had taken place, and said to his sister, 'Has Amnon your brother been with you? Sister, say nothing; he is your brother, don't take this thing to heart.' Tamar remained in Absalom's house, distraught and inconsolable. When King David heard what had happened, he was furious, but because he loved his first-born son, he had no wish to punish Amnon. But Absalom refused to speak to Amnon, because he hated him for having raped his sister. It wasn't until two years later that Absalom avenged the rape of Tamar when he ordered his men to kill Amnon. (2 Samuel 13:1–29)

THE WISE WOMAN OF TEKOAH

The wise woman who brought about a reconciliation between David and Absalom.

† BIBLICAL REFERENCE: 2 Samuel 14:1–20

After he had killed his half-brother Amnon, Absalom fled to Geshur, where he lived for three years. Meanwhile, David's nephew Joab observed that the king had grown to accept the death of Amnon, his first-born son, and was no longer angry with Absalom. Thinking that it was time for a reconciliation between the king and his estranged son, Joab sent for a wise woman from the town of Tekoah. Joab rehearsed her carefully for her appearance before the king, saying, 'You're to pretend to be in mourning, so dress in mourning clothes and don't put on any perfume. Act like a woman who has been in mourning for a long time.' Joab then coached her in what she was to say to the king. When the woman appeared before the king, she told him that she was a widow who had had two sons. Her sons had quarrelled and one had killed the other. Her dead husband's clan had come to her asking for the surviving brother so that his life could be taken to atone for the life of his brother. 'They would thus destroy the heir, too,' continued the woman, 'and extinguish the remaining ember, leaving my husband with neither his name nor a surviving son anywhere in the land.' When the king told the woman to go home while he looked into her case, she asked him to petition God that the blood-feud would end and her surviving son would be allowed to live. 'As the Lord lives,' replied the king, 'not one hair of your son's head shall fall to the ground.' The woman told David that he had just condemned himself with his own words, for he had not yet brought home his own banished son. 'Tell me,' said the king, 'is Joab behind this?' And when the woman replied that he indeed was, the king said that his petition was granted, and he then summoned Joab and sent him to Geshur to bring Absalom back to Jerusalem. However, the king laid down one condition: Absalom was to live apart, in his own house, and not appear in the king's presence. For two years Absalom lived in Jerusalem without seeing the king, during which time he fathered a daughter, to whom he gave his sister's name of Tamar, and three sons. (2 Samuel 14:1–27)

THE TEN CONCUBINES OF DAVID

The king's concubines who became the 'widows' of a living man.

† BIBLICAL REFERENCE: 2 Samuel 15:16; 16:22; 20:3

Some four years after Joab had brought about the reconciliation between David and Absalom, Absalom moved south to Hebron from where he conspired against his father (15:7–12). Absalom then instigated an armed revolt and so many people sided with him that David fled Jerusalem, followed by all the city's inhabitants, but David left behind ten concubines to look after the palace during his

absence. (15:16) When Absalom entered Jerusalem, he was advised by Ahithophel (a former advisor of David's who had sided with Absalom) that the best way to provoke the king would be to sleep with the ten concubines he had left behind. Since the concubines were regarded as royal property, Absalom would also be sending out the clear message that he now considered himself to be king and would thus strengthen the resolve of his followers. Absalom followed Ahithophel's advice and slept openly with his father's concubines. (16:20–22) When David returned to his palace in Jerusalem after Absalom had been killed by Joab, he had the ten concubines placed under house arrest and ensured they were well provided for. But he never went near them again, and they remained shut away – like the widows of a living man – until the day they died. (20:3)

THE GO-BETWEEN AND THE QUICK-WITTED WOMAN

Two women who aided David's spies during his campaign against Absalom.

† BIBLICAL REFERENCE: 2 Samuel 17:17–20

When David fled from Jerusalem, he had instructed his friend and advisor Hushai the Archite to remain in the city and offer his

services to Absalom so that he would then be in a position to undermine the advice given to the king's son by Ahithophel. (2 Samuel 15:32–37) Hushai also acted as a spy for David, employing a young girl as a go-between to take messages to two of David's men – Jonathan and Ahimaaz – who waited for the girl near a brook outside the city walls. On one occasion, however, Jonathan and Ahimaaz were sighted by a youth who reported to Absalom what he had seen. Knowing they had been discovered, the two men quickly left. When they arrived at Bahurim, a village near the Mount of Olives, they hid in an underground cistern in the courtyard of a house. The woman of the house spread a sheet of heavy cloth over the mouth of the cistern to conceal it, and then covered it with grain so that nothing showed. When Absalom's men arrived in pursuit, they asked the woman if she had seen Jonathan and Ahimaaz. She told them the two men had gone further along the brook. Absalom's men went off in that direction, but finding nothing they returned to Jerusalem. Once the men had gone, the woman released Jonathan and Ahimaaz from their hiding place and the two men took Hushai's message to David. When he received the message, David led his people across the Jordan to safety. (2 Samuel 17:17-22)

THE WISE WOMAN FROM ABEL

The woman whose quick thinking saved her town from destruction.

† BIBLICAL REFERENCE: 2 Samuel 20:16–22

When David returned to Jerusalem after the death of Absalom, he faced a revolt led by a man named Sheba. By the time Joab and his army caught up with Sheba at the town of Abel Beth-Maacah, most of Sheba's supporters had deserted him. Joab laid siege to the town, and while he and his men were mining under its walls a woman called out, asking to speak with Joab. When Joab went to her, she told him how in former years the town had a reputation for the wisdom of its inhabitants, and throughout Israel people would say, 'If you want sound advice, go to Abel.' 'That's how disputes were settled,' said the woman. 'And now,' she continued, 'you want to destroy a town of Israel, laying waste to part of the Lord's heritage?' Joab protested that this was not his intention, and said, 'All I want is Sheba, the man who led the revolt against King David. If you hand him over, I shall withdraw my troops.' The woman replied, 'Look, his head will be thrown over the wall to you.' And the woman went and spoke wisely to the people, and they cut off Sheba's head and threw it over the wall to Joab, at which Joab had the trumpet sounded for his forces to withdraw. (2 Samuel 20:15–22)

ABISHAG

MEANING: GIVEN TO ERROR

The Shunammite girl who nursed King David and kept him warm in his old age.

† BIBLICAL REFERENCE: 1 Kings 1:1–4; 15; 2:13–25

When King David was very old he was unable to keep warm, even when covered with bed-clothes. His servants suggested that they found him a young girl to nurse him and lie beside him to keep him warm. They searched throughout the entire kingdom of Israel, and found Abishag, a beautiful girl from Shunem. She served David, nursed him, and although she lay with him to keep him warm she remained chaste. (1:1–4) Abishag was present when Bathsheba and Nathan petitioned David to make his son Solomon king. (1:15; *see* Bathsheba) After David's death, Adonijah (another of David's sons) sought to make Abishag his wife and asked Bathsheba to petition Solomon on his behalf. Solomon saw this as an attempt to usurp his own right to rule in favour of his half-brother Adonijah, and he had Adonijah killed that same day. (2:13-25; *see* Bathsheba)

THE DAUGHTER OF PHARAOH

The first of Solomon's foreign wives.

† BIBLICAL REFERENCE: 1 Kings 3:1; 7:8; 9:16, 24

Solomon married the daughter of an unnamed Pharaoh of Egypt and took her to Jerusalem where she remained while he finished building his palace, the temple and the ramparts around the city. (3:1) For her dowry, Pharaoh had given his daughter the town of Gezer, which he had captured from the Canaanites and razed to the ground. The town was rebuilt by Solomon during his extensive rebuilding programme. (9:16) While Solomon was building his palace in Jerusalem he also built his wife a house that was similar to his palatial Hall of the Throne. (7:8) When her palace was finished, Pharaoh's daughter moved out of Jerusalem to live there. (9:24) She was not the only foreign woman Solomon was to take as his wife, for he married many more foreign wives later in his reign (*see below*, The foreign wives of Solomon).

THE TWO WOMEN JUDGED BY SOLOMON

The two women who both claimed to be the mother to the same child.

† BIBLICAL REFERENCE: 1 Kings 3:16–28

Early in his reign, before he had

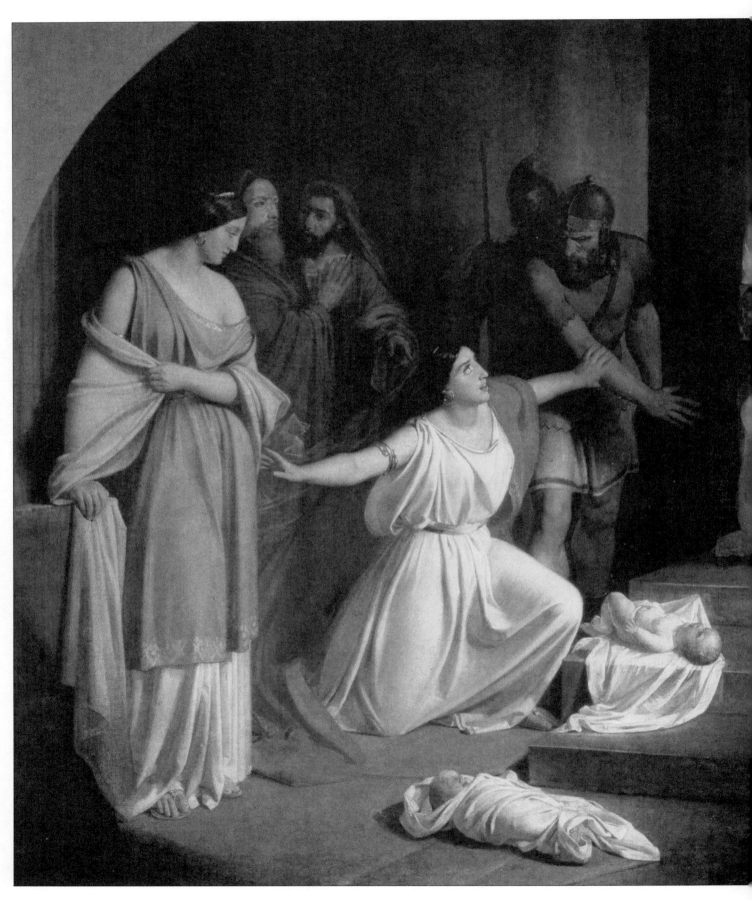

ABOVE
The judgement of Solomon: the mother of the surviving child pleaded with
the king to spare her son's life by giving him to her rival

built the temple in Jerusalem, Solomon went to the shrine at Gibeon to make a sacrifice. While he was there God appeared to him in a dream and enquired what he could give him. Solomon asked for an understanding mind that would help him to govern God's people, and also enable him to discern between good and evil. God was pleased with this answer because Solomon had asked for understanding rather than a long life and riches, and so he gave him a wise and discerning mind. And, because Solomon had *not* asked for them, God also gave him riches and honour. When Solomon awoke, he realized that he had been dreaming. (3:4–15) Nevertheless the things revealed to him in his dream came true and he acquired wisdom, wealth and a long life – he reigned over Jerusalem for forty years. The account of Solomon's dream is followed almost immediately by what has become the most often quoted example of Solomon's wisdom.

One day two prostitutes who shared a house brought their dispute before Solomon for judgement. One of the women explained that she had given birth to a child, and three days later her housemate had also given birth. 'We live all alone in the house,' continued the woman, 'and during the night the other woman's child died because she lay on it in her sleep. At midnight she got up, and while I was asleep she took my child from my bed and put her dead child in its place. When I awoke in the morning to feed my child, it was dead; but when I saw it more clearly in the light of day I could see that it was not the child I had given birth to.' The second woman then spoke up, 'No! The living child is mine; the dead one is yours!' But the first woman retorted, 'That's not true! Yours is the dead one; mine's the one that's alive!' When the two women had finished putting their case to him, Solomon asked for a sword. And when the sword was brought before him he said, 'Cut the living child in half, and give half to one mother and half to the other.' Prompted by her love for her child, the mother of the living son pleaded with Solomon, 'My lord, I beg you not to kill the child. Give him to her.' But the other woman cried out, 'Neither of us shall have him. Cut him in half!' Then Solomon delivered his judgement, 'Do not kill the child. Give it to the first woman, for she is his mother.' All Israel heard about the judgement of Solomon, and they held the king in awe for it was evident that in matters of justice he possessed divine wisdom. (3:16–28) After this Solomon organized his kingdom by appointing officials and administrative districts. With the support of King Hiram of Tyre he began to build the temple in Jerusalem, and he employed a craftsman from Tyre – also named Hiram – to do all the casting in bronze. God appeared again to Solomon after the consecration of the temple, warning him of the dire consequences if he failed to follow his commandments and were to serve other gods.

The 'Judgement of Solomon' in art

Solomon's judgement of the two prostitute-mothers became a popular subject in Christian art. Because Solomon was regarded as an Old Testament 'type' for Christ, the subject came to be associated with the Last Judgement at which Christ will preside as judge. It was also interpreted as an allegory for divine justice and wisdom, and as a symbol for Justice in a more general sense. Visually, the subject provided artists with a potentially dramatic scenario in which the tension was often heightened through the emotionally charged gestures of the two mothers (one pleading, the other accusing) and the dramatic pose of the executioner, who is frequently depicted holding a raised sword in one hand while from the other he dangles the living child he is about to cut in two. The dead child lies inanimate on the ground within this highly charged scene, while over it all presides the figure of Solomon, calmly delivering his judgement from the raised Throne of Justice.

THE QUEEN OF SHEBA

The queen who travelled from afar to test for herself the wisdom of Solomon.

† BIBLICAL REFERENCE: 1 Kings 10:1–13 (duplicated in 2 Chronicles 9:1–12)

When reports of Solomon's fame as a wise and just ruler reached the ears of the Queen of Sheba,

she travelled to Jerusalem with a very large retinue – including camels laden with quantities of gold, precious stones and spices – to see for herself whether or not the reports were true. During her visit the queen questioned Solomon on every subject that came to mind, and he answered all her questions for there was no subject that he could not explain to her, however obscure. When the Queen of Sheba had seen the extent of Solomon's wisdom, the palace he had built, the food served at his table, the way his officials had been organized, the dress and bearing of his servants, his cupbearers and the sacrifices he offered in the temple dedicated to the Lord, she was overwhelmed. And she said to the king, 'The reports I heard in my own country about your wisdom and the way you organize your affairs were true, but I did not believe them until I had seen things with my own eyes. I then discovered that they only painted half the picture, for your wisdom

ABOVE
Putting Solomon to the test: the Queen of Sheba travelled to Jerusalem to see if the king was as wise as he was said to be

and wealth far surpass what I was told. How happy your wives must be! And how happy the servants who are continually in your presence and benefit from your wisdom. Blessed be the Lord, your God, who has shown his approval of you by placing you on the throne of Israel! Because of his eternal love for Israel, he has made you king so that you may dispense order and justice.' She then gave Solomon a hundred and twenty talents of gold, and vast quantities of precious stones and spices. Never again was the king to receive such an abundance of spices as those he received from the Queen of Sheba. In return, King Solomon gave the queen everything she asked of him in addition to the presents he gave her out of his kingly generosity. She then returned to her own country with her retinue.

The account of the Queen of Sheba's visit to Solomon is followed by a description of the great wealth he had accumulated. We are told that he 'surpassed all the kings of the earth in riches and wisdom. The whole world came to Solomon to hear the wisdom with which God had endowed him, and everyone brought with them a present for him: articles made of silver and gold, robes, spices, horses and mules. And this continued for many years.'

(10:23–5) The image thus created of a king who, because he found favour with God, was blessed with immense wisdom and wealth, amplifies his subsequent fall from favour when he turned away from God and took to worshipping other gods.

The Queen of Sheba in art

The subject of the Queen of Sheba's visit to Solomon is fairly widespread in Christian art as Christians saw it as prefiguring the Adoration of the Magi. It was of particular appeal to post-Renaissance and Baroque artists for whom the setting of Solomon's court provided a sumptuous background for the meeting of the king and his regal visitor. The event was also commemorated by Handel in his *Arrival of the Queen of Sheba*. The Queen of Sheba's visit was also part of the extra-biblical legend of the True Cross, according to which the queen came across a beam made from the Tree of Knowledge while she was travelling to Jerusalem, and in a vision she saw that it would later be used for the cross on which Jesus was crucified. The fifteenth-century fresco cycle, *The Legend of the True Cross*, by Piero della Francesca in the church of San Francesco at Arezzo includes scenes of the journey of the Queen of Sheba and her meeting with Solomon.

THE FOREIGN WIVES OF SOLOMON

The women whose worship of foreign gods led to Solomon turning away from the Lord.

† BIBLICAL REFERENCE: 1 Kings 11:1–8

Pharaoh's daughter was not the only foreign woman to be loved by Solomon. He took other wives from among the Moabite, Ammonite, Edomite, Sidonian and Hittite women; in fact, from the very people that God had told the Israelites not to get involved with because they would turn them towards their own gods. But Solomon was attached to his wives, of whom he had seven hundred. He also had three hundred concubines. As Solomon advanced into old age, his wives turned his heart towards other gods so that he was no longer as wholly dedicated to the Lord as his predecessor David had been. He became a follower of the Sidonian goddess Astarte and the Ammonite god Milcom, and he built hilltop shrines dedicated to Chemosh of the Moabites and Molech of the Ammonites. He did the same for all his foreign wives. (11:1–8) And so God became angry with Solomon and told him that, because he had broken both the covenant and the commandments, his son would lose the kingdom. He would, however, retain one tribe.

The foreign wives of Solomon in art

Solomon's foreign wives feature prominently in paintings bearing the title *The Idolatry of Solomon*, in which the king is depicted in old age surrounded by varying numbers of his wives and concubines. One or more statues of pagan gods complete the scene. Solomon is shown either burning incense to the gods or kneeling down in worship before their idols, while the women encourage him in his idolatry. These women possibly include Solomon's Ammonite wife Naamah (*see below*), mother of his successor Rehoboam. The visual drama of the scene is heightened by the contrasting costumes of the protagonists: Solomon, the divinely appointed ruler, is crowned and in full regal dress, while many of the pagan women around him are scantily clothed. The subject was popular in post-Reformation Europe since it gave visual expression to Protestant criticism that the Roman Church's extensive use of religious imagery was idolatrous.

TAHPENES AND HER SISTER

MEANING: THE HEAD OF THE AGE

The wife of Pharaoh, and her sister who married Hadad the Edomite.

† BIBLICAL REFERENCE: 1 Kings 11:19–20

While David was still king, his commander Joab 'slew every male in Edom'. Among the Edomites to escape Joab's purge was a young boy named Hadad, a member of the royal house of Edom, who was taken by his father's servants to Egypt. Hadad found great favour with Pharaoh, who gave him his sister-in-law – the sister of Queen Tahpenes – as a wife. Tahpenes' unnamed sister bore Hadad a son named Genubath, whom Tahpenes raised in the royal palace among Pharaoh's own sons. When Hadad heard that David and Joab had died, he returned to Canaan and became an adversary of Solomon.

ZERUAH

MEANING: LEPROUS OR STRICKEN

The woman whose son became king of the ten tribes of Israel.

† BIBLICAL REFERENCE: 1 Kings 11:26

Zeruah, the wife of Nebat, an Ephraimite in the service of Solomon, is given only the briefest of mentions, but her importance lies in the fact that she was the mother of Jeroboam. As a young man Jeroboam found favour with Solomon, but he later rebelled against him after the prophet Ahijah had told him that Solomon's kingdom was about to be taken away from him because he had turned to worshipping foreign gods. Ahijah prophesied that Solomon's son would be left to rule only one of the tribes of Israel and that Jeroboam would become ruler of the ten tribes that were to be taken away from him. When Solomon sought to kill him, Jeroboam fled to Egypt where he remained until Solomon died.

ABOVE
From wisdom to folly: surrounded by his wives, Solomon knelt in worship of alien gods, provoking the Lord's anger

Following Solomon's death, Jeroboam rejoined the people of Israel when they assembled at Shechem to install Solomon's son Rehoboam as their king. The people, who had been subjected to forced labour under Solomon, demanded that Rehoboam treat them more leniently. When he refused to listen to them, they chose Jeroboam to be their king in his place. However, two of the twelve tribes remained loyal to Rehoboam. These were the tribes of Judah and Benjamin. The ten other tribes followed Jeroboam, thus dividing in two the kingdom that had been united under David. (11:26–12:20)

THE WIFE OF JEROBOAM

The queen who disguised herself when she consulted a prophet.

† BIBLICAL REFERENCE: 1 Kings 14:2–17

When Jeroboam became king he feared that if his people journeyed to Jerusalem to offer sacrifices in the temple their loyalty would revert to Rehoboam, and so he established rival shrines and feast days. He made two golden calves, which he set up in Bethel and Dan, proclaiming them to be the 'gods of Israel'. He also appointed priests from among the common people and not from the Levites to whom the Lord had granted the priesthood in perpetuity (*see above*, Cozbi, page 56). (12:26–32) When Jeroboam's son

Abijah fell ill as a consequence of these heresies, he told his wife to disguise herself and go to Shiloh to consult Ahijah, the prophet who had told him he would be king of Israel. God forewarned Ahijah, who was now blind, of her impending visit, and when she arrived at the prophet's house he greeted her, saying, 'Come in, wife of Jeroboam; why pretend to be someone else?' He then told her of the imminent destruction of Jeroboam and his household,

ABOVE
Unwelcome news: the blind prophet Ahijah forewarned Jeroboam's wife of the imminent destruction of her husband and his household

return home. Having heard all this, Jeroboam's wife left Ahijah and returned to Tirzah. As she crossed over the threshold of her house, her son breathed his last. However, Jeroboam and his wife had another son, Nadab by name, who became king of Israel when his father died after reigning over the northern kingdom for twenty-two years. (14:1–20)

NAAMAH

MEANING: PLEASANT

Wife of King Solomon and mother of his successor, Rehoboam.

† BIBLICAL REFERENCE: 1 Kings 14:21

As an Ammonite, Naamah was one of the 'foreign wives' who led Solomon to turn away from the Lord to other gods, for he set up shrines for the Ammonite god Molech. Solomon's action brought about the division of the previously united kingdom into two: the southern kingdom of Judah, which was ruled by Rehoboam, Solomon's successor and a descendant of King David, and the northern kingdom of Israel, ruled by Jeroboam. The hostility between the two rulers that had broken out at the beginning of Rehoboam's reign was to continue until his death. Like his northern counterpart, Rehoboam also turned away from the Lord to worship other gods, including the Canaanite

Asherah. He might have been influenced in this by his mother, who had similarly influenced his father before him. He may also have been influenced by his wife Maacah.

MAACAH

MEANING: OPPRESSION

The wife of King Rehoboam, and mother of King Abijam.

† BIBLICAL REFERENCE: 1 Kings 15:2, 13

Maacah was a descendant of Absalom, probably his granddaughter, and shares the same name as David's fourth wife, the mother of Absalom and Tamar. She was the mother of Abijam, who became king of Judah on his father's death. He followed in his father's footsteps in other ways too, for we are told that 'he followed the sinful example of his father before him, and his heart was not wholly true to the Lord.' (15:2–3) Abijam was succeeded by his son Asa, who stripped Maacah of her position at court because she had an idol made of the Canaanite goddess Asherah. Asa burnt the offending article by the brook Kidron. (15:9–13) Versions of the Bible differ as to whether the Maacah referred to in verse 13 was Asa's grandmother (NJB) or his mother (RSV). If the latter, it would mean that the wives of Rehoboam and his son Abijam both shared the name Maacah.

and that the Lord would abandon the people of Israel because they had followed Jeroboam in turning away from him to worship the goddess Asherah. He also told her that her sick son would die upon her

Women from the time of the decline of Judah and Israel

It was during Asa's reign as king of Judah that Jeroboam, king of the northern kingdom of Israel, died. He was succeeded by his son Nadab, who was plotted against and killed by Baasha after a reign of only two years.

Baasha was killed in his turn, as were Elah and Zimri, the two kings who succeeded him. These were followed by Omri, who emulated his predecessors in their worship of pagan gods. In spite of Omri's allegedly ignominious reign, it is worth mentioning here that he bought the hill of Samaria from a certain Shemer, and on it built the fortified town of Samaria, which he named Samaria after Shemer, the owner of the hill. Asa was still reigning over the kingdom of Judah when Omri died and was succeeded as king of Israel by his son Ahab, who married Jezebel (*see below*), the daughter of Ethbaal, king of Sidonia (Phoenicia). Ahab took to worshipping the god Baal, and built a temple for him in Samaria, but the prophet Elijah came to him and foretold of the drought and famine that were to afflict his country in the coming years. (15:29–17:1) After Elijah had delivered his warning to Ahab, God told him to go into hiding east of the Jordan, by the Cherith, described as a 'brook'

(RSV) or 'torrent' (NJB). When the watercourse dried up because of the drought, God instructed him to go to Zarephath in Sidonia, where he had arranged for a widow to feed him. (17:2–9)

THE WIDOW OF ZAREPHATH

The woman who was saved from starvation and whose son was raised from the dead.

† BIBLICAL REFERENCE: 1 Kings 17:10–24; Luke 4:25–6

When Elijah entered the city of Zarephath, he encountered a widow collecting sticks by the city gate. He asked her to bring him some water to drink, and as she left to fetch the water he called after her to bring him a piece of bread as well. She replied that she had no baked bread, only a handful of flour in a jar and a small quantity of oil in a cruse (an earthenware vessel), and that she was just gathering some kindling so that she could prepare the food for herself and her son to eat. And she added,

'Then we shall die.' Elijah told the widow not to be afraid. She was to go and do as she had said; but first she should use her supplies to make him a small scone, after which she should make something for herself and her son. He then said, 'The Lord, God of Israel, says, "The jar of flour shall not be used up, and the cruse of oil shall not run dry, until the day that the Lord sends rain to fall on the land."' The widow went and did as Elijah had told her, and the jar of flour was not used up, nor the cruse emptied, just as the Lord had told her through Elijah. After this the widow's son became seriously ill and died. The widow challenged Elijah, saying, 'O man of God, what have you got against me? Have you come here to make me realize my sins and to cause the death of my son?' Elijah told her to give him her son, and he carried him into the upper room where he was lodging and laid the child on his own bed. Elijah then cried out to the Lord, and stretched himself on

ABOVE
A mother's dilemma: Elijah asked the widow of Zarephath to give him the
last of her provisions when she and her son were starving

the child three times, calling out to the Lord each time. The Lord heard Elijah's prayer, and the child's soul came back into his body, and he began to breathe again. Elijah picked up the child, took him downstairs, and gave him back to his mother, saying, 'Look, your son is alive.' 'Now I know you are a man of God,' she replied, 'and the word of the Lord in your mouth is truth itself.' (17:10–24)

The miracles performed by God through Elijah and the concluding words 'you are a man of God' spoken by the widow of Zarephath serve both to introduce Elijah and to pave the way for his denunciation of Ahab and Jezebel and the miracle that occurred during his confrontation on Mount Carmel with the priests of Baal. (18:19–40)

The widow of Zarephath also appears in the New Testament,

where she is mentioned by Jesus in his address to the congregation in the synagogue at Nazareth following his temptation in the wilderness. Anticipating his audience's hostile reaction after he had read a passage from the writings of the prophet Isaiah, he said, 'I am telling you a truth when I say to you that no prophet is acceptable in his own country. And it is true to say there were many widows in Israel in Elijah's time [...] when there was a great famine throughout the country; but Elijah was sent to none of these except for a widow at Zarephath.' (Luke 4:16–26)

The widow of Zarephath in art

The widow of Zarephath and her son sometimes feature as secondary figures in scenes depicting the life of the prophet Elijah. She

may either be collecting sticks or offering him the food she has made with her last flour and oil. The presence of her son serves as a visual reminder that Elijah raised him from the dead.

JEZEBEL

MEANING: CHASTE

The woman who, having slaughtered all who got in her way, was thrown to her death from a window and eaten by dogs.

† BIBLICAL REFERENCE: 1 Kings 16:31; 18:4, 14, 19; 19:1–2; 21:5–15, 23, 25; 2 Kings 9:7, 10, 22, 30–37.

When Jezebel, the daughter of Ethbaal, king of Sidonia (Phoenicia), married Ahab, king of Israel, her husband took to worshipping the Canaanite/ Phoenician god Baal and built a temple dedicated to him in Samaria. (16:31–2) After Elijah had been away from Israel for three years, God instructed him to return there and make himself known to Ahab. During Elijah's absence, Jezebel had slaughtered the prophets of the Lord; but Obadiah, a man who revered God, had managed to save one hundred of them by hiding them in a cave. Now it happened that Elijah met Obadiah while he was on his way to see Ahab. The two men already knew each other, but Obadiah's initial pleasure at seeing Elijah again was short-lived, for the prophet told him

ABOVE
Life restored: the Lord answered Elijah's prayers and the widow's son began to breathe again

to go to Ahab and say, 'Elijah is here.' At first Obadiah protested, not only afraid that he would be killed because he had saved a hundred prophets from Jezebel's massacre but also that as soon as he left him Elijah might go into hiding again. In spite of his protests, Elijah persuaded him to do as he had said. When Elijah met Ahab later that day, he con-demned him for having forsaken God to follow Baal, and he told him to assemble all the people of Israel on Mount Carmel together with the 'four hundred prophets of Baal who eat at Jezebel's table.' In the ensuing confrontation, Elijah the prophet of the Lord defeated the prophets of Baal and the people prostrated themselves before the might of God. Elijah then told the people to seize the prophets of Baal, and they took them down to the brook of Kishon where they slaughtered them all. Shortly afterwards the heavens opened, bringing the drought to an end. (18:1–45) When Ahab returned from Mount Carmel to Jezreel he told Jezebel everything that Elijah had done, and how he had slaughtered the

ABOVE
Worship of false idols: Elijah met Ahab and Jezebel and condemned them for forsaking God to follow Baal

ABOVE
Grisly end: the eunuchs threw Jezebel from the window
to be trampled under horses' hooves

prophets of Baal. And so Jezebel sent Elijah a message, saying, 'May the gods do their worst to me, and more, if by this time tomorrow I have not done with your life as you did with theirs.' Fearing for his life, Elijah fled south to Judah and went into the wilderness. (19:1–3) It was while he was in the wilderness that he heard the 'still small voice' of God instructing him to appoint Elisha, the son of Shaphat from Abel-Meholah, as the prophet who would succeed him in ridding the land of all who had become followers of Baal. And when the elderly prophet met Elisha, the young man followed him and became his servant. (19:13–21) While Elijah was in Judah, the kingdom of Israel was attacked by Ben-Hadad, king of Aram (Syria). He besieged Samaria, but the Lord sent a prophet to Ahab and told him how he might raise the siege. The prophet came to Ahab a second time, and told him that the Lord would ensure his victory over the Aramaeans and the capture of their army. After Ahab had defeated Ben-Hadad, he made a treaty with him and let him go. The prophet then came to Ahab again and told him that because he had allowed Ben-Hadad to escape the destruction that God had intended for him, Ahab would pay with his life. Filled with resentment and in a foul temper, the king went back to Samaria. (20:1–43)

It was while Ahab was still in this bad mood that he went to see a certain Naboth, who owned a vineyard next to the royal palace, and demanded that he give him the vineyard so that he could turn it into the palace vegetable garden. In exchange Ahab offered him a better vineyard or, if Naboth preferred, its value in money. This went against the tradition established when the Israelites entered Canaan, that the ancestral property allocated to each family at the time of the occupation should remain permanently within that family, and so Naboth replied, 'The Lord forbid that I should give you the inheritance of my fathers.' This reply greatly displeased Ahab, who returned to his palace in such a foul temper that he took to his bed and refused to eat. When Jezebel asked him what had annoyed him so much that he would not eat, Ahab told her about his visit to Naboth and his refusal to part with his vineyard. 'Aren't you the king of Israel?' she said, 'Get up and eat, and don't worry yourself about it. I shall get you Naboth's vineyard myself.' And Jezebel wrote letters in Ahab's name to the elders of the city telling them to summon an assembly at which Naboth was to be present. He was to be confronted by a couple of rogues who would accuse him before the assembly of having cursed both God and the king, and then taken outside and stoned to death. She sealed the letters with the king's seal and sent them to the elders. The elders followed Jezebel's instructions and then sent word to her that Naboth had been stoned and was now dead. As soon as she received this news, Jezebel told Ahab to go and take possession of the dead man's vineyard, and he went and took possession of it. Then the word of God came to Elijah telling him to go to Ahab, whom he would find in Naboth's vineyard, and say to him, 'The Lord says, "You have committed murder and now you take possession as well?"' Elijah was then to tell Ahab that the dogs would lick up his blood in the same place that they had licked up the blood of Naboth, and Jezebel would be eaten by dogs in the field of Jezreel. And when Elijah came to Ahab and told him these things, the king tore his robes, put on sackcloth, and moped around his palace. (21:1–27)

The story of Jezebel is continued in the Second Book of Kings, but several relevant events happen in the interim. Ahab was killed in battle and the dogs licked up his blood from the ground, as Elijah had prophesied. He was first succeeded as king of Israel by his son Ahaziah who, like his father before him, worshipped Baal. Ahaziah died two years later, but since he had no sons he was succeeded by his brother Jehoram (known as 'Joram' to avoid confusion with Jehoram, king of Judah, who became Joram's brother-in-law when he married Athaliah the daughter of Jezebel and Ahab (*see below*, Athaliah). (22:29–40, 51–3) When the Moabite king Mesha rebelled against King Joram of Israel because of the annual tribute he had to pay, Joram appealed for help to the king of Edom and to Jehoshaphat, king of Judah. The three kings were on the point of defeating the Moabites when the Moabite king made a burnt offering of his eldest son and heir on top of the city walls. The besieging forces of the alliance were filled with fear at the wrath of Chemosh, the Moabite god, and withdrew to their own countries. (3:26–7) It was around this time that Elijah was taken up into heaven and Elisha took on both his mantle and his prophetic mission. (2 Kings 1:17; 2:9–13) When Jehoshaphat king of Judah died he was succeeded by his son Jehoram, who married Ahab's daughter Athaliah. He died after reigning for eight years and was succeeded by his son Ahaziah. (8:16–17, 25) While Joram was still king of Israel, Elisha instigated a rebellion against him by arranging for a disciple of his to anoint Jehu, son of Jehoshaphat, as a rival king. And the disciple told Jehu that it was the will of the Lord that he should wipe out the house of Ahab, and he repeated the prophecy that

Jezebel would be eaten by dogs. (9:1–10). Jehu then made his way to Jezreel, where King Ahaziah was visiting King Joram. The two kings rode out in their chariots to meet Jehu, and when Joram asked him if he had come in peace, Jehu replied, 'How can I come in peace while the prostitutions and sorceries of your mother Jezebel continue?' When Joram heard this he turned his chariot around and fled, but Jehu drew his bow and shot him between the shoulders, and killed him. Jehu turned to his equerry, and told him to take Joram's body and throw it onto Naboth's vineyard. He then set off in pursuit of Ahaziah, and shot him too, but he fled to Megiddo where he died from his wound. When he headed back to Jezreel, Jezebel was told of his approach. She put mascara on her eyes, adorned her hair, and looked out of her window. As Jehu came in through the gateway, she called down to him, 'Do you come in peace, you murderer of your master?' Jehu looked up at the window and called out, 'Who is with me? Who?' When two or three eunuchs peered down at him, he shouted to them, 'Throw her down!' They threw her out of the window, and her blood splattered over the walls and over the horses, and she was trampled under their hooves. Jehu went into the palace, and ate and drank, and then said, 'Deal with

this accursed woman and see that she is buried, for she is the daughter of a king.' But all that they found left of her was her skull, her feet and her hands. When they told Jehu, he said, 'This is the word of the Lord which he spoke through his servant Elijah the Tishbite, "In the field of Jezreel the dogs will eat the flesh of Jezebel, and her corpse will be like dung spread on the fields, so that no one will be able to say, "This was Jezebel."' (9:16–37) Jehu then ordered the assassination of Ahab's seventy sons who were being educated in Samaria, and he killed all of Ahab's household in Jezreel, his officials, his friends and his priests. (10:1–11) From Jezreel, Jehu went to Samaria where he killed the surviving members of Ahab's family. He tricked all the devotees of Baal into assembling in Baal's temple where his men massacred them. They then destroyed the statue of Baal and demolished his temple, which they turned into a latrine. (10:17–27) Jehu thus eradicated all traces of Jezebel and her influence, after which God appointed him king of Israel. (10:30)

Jezebel in art

The story of Jezebel is inseparable from the story of Elijah. Legend relates that Elijah lived as a hermit on Mount Carmel, and since the early Carmelites regarded him as the founder of their Order he features prominently in the decoration of Carmelite churches. Jezebel is sometimes present in works depicting the miracles performed by Elijah, such as his defeat of Jezebel's priests of Baal on Mount Carmel. Other works show her about to be thrown to her death by two eunuchs.

THE WIDOW AND THE JAR OF OIL

The woman whose children were saved from slavery by a miraculous jar of oil.

† BIBLICAL REFERENCE: 2 Kings 4:1–7

The wife of a member of the prophetic community came to Elisha and told him her husband had died and that one of their creditors was coming to take her two children to be his slaves. He asked the widow what she had in the house, and she replied, 'Nothing, except for a jar of oil.' So Elisha said, 'Borrow as many empty vessels as you can from your neighbours and then go into your house with your sons. When you have closed the door, pour the oil into these vessels; and when each one is full put it to one side.' The widow returned home and borrowed as many vessels as possible from her neighbours. She then went into her house and closed the door behind herself and her sons. She began to pour the oil from her jar into the empty vessels passed to her by her sons, and when each vessel was full they put it to one side. The time came when she asked her son to pass her another vessel, and he replied, 'There aren't any more.' And the oil stopped flowing. She then went to Elisha, who said, 'Go and sell the oil, and pay off your debt. You and your children can live off the rest.' (4:1–7) This incident, which parallels the story of Elijah and the widow of Zarephath, follows immediately after the Moabite king's sacrifice of his eldest son. Together the two episodes give an insight into the treatment of children in the lands of the Middle East in the ninth century BC.

THE SHUNAMMITE WOMAN

The woman whose son was raised from the dead by Elisha.

† BIBLICAL REFERENCE: 2 Kings 4:8–37; 8:1–6

On one occasion when Elisha was travelling to Shunem, a wealthy townswoman urged him to stay and eat some food. From then on, whenever he passed that way he would break his journey and stop there for a meal. The woman said to her husband, 'I am sure that the man who passes this way so often is a man of God. Let us build a small room for him, and furnish it with a bed, a table, a chair and a lamp. Then whenever he comes here he will have somewhere to stay.' One day while Elisha was resting in this room, he told Gehazi his servant to fetch the Shunammite woman. When the woman came, he said, 'Now say to her, "Look, you have gone to all this trouble for us. What can we do for you? Would you like me to say something on your behalf to the king or to the commander of the army?"' She replied, 'I live among my own people.' Elisha asked, 'What can we do for her then?' Gehazi answered, 'Well, she has no son, and her husband is old.' Elisha said to the woman as she stood in the doorway, 'This time next year you will be cradling a son in your arms.' The woman replied, 'No, my lord, do not mislead me.' But the woman conceived and gave birth to a son in the spring, as Elisha had foretold. One day, when the child had grown up, he went out to his father who was in the fields with the reapers and complained that his head hurt. His father told a servant to take the child to his mother; and the child lay in her lap until noon, when he died. The woman took the child to Elisha's room where she lay him on the holy man's bed. She left the room, closing the door on her son. She then said to her husband, 'Get me a servant and a donkey, for I must go quickly to the holy man and back.' Her husband protested, but she saddled up the donkey. Telling the servant

ABOVE
Raised from the dead: Elisha repaid the Shunammite woman's generosity
by bringing her son back to the land of the living

not to let the beast slacken its pace, she set off to Elisha on Mount Carmel. When Elisha saw the woman approaching in the distance, he said to Gehazi, 'Look, here comes our Shunammite. Run to meet her, and ask her, "Are you well? Is your husband well? Is your son well?"' And when he asked her these things, she replied, 'All is well.' But when she came to Elisha, she fell to the ground and held on to his feet. Gehazi tried to push her away, but Elisha said, 'Leave her alone, for her soul is deeply distressed, and the Lord had not told me.' The woman then said to Elisha, 'Did I ask my lord for a son? Did I not say, "Do not mislead me?"' And Elisha told Gehazi, 'Hurry, take my staff with you and go. If you meet any one on the way, do not greet them. If any one greets you, do not return their greeting. And place my staff on the child.' When Gehazi arrived at the woman's house he placed the staff on the child, but the child gave no sign of life. So he went to meet Elisha, who was following with the mother, and said, 'The child has not stirred.' Elisha went into the house and saw the child lying on his bed, dead. Closing the door behind him, he prayed to the Lord. Then he climbed on to the bed and lay down on top of the child, putting his mouth to his mouth, his eyes to his eyes, and his hands on his hands; and as he lay like this the child's body began to warm. Having done this, he got up and walked back and forth in the house. He then went back and lay down on top of the child again. When he had repeated this seven times, the child sneezed and opened his eyes. Summoning Gehazi, he told him to fetch the Shunammite. When she entered the room, Elisha said, 'Pick up your son.' And she prostrated herself at his feet, then picked up her son and left the room. (4:8–37)

Some time later Elisha warned the Shunammite woman that the land was to be struck by a famine lasting seven years, and he told her to take her family and go and live in another country. This she did, and for seven years she lived in the land of the Philistines. When seven years had passed she came home and went to the king to appeal for the return of her house and land. It so happened that when she went into the king he was talking with Gehazi. The king had asked him about the wonders Elisha had performed, and Gehazi was just telling the king how Elisha had raised the child from the dead when the Shunammite woman lodged her appeal. Gehazi told the king that this was the very woman whose son had been raised from the dead by Elisha. The woman then told her story to the king, after which he ordered his officials to restore all her property to her,

together with all the revenue that had come from her land since the day she had left the country. (8:1–6)

The Shunammite woman in art

The raising of the Shunammite woman's son sometimes features in works showing the miracles performed by Elisha. Christians saw it as prefiguring the Raising of Lazarus, thus assuring its place in Christian art.

NAAMAN'S WIFE AND HER LITTLE MAID

The Israelite girl who instigated one of Elisha's miracles.

† BIBLICAL REFERENCE: 2 Kings 5:2–5

In one of their raids on Israelite territory, the Aramaeans (Syrians) had carried off a young girl who became the servant of the wife of Naaman, commander of the king of Aram's army. Naaman was held in high regard by the king because of the victories he had won for Aram, but he was a leper. One day the little maid said to her mistress, 'If only my lord would go to the prophet of Samaria, he would cure him of his leprosy.' When Naaman told the king what the little Israelite maid had said, the king said, 'Go to Israel, and I shall give you a letter to take to the king.' Naaman went to Israel and was healed by Elisha, but when he tried to pay him for his cure, the

prophet refused. Elisha's servant Gehazi witnessed his master's refusal and ran after Naaman, determined to extract some kind of payment from him. Naaman gave him two of bags of silver and two fine robes, which Gehazi took home and hid. But Elisha knew in his heart what Gehazi had done, and when he next saw him he told him that he and his descendants would thenceforth be afflicted with Naaman's leprosy. When Gehazi left Elisha, he was a leper, with his skin as white as snow. (5:1–27)

TWO WOMEN CANNIBALS

The women whom famine drove to eat one of their children.

† BIBLICAL REFERENCE: 2 Kings 6:26–30

When the city of Samaria was besieged by the Aramaeans (Syrians), food became so scarce that donkeys' heads were selling for eighty silver shekels each. During the famine the king was walking around the city's ramparts one day when a woman called out to him, asking for his help. He asked her what the matter was, and she answered, 'This woman here said to me, "Give up your son so that we may eat him, and tomorrow we shall eat my son." So we cooked my son and ate him. The next day I said to her, "Give up your son so that we may eat him." But she has hidden her son.' This

ABOVE
Naaman's wife and her servant: at the maid's suggestion, Naaman went
to Israel and was cured of his leprosy

brief episode concludes with the narrator telling us that when the king heard these words he tore off his clothes, and the people saw that he was wearing sackcloth next to his skin.

ATHALIAH

MEANING: WHOM GOD HAS AFFLICTED

The woman who ruled Judah after murdering the royal family.

† BIBLICAL REFERENCE: 2 Kings 8:18, 26; 11:1–20 (duplicated in 2 Chronicles 22:2, 10–12; 23:12–15, 21, 24:7)

Athaliah was the daughter of Jezebel and Ahab. She married Jehoram son of Jehoshaphat, who became king of Judah on his father's death. Athaliah's influence meant that Jehoram turned away from the Lord to worship other gods. (8:16–18) On his death, Jehoram was succeeded as king of Judah by his son Ahaziah (not to be confused with the king of Israel of the same name; *see above*, Jezebel). While Jehu was travelling to Samaria to wipe out the surviving members of Ahab and Jezebel's family (*see above*, Jezebel), he met King Ahaziah's brothers who were on their way to pay their respects to the sons of King Ahaziah and the sons of Athaliah the queen mother. Jehu made them his prisoners and then slaughtered them all. Meanwhile, when Athaliah learned of the death of her son, who had been killed while fleeing from Jehu

 ABOVE
Last moments of a queen: Athaliah was taken out of the temple and put to death at the horses' entrance to the palace

(*see above*, Jezebel), she ordered the murder of the entire royal family and took the throne for herself, thus becoming the only woman to rule over Judah as its queen. However, one child was saved from the massacre and hidden by Jehosheba, Ahaziah's half-sister (*see entries below*, Zibiah and Jehosheba). The child's name was Joash (sometimes referred to as Jehoash). In the seventh year of Athaliah's reign, Jehoida the priest summoned the captains of the guard to the temple of the Lord. Having made a pact with them and put them under oath, he brought the seven-year-old Joash out of hiding and showed him to them. Jehoida then arranged for them to secure the temple with guards later that same week. When the guards were all in place both inside and outside the temple, he crowned Joash king of Judah, and the people clapped their hands and shouted, 'Long live the king!' On hearing all the shouting, Athaliah made her way to the temple where she saw the young king surrounded by the people, and she tore at her clothes while shouting, 'Treason! Treason!' Jehoida had told the guards that she was not to be killed in the temple of the Lord, so they took her outside and killed her at the horses' entrance to the palace.

ZIBIAH

MEANING: GAZELLE

The wife of Ahaziah, king of Judah, and mother of Joash.

† BIBLICAL REFERENCE: 2 Kings 12:1 (duplicated in 2 Chronicles 24:1)

Zibiah was from Beersheba. Her son Joash was the only one of Ahaziah's children to escape Athalia's massacre. He was saved by Jehosheba (King Ahaziah's half-sister and Zibiah's sister-in-law), who raised him in safety within the confines of the temple (*see below*, Jehosheba).

JEHOSHEBA

MEANING: JEHOVAH IS HER OATH

The woman who saved the life of a future king.

† BIBLICAL REFERENCE: 2 Kings 11:2 (duplicated in 2 Chronicles 22:11)

Jehosheba was the daughter of King Jehoram (but not by his wife Athaliah) and half-sister to King Ahaziah. She saved the life of Ahaziah's baby son Joash by hiding him and his nurse in a bedroom when Athaliah massacred the rest of the king's sons. Joash was raised secretly in the temple of the Lord, where he received religious instruction from Jehoida the priest, Jehosheba's husband, who staged the coup against Queen Athaliah when Joash was seven years old. (For the story of Jehoida's coup, *see* page 125.)

JEHOADDIN

MEANING: JEHOVAH IS HER ORNAMENT

The wife of Joash, king of Judah, and mother of Amaziah.

† BIBLICAL REFERENCE: 2 Kings 14:2 (duplicated in 2 Chronicles 25:1)

Jehoaddin was from Jerusalem. As with other royal wives named in the closing chapters of the Second Book of Kings which recount the demise of the kingdoms of Judah and Israel, Jehoaddin is mentioned solely in her capacity as the mother of Joash's successor as king of Judah, his son Amaziah. It was during her husband's reign that Hazael king of Aram (Syria) attacked Judah. When Hazael was about to attack Jerusalem, Joash sent him the contents of the temple treasury, and the Aramaeans withdrew. (12:18–19) After Joash had given Hazael the contents of the Temple treasury, some of his own servants rebelled against him and killed him. Meanwhile, in the northern kingdom of Israel the throne had passed from Jehu to his son Jehoahaz, and from Jehoahaz to his son Jehoash, who was provoked into war by Jehoaddin's son Amaziah.

JECOLIAH

MEANING: POWERFUL, OR ABLE THROUGH JEHOVAH

The wife of Amaziah, king of Judah, and mother of Azariah.

† BIBLICAL REFERENCE: 2 Kings 15:2 (duplicated in 2 Chronicles 26:3)

After Jecoliah's husband, King Amaziah, had defeated the Edomites he brought their idols back to Judah, set them up as his gods and worshipped them. (2 Chronicles 25:14) He then provoked Jehoash king of Israel to declare war against him, but Jehoash defeated him and took him back to Samaria as his prisoner. When he returned to Jerusalem he was plotted against and fled to Lachish, where he was murdered. He was succeeded by his sixteen-year-old son who is known under two different names: Azariah (RSV) and Uzziah (NJB).

JERUSHA

MEANING: MARRIED OR POSSESSION

The wife of Azariah, king of Judah, and mother of Jotham.

† BIBLICAL REFERENCE: 2 Kings 15:33 (duplicated in 2 Chronicles 27:1)

Jerusha was the daughter of Zadok. Her husband, King Azariah, was afflicted with leprosy and lived in confinement. His kingdom was governed by Jotham, the son of Azariah and Jerusha, who acted as regent. Jotham became king of Judah on the death of his father. He was succeeded in turn by his son Ahaz, but the name of his wife is not recorded.

ABI/ABIJAH

MEANING: GOD IS MY FATHER

The wife of Ahaz, king of Judah, and mother of Hezekiah.

† BIBLICAL REFERENCE: 2 Kings 18:2 (duplicated in 2 Chronicles 29:1)

Abi or Abijah, was the daughter of Zechariah. During her husband Ahaz's reign, the kingdom came under attack from the Aramaeans (Syrians). At the same time, the Assyrians invaded the northern kingdom of Israel and deported the people of Naphtali to Assyria. Jotham was succeeded by his son Ahaz. It was during his reign that the Assyrians laid siege to Samaria, captured it, and deported the Israelites to Assyria. The Assyrian king Sargon II then resettled the country with people drawn from a variety of locations. These events effectively brought to an end the kingdom of Israel. From here onwards the country is known as Samaria, and its inhabitants as the Samaritans. The author of this chapter of the Second Book of Kings comments that although the Samaritans worshipped the Lord, they also served their own gods at the same time. (17:5–33) They were therefore 'to be considered beyond the pale of religiously proper persons … [a] Jewish attitude toward the Samaritans [that] continued into New Testament times'. (NOAB, 480) Abijah was the mother of Hezekiah, who became king of Judah on his father's death.

HEPHZIBAH

MEANING: SHE IS MY DELIGHT

The wife of Hezekiah, king of Judah, and mother of Manasseh.

† BIBLICAL REFERENCE: 2 Kings 21:1

Unlike his predecessors, particularly his father, who had allowed the worship of pagan gods to continue, Hezekiah was devoted to the Lord and carried out religious reforms that included the destruction of the pagan shrines. (18:1–6) The author of this eighteenth chapter of the Second Book of Kings places the catastrophic fall of Samaria to the Assyrians in his reign, whereas the preceding chapter places it in the reign of Ahaz (*see above*, Abi/Abijah). It was during Hezekiah's reign, however, that the Assyrian king Sennacherib invaded Judah. (18:13) After Sennacherib's assassination by his sons, Hezekiah received an embassy from the king of Babylon, and the prophet Isaiah warned him that the time would come when the people of Judah, including some of Hezekiah's own sons, would be taken in captivity to Babylon. (20:12-18) When Hezekiah died, he was succeeded by his twelve-year-old son Manasseh. (20:21-21:1)

MESHULLEMETH

MEANING: RETRIBUTION OR FRIEND

The wife of Manasseh, king of Judah, and mother of Amon.

† BIBLICAL REFERENCE: 2 Kings 21:19

Meshullemeth was the daughter of Haruz of Jotbah. Her husband Manasseh undid his father's religious reforms and shed much innocent blood. He was condemned by the prophets for his wickedness and apostasy. On his death he was succeeded by his son Amon.

JEDIDAH

MEANING: BELOVED

The wife of Amon, king of Judah, and mother of Josiah.

† BIBLICAL REFERENCE: 2 Kings 22:1

Jedidah was the daughter of Adiah of Bozkath. Her husband Amon emulated his father in that he forsook the Lord and served pagan gods. His servants plotted against him and killed him in his palace, but the people killed those who had conspired against him and appointed his son Josiah as his successor.

HAMUTAL

MEANING: KINSMAN OF THE DEW

The wife of Josiah, king of Judah, and mother of Jehoahaz and Zedekiah.

† BIBLICAL REFERENCE: 2 Kings 23:31

(repeated in 2 Kings 24:18 and Jeremiah 52:1)

Hamutal was the daughter of Jeremiah of Libnah. Unlike his father and grandfather, her husband King Josiah was devoted to the Lord. He set about repairing the temple of the Lord, and while the temple was being repaired the high priest found the Book of the Law, which he sent to Josiah. When the book was read to him, the king tore his clothes for he was concerned that the failure of previous generations to obey the laws set out in the book would incur God's wrath. Josiah's concern was such that he sent out a deputation led by the high priest to discover what fate awaited the people of Judah. They went to Huldah, a prophetess who lived in Jerusalem, and the message she gave them to take back to Josiah caused him to pursue his religious reforms with renewed zeal (*see below*, Huldah). Josiah also rebelled against the Assyrians. When he heard that Pharaoh Necho of Egypt, an ally of the Assyrians, was on his way to Assyria, Josiah intercepted him at Megiddo and was killed in the battle. His body was taken back to Jerusalem and the people anointed his son Jehoahaz as his successor. As a consequence of Josiah's defeat, the kingdom of Judah became a vassal of Egypt. Pharaoh Necho put Jehoahaz in chains and took him to Egypt where he died. Mattaniah,

another of Hamutal's sons, was later appointed king of Judah by Nebuchadnezzar when he captured Jerusalem (*see below*, Nehushta).

HULDAH

MEANING: WEASEL

The prophetess who was consulted by King Josiah and prophesied the destruction of Jerusalem and Judah.

† BIBLICAL REFERENCE: 2 Kings 22:14–20

The name Huldah is supposedly derived from an old clan name. (Lockyer, 70–71) She was indirectly responsible for the religious reforms carried out by King Josiah for she prophesied that the Lord's wrath would be unleashed because the people had forsaken him and turned to worshipping other gods. She also prophesied that because Josiah had humbled himself before God he would not live to see the destruction of Jerusalem. As a result of Huldah's prophecy, Josiah carried out sweeping reforms that led to the destruction of all vestiges associated with the cults dedicated to Baal, Molech, Ashtoreth and other pagan gods, and to a renewal of the covenant between the people of Judah and their God. Huldah's prophesied destruction of Jerusalem and Judah occurred at the hands of Nebuchadnezzar during the reigns of Josiah's successors. It is

perhaps significant that Huldah was consulted rather than Jeremiah, her contemporary, whose prophecies concerning the destruction of Judah and Jerusalem are recorded in the biblical book that bears his name.

ZEBIDAH

MEANING: A GIFT

The mother of Jehoiakim, king of Judah.

† BIBLICAL REFERENCE: 2 Kings 23:36

Zebidah was the daughter of Pedaiah of Rumah. Her son, who was originally named Eliakim, was appointed king of Judah by Pharaoh Necho in place of Josiah's son Jehoahaz.

NEHUSHTA

MEANING: A PIECE OF BRASS

The wife of Jehoiakim, king of Judah, and mother of Jehoiachin.

† BIBLICAL REFERENCE: 2 Kings 24:8, 12, 15

Nehushta was the daughter of Elnathan of Jerusalem. It was during the reign of her husband Jehoiakim that Nebuchadnezzar, king of Babylon, first invaded Judah. He was succceeded by his son Jehoiachin, who had reigned for only three months when Nebuchadnezzar captured Jerusalem in 597BC. King Jehoiachin, his mother Nehushta, and the court nobles and officials surrendered, and together with several thousand others were deported to Babylon. Nebuchadnezzar installed Jehoiachin's paternal uncle Mattaniah as king, and changed his name to Zedekiah. When Zedekiah rebelled, Nebuchadnezzar besieged Jerusalem. Zedekiah escaped, but was captured by Chaldean soldiers who took him to Nebuchadnezzar. His sons were killed in front of him, his eyes were gouged out, and he was put into chains and carried off to Babylon. Nebuchadnezzar's forces then destroyed the temple of the Lord, sacked Jerusalem, and deported yet more of the population of Judah to Babylon. The rise of the Persian empire under Cyrus the Great and its conquest of Babylonia in 539BC brought with it the release of the Jews from exile when Cyrus allowed them to return to Judah. The return from exile, the re-establishment of the Jewish community in Jerusalem, and the rebuilding of the Temple are recounted in the Books of Ezra and Nehemiah.

NOADIAH

MEANING: ONE TO WHOM THE LORD REVEALED HIMSELF

The prophetess who opposed Nehemiah.

† BIBLICAL REFERENCE: Nehemiah 6:14

Noadiah is mentioned briefly by Nehemiah as one of the people who made threats against him in order to halt his re-building of the temple in Jerusalem. Two others named with her are Sanballat, the Samaritan leader, and Tobiah the Ammonite.

WIVES FROM ASHDOD, AMMON AND MOAB

The foreign wives condemned by Nehemiah.

† BIBLICAL REFERENCE: Nehemiah 13:23–27

At the end of his book, Nehemiah speaks out against the Jews who had taken foreign wives from Ashdod, Ammon and Moab. He remarks that half of the children of Jews who had married women from Ashdod, Ammon and Moab, spoke a foreign language and could no longer speak the language of Judah. He had scolded them, cursed them, hit several of them, torn out the hair of others, and had forced them to take an oath, saying to them, 'You are not to give your daughters in marriage to the sons of non-Jewish men, or let their daughters marry your sons, or marry them yourselves!' Nehemiah then reminds his readers that, although Solomon had been one of the greatest kings who ever lived, his foreign wives were able to cause even him to sin against God. (For more on Solomon and his foreign wives, *see* pages 108–9.)

QUEEN VASHTI

MEANING: BEAUTIFUL WOMAN

The beautiful queen who defied her drunken husband.

† BIBLICAL REFERENCE: Esther 1:9–2:4, 17

Vashti was the wife of King Ahasuerus (Xerxes). Not only was she beautiful and 'fair to behold', but her name itself means 'beauty' or 'beautiful woman'. In the third year of his reign, King Ahasuerus held a great feast to which he invited all his princes and servants, his army chiefs, and the nobles and governors of his provinces. The feast lasted 180 days, and was followed by another to which he invited all who were in Susa, the capital of his empire. The wine flowed freely. Queen Vashti also gave a feast. On the seventh day of the feast, when the king was 'merry with wine', he ordered the seven eunuchs who served him to fetch Queen Vashti so that he could show off his beautiful wife to his guests. When the queen refused to come to him, the king was beside himself with rage and consulted his legal advisers as to what could lawfully be done to Queen Vashti for not obeying his command. The adviser named Memucan replied that the queen had not only wronged the king, she had also wronged all of Ahasuerus's subjects, for news of what she had done would soon

ABOVE
Act of defiance: when Queen Vashti refused to obey her husband, he issued an
edict that all women should submit to the authority of their husbands

reach the ears of all the women and they would adopt a similarly contemptuous attitude towards their husbands. Memucan then advised Ahasuerus to issue a royal edict banishing Vashti, and to find a woman more worthy of being his queen. The edict, which was to be proclaimed throughout the empire, would command that 'all women will henceforth submit to the authority of their husbands, both high and low alike.' This pleased the king, who did as Memucan advised, and letters were sent to all the provinces to ensure that every man would be master in his own house. When the king's anger eventually abated, his courtiers suggested that a search be made throughout all the provinces for beautiful young virgins, and these virgins should be brought to Susa where they would be placed in the care of Hegai, the king's eunuch in charge of the harem. The girl who pleased the king most would take Vashti's place as queen.

ESTHER/HADASSAH

MEANING: ESTHER, STAR; HADASSAH (HER HEBREW NAME), MYRTLE

The Jewish girl who became Queen of Persia and saved her people from annihilation.

BIBLICAL REFERENCES: Esther 2:7–9:32

Esther was a beautiful Jewish girl living in Susa in the time of King Ahasuerus. She was the daughter of Abihail, but both her parents had died while she was young and she had been raised by her cousin Mordecai, a Jew deported to Susa during the reign of King Jehoiachin of Judah, who had adopted her as his own daughter. When the royal edict went out to the provinces, a great number of girls were brought to Susa and placed in Hegai's care. Esther was also taken to the palace and entrusted to Hegai, but she did not tell anyone about her race or parentage, for Mordecai had told her not to. And every day he passed in front of the harem to find out how Esther was faring. She soon found favour with the king, who gave her seven maids and moved her into the best quarters in the harem. For twelve months the girls remained in the harem, taking it in turns to appear before the king. When it was Esther's turn to go into the king's presence, he found her more to his liking than any of the other girls, and so he crowned her as his queen in place of Vashti. He then gave a great banquet – Esther's banquet – for the entire court, proclaimed a holiday for all the provinces, and distributed gifts with royal largesse. It was around this time that Mordecai heard that two officers in service in the royal household were plotting to assassinate the king. Mordecai told Queen Esther, who informed the king on Mordecai's behalf. When the affair was investigated, the men were found guilty and hanged. Shortly after this, the king promoted Haman son of Hammedatha to the office of grand vizier, and the king commanded that everyone bow low or prostrate themselves in his presence. Mordecai refused to do either, and so some of the officials reported him to Haman. They also told Haman that Mordecai was a Jew. When Haman saw for himself that Mordecai refused to bow to him, he was furious. But rather than merely eliminate Mordecai, he determined to rid the whole kingdom of Mordecai's race – the Jews.

Lots were cast in Haman's presence to establish an appropriate date for the purge. When a date had been determined for the month of Adar, the twelfth month of the year, Haman went to the king and proposed that the king issued a decree for the annihilation of the Jews. He also offered the king an inducement of ten thousand silver talents for the royal treasury, but the king said, 'The money is yours to keep. You can have the people too, to do with them as you wish.' Letters sealed with the king's seal were duly sent out to all the provinces ordering the slaughter of the Jews and the seizure of all their property on the 13th day of Adar. The news created great distress throughout the Jewish community. When Mordecai tore off his robes and

put on sackcloth, the grief-stricken Esther sent him new robes to replace the sackcloth but he refused to put them on. She then summoned Hathach, one of her attendants, and sent him to Mordecai to find out why he was behaving in this way. Mordecai told him about his confrontation with Haman, and about the inducement Haman had offered the king. He also gave him a copy of the decree issued in Susa for the annihilation of the Jews to give to Esther, and urged her to intervene with the king on behalf of her people. After Hathach had spoken with her, Esther sent a message back to Mordecai telling him of the law that applied to anyone who approached the king in his inner court without having been summoned: they were condemned to death, unless the king pointed his golden sceptre at them to grant them their life. Moreover, the king had not summoned her once in the past thirty days. Mordecai replied that Esther was no safer in the royal palace than any of the other Jews. For if she maintained her silence at such a time, the Jews would be saved by other means while Esther and her father's entire family would perish. 'Perhaps,' concluded Mordecai, 'it is no coincidence that you have been made queen at just such a time as this.' Esther then sent word to Mordecai, saying, 'Gather together all the

Jews in Susa and fast for three days on my behalf. My maids and I shall keep the same fast. Then I shall go to the king, in spite of the law; and if I perish, I perish.' And Mordecai did as Esther had instructed.

On the third day, after the fast had finished, Esther put on her royal robes; the image of beauty and regal splendour, she then went and stood in the presence of the king. When the king saw her standing before him in the inner court, he looked on her favourably and held out towards her the golden sceptre in his hand. He then said, 'What is it, Queen Esther? Whatever you request shall be granted you, even if it is half my kingdom.' She replied, 'If it please the king, let the king and Haman come to a banquet I have prepared for them.' The honour of being invited to dine alone with the king and queen left Haman feeling elated. His elation was short-lived, however, for it turned to anger as soon as he saw Mordecai who, yet again, refused to bow down to him. When he got home he called together his wife, his family and his friends and boasted about his wealth and the high favour he enjoyed with the king, but he confessed that it all meant nothing as long as he saw Mordecai working in the Chancellery. His wife Zeresh and his friends suggested that he order a gallows 50 cubits (about 22 metres) high to be erected,

 ABOVE
Royal request: Queen Esther risked her life by seeking an audience with the
king in his inner court, but she was spared

and in the morning ask the king to hang Mordecai on it. This idea pleased Haman, and he had the gallows set up. But the king was unable to sleep that night. He called for the Chronicles – the book of memorable deeds – to be brought and read to him. He heard the account of how Mordecai had denounced the two men who had plotted to kill the king, and he asked what honour

ABOVE
Deadly words: during Esther's banquet for the king and Haman, she pleaded with her husband to spare the Jews and named Haman as their persecutor

had been conferred on him for this act. 'None,' came the reply. The king then asked who was in the outer chamber. It so happened

that Haman had just entered the court to speak to the king about hanging Mordecai on the gallows he had erected, and so the king's servants replied, 'Haman is there.' The king said, 'Show him in.' When Haman entered, the king asked him how he should treat a man whom he wished to honour. Thinking that the king was talking about him, Haman replied that he should be given royal robes of honour, a horse from the king's stable and a royal crown, and he should be led on horseback around the central square of Susa by one of the king's dignitaries, who would proclaim that this was how the king treated those he chose to honour. Then the king said, 'Go quickly and take the robes and horse, and do everything just as you have described to Mordecai the Jew who works in the Chancellery.' And so Haman went and did for Mordecai all the things he had envisaged for himself. Afterwards, when he related to his wife and friends what had happened, they warned him that his influence was on the wane while Mordecai's was on the rise, and they said to him, 'You are sure to fall before he does.' While they were still talking, the king's servants arrived to take Haman to the banquet.

The king and Haman went to Queen Esther's banquet, and on the second day the king again asked Esther what she wished to

request of him. She replied, 'If I have found favour with you, and if it so pleases the king, let my life and the lives of my people be spared. For I and my people have been marked out to be slaughtered. Had we merely been sold into slavery, I would have said nothing; but as things stand, it is beyond our persecutor's means to recompense the king for the loss he is about to suffer.' The king interrupted her, 'Who is he? Where is the man that would do this?' Esther said, 'Our persecutor? It's this vile man Haman!' On hearing these words Haman was overcome with fear. The king was so angry that he left the banquet and went out into the garden. Haman realized that all was lost, and so he stayed behind to plead for his life with the queen. When the king came back from the garden, he found Haman draped over the couch on which his wife was reclining. 'What!' exclaimed the king, 'Would this man even rape the queen in my presence, and in my palace?' And at these words they covered the doomed man's face with a veil. Harbona, one of the king's officers, told the king about the gallows that Haman had prepared for Mordecai. The king said, 'Hang him on it!' And so Haman was hanged on the gallows on which he had intended to hang Mordecai. The king gave Haman's house to Esther, and he gave Mordecai the ring of office that he had taken away from Haman. Then Esther asked the king to revoke the decree by which Haman had contrived the elimination of her people, and the king told her to write the necessary letters in the king's name and to seal them with the king's seal. Mordecai dictated the letters, which gave the king's permission to the Jews to defend themselves against anyone who might attack them on the day allotted by Haman for their elimination. As soon as they were written, couriers sped off on horseback to deliver them to all the provinces. Mordecai left the palace in his magnificent royal robes, and in Susa and throughout the entire realm the Jews celebrated the new decree with feasting and a holiday.

On the 13th day of Adar, the twelfth month, the king's decree came into force. This was the day on which the enemies of the Jews had hoped to slaughter them, but the opposite happened: it was the Jews who slaughtered their enemies, and among the dead in Susa were the ten sons of Haman. Then Esther went to the king and asked him to extend his decree to the next day too, the 14th day of Adar, and on the 15th the Jews of Susa rested and spent the day feasting. But in the villages they rested on the 14th. Mordecai wrote all this down, and sent letters to all the Jews in the provinces, instructing them that the 14th and 15th days of Adar should be kept as an annual festival to celebrate the days on which the Jews had eliminated their enemies, and the month in which their sorrow had been turned into joy. These days were to be called Purim (from the word *pur*, meaning 'lot', for the date had been fixed by the casting of lots). Queen Esther then wrote letters to all the provinces, endorsing what Mordecai had written and urging the Jews to observe the days of Purim at the appointed time. Her command fixed the practices of Purim.

Esther in art

Esther's popularity as one of the great biblical heroines is perpetuated by the festival of Purim. Her popularity as a subject in Christian art was assured by the early Church which saw the act of her pleading with the king for the lives of her people as prefiguring the intercession of the Virgin (herself a figure of the Church) on the Day of Judgement. Images portraying Esther before the king are therefore widespread and include notable examples by the seventeenth-century artists Rubens, Rembrandt and Poussin. Many of these show the king holding out his golden sceptre to Esther. Another fairly common subject is the banquet Esther gave for her husband the king and Haman, with some works depicting Esther's denunc-iation of the grand vizier. In a more secular vein, the theme of Esther beautifying herself before going into the presence of the king gave artists the opportunity to portray the female nude. *Esther at Her Toilette* by the nineteenth-century French painter Théodore Chassériau is a particularly sensuous example of the latter. Esther has also been immortalized in plays by Sachs and Racine, and in music by Handel.

ZERESH

MEANING: STAR

The wife of Haman, King Ahasuerus's grand vizier.

† BIBLICAL REFERENCE: Esther 5:10–14, 6:13

When Haman complained about the disrespect shown him by Mordecai the Jew, his wife Zeresh suggested that he erect a gallows on which to hang him. (5:14) Later, when Haman told Zeresh that Mordecai had gained the king's favour, she warned him, 'If Mordecai is Jewish, you will never win against him. You are sure to fall before he does' (*see above*, Esther).

3 The Writings, the Prophets and the Apocrypha

The Pentateuch and Historical Books set forth the spiritual, legal and historical traditions of the Jewish people and their religion, whereas the biblical books that comprise the Writings are very different in both form and style, for they include wisdom literature (books of proverbs and teachings relating to the quest for wisdom), poetry and songs. The books of the Prophets, which contain the pronouncements of those who served as a mouthpiece for God, frequently make use of allegory as they urge the people of Israel to return to the Way of the Lord or face the consequences of their erring. The earlier prophets also contain some historical writings. The books known as the Apocrypha (by Protestants) or the Deuterocanon (by Catholics and Orthodox Christians), generally dated to between the third century BC and the first century AD, comprise several different literary genres, including wisdom literature, historical works, novelistic stories and apocalyptic writings. The selection and order of the books that comprise these three collections differ in the Protestant, Catholic and Orthodox Bibles. The order followed here is that of the Revised Standard Version.

Women in the Books of the Writings

THE DAUGHTERS OF JOB

Three young women who died while eating and drinking.

† BIBLICAL REFERENCE: Job 1:2–4; 13–19

The opening verses of the Book of Job describe Job as an honest and upright man who feared God. He had three daughters and seven sons, and was a man of considerable wealth, owning several thousand sheep and camels, a few hundred donkeys and many servants. His three daughters would spend their days eating and drinking with their brothers, who each took it in turn to invite their sisters and other brothers to their house. (1:2–4) On the fateful day that Satan began to test Job's faith in God, a succession of messengers ran to Job with news of the

 ABOVE
In happier days: Job was a wealthy man with three daughters and seven sons who feared God

ABOVE
Reversal of fortune: top left, Satan asks God to release him from his chains so
he can test Job's faith in God; below, a messenger appears to bring bad news

JEMIMA, KEZIA AND KEREN-HAPPUCH

MEANING: JEMIMA, DOVE; KEZIA, CASSIA; KEREN-HAPPUCH, HORN OF EYE-PAINT

The three daughters born to Job after his trials were over.

† BIBLICAL REFERENCE: Job 42:13–15

When Job's trials were over, God restored to him the wealth he had lost earlier, and doubled it. The three daughters born to him late in life are described as the most beautiful in the land. Moreover, their father gave them the same rights of inheritance as their seven brothers.

THE PRINCESS OF TYRE

A royal wedding song for a foreign princess.

† BIBLICAL REFERENCE: Psalm 45

The psalmist urges the foreign bride to forget her people and her former heritage in preparation for her marriage to an unnamed king of Israel. If she does, her kingly bridegroom will love her all the more. With the bride dressed in robes of gold brocade and accompanied by a retinue of virgin bridesmaids, the wedding procession makes its way to the palace, which it enters amidst great joy and rejoicing.

The song ends with the psalmist saying that her ancestors will be replaced by her sons, who

sequence of catastrophes that had befallen him. The last messenger of the day announced that Job's sons and daughters had been eating and drinking in his eldest son's house when a mighty wind roared out of the desert and blew the house down on top of them, killing them all. Job tore his robes, shaved his head, prostrated himself on the ground, and said, 'Naked I came from my mother's womb, and naked I shall return. The Lord gave, and the Lord has taken away. Blessed be the name of the Lord!' (1:13–21)

THE WIFE OF JOB

The mother of Job's twenty children.

† BIBLICAL REFERENCE: Job 2:9–10; 19:17; 31:9–10

Job's wife makes only three brief appearances in the entire Book of Job. We first meet her when, having failed to dent Job's faith in God, Satan has covered Job's whole body with sores. Taking up a piece of broken pot to scrape his skin, Job went and sat on a heap of ashes. His wife said to him, 'Why are you clinging to this integrity of yours? Curse God, and die.' Job answered, 'That is what a fool of a woman would say. If we receive good from God's hand, shall we not also receive evil?' (2:9–10) Later, when Job had become a social outcast and his physical body had deteriorated, he says (19:17), 'I am repulsive to my wife' (RSV) or 'My breath is unbearable to my wife'. (NJB) The last reference to his wife comes when Job reviews his past conduct, and says, 'If my heart has been seduced by a woman, or if I have lurked at my neighbour's door, let my wife go and grind for someone else, let others have intercourse with her!' (31:9–10, NJB) Although she is not mentioned again, when Job's trials were over she bore him another seven sons and three daughters.

ABOVE
Test of faith: Satan inflicted a series of catastrophes upon Job including the death of all his children

will become rulers of the world.
Like the Song of Songs (*see below*,
The Shulammite woman), this
psalm is possibly an allegory for
spiritual union with God: the bride
personifies the human soul, the
unnamed bridegroom God.

WISDOM AND FOLLY

*The personification of what is
most desirable and what is not.*

† BIBLICAL REFERENCE: Wisdom
Proverbs 1:20–2; 3:14–18; 4:6–9;
5:18–19; 9:1–6; 11:16; 12:4; 14:1;
18:22; 19:14; 29:3. Folly 5:3–6, 5:20;

6:23–6, 29; 7:10–27; 9:13–18; 11:22;
14:1; 19:13; 21:9, 19; 23:27–8; 25:24;
27:15; 29:3; 30:20

The Book of Proverbs was
compiled so that its readers may
attain 'wisdom and discipline,
understand words of insight,
acquire a disciplined approach to

ABOVE
Two contrasting women: on the left is Wisdom who is 'more precious than
rubies'; on the right is Folly 'dressed like a prostitute, cunning of heart …'

life, doing what is upright, just and honest ...' (1:2–3) To achieve this end the authors drew on the traditional maxim that we get to know a thing through its opposite; they also employ the ancient literary device of person-ification. And so we find two contrasting women frequenting its pages: the one represents wisdom, who is 'more precious than rubies, and nothing you desire can compare with her' (3:15); the other, representing folly, is 'dressed like a prostitute, cunning of heart ... loud and brazen.' (7:10–11) Together they personify our human predica-ment, which the Persian poet Rumi likened to 'an angel's wing tied to an ass's tail'. One aspect of us is drawn towards the things that promote our spiritual evolution; the other is drawn towards the things that impede it. We can approach the personifications of Wisdom and Folly with these two aspects in mind.

Wisdom calls aloud in the streets, she raises her voice in the market squares; she calls out at noisy street corners, and delivers her message at the city gates. 'O simple people, how much longer will you cling to your simple ways? How much longer will mockers delight in their mockery, and fools hate knowledge?' (1:20–2)

[Wisdom] is more profitable than silver, her yield is greater than gold. She is more precious than rubies, and nothing you desire can compare with her. Long life is in her right hand; in her left are riches and honour. Her ways are pleasant ways, and all her paths are peace. She is a tree of life to those who embrace her; those who hold her fast live happy lives. (3:14–18)

Do not forsake wisdom, and she will protect you; love her, and she will watch over you. … Hold her close, and she will exalt you; embrace her, and she will honour you.
(4:6, 8)

My son, pay attention to my

wisdom, … for the lips of an adulteress drip with honey, and her speech is smoother than oil; but in the end she is as bitter as wormwood, sharp as a two-edged sword. (5:1, 3–4)

May your fountain be blessed, and may you rejoice in the wife of your youth, a loving hind, a graceful doe – may you always delight in her breasts. May you always be captivated by her love. Why be seduced, my son, by someone else's wife? Why fondle the breasts of an adventuress? (5:18–20)

My son, keep your father's commandment, and do not reject your mother's teaching. … For the commandment is a lamp, the teaching is a light; the corrections of discipline are the way to life, preserving you from the immoral woman, from the smooth tongue of the adventuress. Do not let your heart lust after her beauty, nor let her captivate you with her eyes; a prostitute can be bought for a loaf of bread, but an adulteress snares life itself. (6:20, 23–6)

Say to Wisdom, 'You are my sister!' and call insight your intimate friend; they will preserve you from the loose woman and the seductive

words of the adulteress. From my window I notice a foolish youth. A woman comes towards him, dressed like a prostitute, cunning of heart. She takes hold of him and kisses him, and brazenly says, 'I have perfumed my bed with aloes and myrrh. Come, let us make love till morning. Let us savour the delights of love.'
(7:4–18, abridged)

Wisdom has built her house, she has hewn her seven pillars. She has slaughtered her beasts, drawn her wine and laid her table. She has sent out her maids, and she calls from the highest points of the city … 'Come, eat my bread, and drink the wine I have drawn. Leave foolishness behind and live, and walk the path of insight.' (9:1–3, 5–6)

Folly acts on impulse; she lacks restraint and has no knowledge. She sits at the door of her house, on a seat at the highest point of the city, and calls out to passers-by, 'Whoever is simple, come in here!' (9:13–16)

A gracious woman acquires honour, but violent people acquire only wealth. … A gold ring in a pig's snout is like a beautiful woman who lacks discretion. (11:16, 22)

An accomplished woman is a crown for her husband. (12:4)

Wisdom builds herself a house; with her own hands Folly tears it down. (14:1)

He who finds a wife finds happiness, and receives favour from the Lord. (18:22)

A quarrelsome wife is like a dripping tap. Houses and wealth are inherited from our fathers, but a prudent wife is from the Lord. (19:13–14)

A prostitute is a deep pit, and a wayward wife is a narrow well. Like a bandit, she lies in wait, and increases the numbers of those without faith. (23:27–8)

It is better to live on the corner of a roof than share a house with a quarrelsome woman. (25:24)

The lover of Wisdom brings joy to his father, but a person who frequents prostitutes fritters away his very substance. (29:3)

The way of the adulteress is to eat, wipe her mouth, and say, 'I have done nothing wrong.' (30:20)

THE PERFECT WIFE

The teaching of Lemuel's mother.

† BIBLICAL REFERENCE: Proverbs 31:10–31

The concluding chapter of the Book of Proverbs is attributed to King Lemuel and contains the teachings his mother taught him. Verses 10 to 31 describe the qualities associated with the perfect wife and take the form of an acrostic (i.e. the first word of each verse begins with a successive letter of the Hebrew alphabet).

> She is clothed in strength and
>   dignity,
> she can laugh at the day to
>   come.
> She speaks with wisdom,
> and kindly instruction is on her
>   tongue.
> Her children stand up and call
>   her blessed;
> Her husband also, and he sings
>   her praises:
> 'Many women have done
>   exemplary things,
> but you surpass them all.'
>   (PROVERBS 31:25–9)

THE WOMAN WHOSE HEART IS SNARES AND NETS

A personification of Folly.

† BIBLICAL REFERENCE: Ecclesiastes 7:26

In his search for wisdom, the author of Ecclesiastes – known as the Preacher – found also the 'folly which is madness'. (7:25) He found 'more bitter than death the woman whose heart is snares and nets, and whose hands are chains. The person who pleases God will escape her, but the sinner is ensnared by her.'

THE SHULAMMITE WOMAN

The woman who is 'as a lily among brambles'.

† BIBLICAL REFERENCE: The Song of Songs

The Song of Songs is a love poem which takes the form of a dialogue between a lover and his beloved. Considered by some to be a celebration of the variety and power of human love, and by others to be an allegory of the desire of the human soul for union with God, the Song of Songs is also in part a hymn to feminine beauty, which is itself a reflection of divine beauty. Whatever interpretation we care to apply to the Song, the beauty of its words is beyond question. So is the sensuality of its poetic imagery, as in the following verses in which the lover describes his beloved.

> How beautiful you are, my
>   beloved.
> Oh, how beautiful you are!
> Your eyes are doves
>   behind your veil;
> your hair is like a flock of goats
> descending the slopes of Mount
>   Gilead.
> Your teeth are like a flock of
>   sheep
> freshly shorn, after the
>   washing.
> Each one has its twin,
> not one is unpaired.
> Your lips are a scarlet thread,

and your mouth enchanting.
Your cheeks behind your veil
are like halves of a
   pomegranate.
Your neck is like the tower of
   David, …

Your two breasts are two
   fawns,
twins fawns of a gazelle
that feed among the lilies.

(SONG OF SONGS 4:1–5)

Women in the Books of the Prophets

THE DAUGHTER(S) OF ZION

A personification of Jerusalem and its inhabitants.

† BIBLICAL REFERENCE: Isaiah 1:8; 3:16

Isaiah delivered most of his prophecies in Judah at a time in the eighth century BC when the northern kingdom of Israel had been annexed by the Assyrians and Judah was itself threatened by foreign rulers. It is clear from his first use of the phrase 'the daughter of Zion' that this is a personification of the city of Jerusalem and its inhabitants, for he writes: 'The daughter of Zion is left like a booth in a vineyard,

like a hut in a cucumber field, like a city under siege.' (1:8) He adds that if it were not for the fact that some had survived the destruction, Jerusalem would be like Sodom and Gomorrah (1:9). Moreover, 'the faithful city has become a harlot'. (1:21) To place Isaiah's second reference to the 'daughters of Zion' in context, it is worth quoting a couple of verses that precede it, for Isaiah says that the downfall of both Jerusalem and Judah came about because their words and actions were an affront to God (3:8), and that human pride and arrogance will have to be abased, and God alone exalted. (2:17) Personifying

the people as the 'daughters of Zion', he says, 'The Lord says, "The daughters of Zion are haughty and walk with heads held high, flirting with their eyes, mincing along with bangles jingling on their feet; the Lord will cover the heads of the daughters of Zion with sores, and lay bare their heads.' (3:16–17)

THE YOUNG WOMAN WHO WILL GIVE BIRTH TO A SON

The mother-to-be of Immanuel.

† BIBLICAL REFERENCE: Isaiah 7:14

God instructed Isaiah to meet King Ahaz and tell him not to be

ABOVE
The Shulammite Woman: a celebration of the woman who was 'a lily among brambles'

afraid: the house of David would not fall to the combined forces of Aram, Ephraim and Samaria. (7:3–6) When Isaiah met Ahaz, he told him to ask God for a sign, but Ahaz refused because he did not want to test God. So Isaiah said, 'The Lord himself will give you a sign: the young woman will conceive and give birth to a son, and will call him Immanuel ['God is with us'].' (7:14) Some authorities suggest that Isaiah was referring to the wife of Ahaz, or to Isaiah's own wife (*see below*), but the evangelist Matthew interpreted this prophecy as applying to Mary, the mother of Jesus (Matthew 1:23; *see below*, Mary, Mother of Jesus, page 164).

ISAIAH'S WIFE

† BIBLICAL REFERENCE: Isaiah 8:3

The unnamed wife of Isaiah is mentioned briefly in connection with the conception and birth of the prophet's second son Maher-shalal-hash-baz. The name, which God had previously instructed Isaiah to write down on a tablet, means 'Speedy-spoil-quick-booty', and is said to predict the destruction of Damascus and Samaria in 722BC. (NJB, 887)

HAUGHTY WOMEN

† BIBLICAL REFERENCE: Isaiah 32:9–20

The prophet says, 'Stand up, you haughty women, listen to my words: you over-confident daughters, pay attention to what I say.' (NJB, 32:9) In another translation, the same verse begins, 'Rise up, you women who are at ease ...' (RSV). As with his earlier mention of 'the daughters of Zion' (*see above*), Isaiah may here be addressing the people as a whole – female and male.

VIRGIN DAUGHTER OF BABYLON

† BIBLICAL REFERENCE: Isaiah 47:1–15

This prophecy – which begins, 'Step down! Sit in the dust, virgin daughter of Babylon. Sit on the ground without a throne, O daughter of the Chaldeans! For never again shall you be called tender and delicate ...' – refers to the as-yet-unconquered (therefore 'virgin') kingdom of Babylon prior to its conquest by the Persians.

THE BRIDE WHO BECAME A HARLOT

† BIBLICAL REFERENCE: Jeremiah 2:1ff

In this lengthy prophecy, the Lord tells Jeremiah to proclaim to Jerusalem, 'I remember your faithful devotion, your love as a bride, and how you followed me through the wilderness, a land not sown ....' (2:1–2) But Judah, God's faithful bride, turned to harlotry, waiting by the roadside for her lovers (other gods), and polluting the land with her prostitution. (3:2) Jeremiah's prophecy continues in the same vein for several chapters, predicting the disaster that awaits Judah at the hands of Nebuchadnezzar.

VIRGIN ISRAEL

† BIBLICAL REFERENCE: Jeremiah 31:21–2

Chapter 31 of the Book of Jeremiah contains the frequently quoted passage (vv.31–4) in which God announces a new covenant, understood by Christians as prophesying the coming of Christ. Prior to this he calls his people to come to him again, saying, 'Come home, O virgin Israel, come home to these cities of yours. How long will you hesitate, O rebellious daughter?' (31:21–2)

THE UNFAITHFUL WIFE

† BIBLICAL REFERENCE: Ezekiel 16:1–59

An allegorical history of Jerusalem in the form of a folk-tale.

OHOLAH AND OHOLIBAH

MEANING: OHOLAH, SHE WHO HAS A TENT; OHOLIBAH, MY TENT IN HER

† BIBLICAL REFERENCE: Ezekiel 23:1–48

An allegorical story of two sisters (Samaria and Jerusalem) and their lovers (foreign gods). The sisters' names are a play on words which implies that although Samaria had a religious sanctuary (Oholah, 'has a tent'), the sanctuary recognized by the Lord was in Jerusalem (Oholibah, 'my tent [is] in her'). (NOAB, 1027)

BELSHAZZAR'S MOTHER

The queen who recommended the prophet Daniel to her son.

† BIBLICAL REFERENCE: Daniel 5:10–12

When King Belshazzar succeeded his father Nebuchadnezzar to the throne, he gave a great feast at which the guests drank from the gold and silver vessels that Nebuchadnezzar had taken from the temple in Jerusalem. As they were drinking, a hand appeared and wrote on one of the walls the Aramaic words, '*Mene, mene, teqel, parsin.*' Belshazzar turned pale with alarm, and began to tremble so much that his knees knocked together. He called for his soothsayers, Chaldeans (meaning 'sorcerers') and astrologers, but none of his sages could either read the writing or explain what it meant. Attracted by the commotion, Belshazzar's mother (Nebuchadnezzar's widow) entered the banqueting hall and told her son to send for Daniel, a man so gifted with the wisdom of the gods that Nebuchadnezzar had made him head of the magicians, soothsayers, Chaldeans and astrologers. (Daniel had previously interpreted two of her husband's dreams: 2:24–45; 4:6–23.)

Women in the Books of the Apocrypha

APAME

The concubine who slapped a king.

† BIBLICAL REFERENCE: 1 Esdras 4:29–31

According to the author of 1 Esdras, Apame was a concubine of King Darius of Persia (reigned 521–485BC). Three of the king's bodyguards held a contest in which they were each to name the strongest thing. The first named wine; the second, the king; and the third, women. But the third, who is identified as Zerubbabel, added that truth was the strongest of all. Each of the men then expanded on their choice before the king, and when it came to the turn of Zerubbabel, he said, 'Although both wine and the king are strong, women are their masters for they give birth to them; they also give birth to the men who plant vineyards and make wine. Women make men's clothes, and bring men glory. Indeed, men cannot exist without women. Everything they do is for women. And many men have lost their minds or perished over women. Is it not true that the king is great and powerful? Yet I have seen him with Apame his concubine, the daughter of Bartacus. She would sit at the king's right hand, and take the crown from his head and put it on her own; and when she slapped him with her left hand, he would look at her open-mouthed. If she smiles at him, he laughs; if she loses her temper with him, he flatters her to placate her. Since women do such things, surely they are strong.' At this Zerubbabel paused, and then began to discourse on the strength of truth.

THE WOMAN WHO MOURNED FOR HER SON

A vision of the old and new Jerusalems.

† BIBLICAL REFERENCE: 2 Esdras 9:38–10:27

Writing towards the end of the first century AD, the author of 2

Esdras, who gives his name as both Ezra and Salathiel, describes a sequence of apocalyptic visions, in the fourth of which he saw a woman, weeping and in mourning. When he asked her why she was weeping, she replied that she had been barren for thirty years, and during those thirty years she had prayed continuously to the Most High that he would consider her distress and give her a son. Her prayers were answered, and when her son grew up she obtained a wife for him and arranged for his marriage feast, but when her son entered the bridal chamber he fell down and died. The grief-stricken woman had fled from the city to the field where Ezra now saw her, and there she would remain, fasting and mourning until she died. Ezra responded angrily, contrasting her mourning for her son with the mourning of Zion (Jerusalem), the mother of them all. The woman might be mourning her son, but the people were mourning their mother, and he asked her, 'Who should be mourning the more, the mother who lost a multitude, or a woman who had lost one son?' Ezra told her to return to her husband in the city, but the woman refused, saying that she would die where she was. He then described to her the desolation of the temple and the suffering experienced by the people, but while he was doing so the woman's face lit up and shone like lightning, and he became frightened. He was wondering what this could mean when the woman let out a fearful cry that shook the earth beneath his feet, and she vanished. In her place he saw a city. Ezra called out to Uriel, the angel who had shown him his earlier visions. Uriel came to him, and interpreted the vision for him. The woman was the city of Zion. The thirty years she had remained barren were the three thousand years that passed before any offerings were made to her. At the end of those three thousand years, Solomon had built the city and made offerings. This was when the woman bore a son, and her son's death was the destruction that had befallen Jerusalem. Because Ezra had sought to console the woman, he had been shown a vision of Jerusalem in the fullness of its heavenly glory. Ezra had therefore been told to remain in the field outside the earthly city, where there were no buildings, because no edifice erected by human hands could endure when the Heavenly City was revealed. (9:38–10:54)

ANNA

MEANING: GRACE

The woman who worked to support her family.

† BIBLICAL REFERENCE: Tobit 2:1, 11; 5:17–21; 10:4–7; 11:5–9; 14:12

Anna was the wife of Tobit, a pious Jew from Thisbe in Galilee, who had been taken captive to Nineveh. She was reunited with her husband when he returned from exile one year at the feast of Pentecost, but Tobit left the family feast to perform the charitable act of burying a recently

ABOVE
Making the blind see again: Tobias with his mother Anna and father Tobit, who lost his sight when the droppings of sparrows went in his eyes

deceased member of his clan. Because his contact with the dead had rendered him ritually unclean (*see above*, Women and the law), he spent the night outside beside a wall in his court-yard. However, the droppings from the sparrows on top of the wall fell into his eyes and he became blind that same night, and so Anna went out to work to support her husband and their son Tobias. One day her employers gave her a kid in addition to her wages, but Tobit refused to believe it was a gift and accused her of having stolen it. Stung by his accusation, Anna replied, 'Where is your charity now? You assume you know everything!' Filled with grief by this reproach and by his blindness, Tobit went and prayed to the Lord to release him from this life. (1:1–2, 2:1–3:6) That same night, in the town of Ecbatana in Media, a young woman named Sarah prayed to the Lord in a similar vein (*see below*, Sarah). While they were both finishing their prayers, the Lord sent the angel Raphael to heal Tobit's sight and to give Sarah in marriage to Tobias (3:16–17). Tobit then remembered some money he had left in trust with a relative in the town of Rages in Media and, since he had prayed to die, he called Tobias to him and explained about the money and charged him to look after his mother when he died. (4:1–4)

When they looked for someone to accompany Tobit on the journey to Media, they found Raphael, who had given himself the name Azarias. (5:4, 12) Anna wept as her son prepared to leave, and said to Tobit, 'Why send our son away? Is he not the stuff of life to us? Money is as nothing compared to our child.' But Tobit told her not to worry, for his guardian angel would watch over him, and Anna stopped weeping. When the two men set off, Tobias's dog went with them too. (5:17–21; *see below*, Sarah, for the story of Sarah's marriage to Tobias) When Tobias and Raphael failed to return from Rages within a certain time, Anna was convinced that her son had perished, and she went into mourning. Tobit endeavoured to reassure her, but she refused to be consoled. Every day she went to wait by the road that Tobias and Raphael had taken when they left, and at night she mourned. (10:4–7) Her roadside vigil was eventually rewarded when she saw Tobias and Raphael coming towards her. She told her husband his son was coming home, then ran to meet the two men on the road, and embraced the son she had presumed dead. (11:5–9; *see below*, Sarah, for the account of Tobias and Sarah's homecoming) When Anna died, Tobias buried her with his father. (14:12)

SARAH

MEANING: PRINCESS

The young woman whose seven husbands were killed by the demon Asmodeus.

† BIBLICAL REFERENCE: Tobit 3:7–15; 7:1, 8; 11–13; 8:1–9

Sarah was the beautiful daughter of Raguel, from Ecbatana in Media. She had been married seven times, but on each occasion her husband had been killed by the demon Asmodeus. When her father's servants reproached her, and accused her of having strangled her husbands, Sarah contemplated hanging herself. But the thought of the disgrace this would bring on her father, and the fact that she was his only child, dissuaded her. Filled with grief by the maids' reproaches and the loss of her seven husbands, Sarah prayed to the Lord to release her from this life or, failing this, command that she be shown more respect and no longer hear the reproaches of others. (3:7–15) While the angel Raphael and Tobias were travelling to Rages (*see above*, Anna, for the reason for their journey), Raphael suggested that they stayed with Raguel, a relative of Tobias, in Ecbatana. He also told him about Raguel's daughter Sarah, and proposed that Tobias marry her on their return from Rages. Tobias told the angel that he had heard Sarah had already had seven husbands, all of whom

had died in the bridal chamber. He feared suffering the same fate because of the demon who was in love with her. But the angel told Tobias what to do to get rid of the demon, adding that Sarah had been destined for Tobias for all eternity. (6:9–17) Sarah came out to meet the two men when they arrived at Raguel's home, greeted them, and took them into the house. When Raguel saw Tobias, he turned to his wife Edna and commented on the resemblance between Tobias and his own cousin Tobit. In the ensuing conversation with his guests, he learned that Tobias was Tobit's son. Sarah and Edna wept when they were told that Tobit had lost his sight. Raphael then told Raguel of the proposed marriage between Sarah and Tobias, and Raguel called his daughter and the marriage contract was sealed there and then. Edna went and prepared the marriage chamber, and comforted Sarah when she began to weep as she entered the chamber (presumably because her seven previous husbands had all died on their wedding night, and she anticipated

ABOVE
Safe and well: Tobias survived the perils of Sarah's bedchamber – her previous seven husbands all died on their wedding night

the same fate for Tobias). Tobias joined Sarah in the bridal chamber and burnt a mixture of incense and fish – it was a man-eating fish that Tobias had caught in the Tigris – as Raphael had instructed him to do, and when the demon Asmodeus smelt the odour, he fled to Egypt where Raphael bound him tight. Sarah and Tobias prayed together, and then went to sleep. (8:1–9) The wedding feast lasted fourteen days, during which Raphael went to Rages to collect Tobit's money, and when the feast was over Tobias and Sarah set off on the homeward journey to Thisbe. As they neared the town, Tobias and Raphael went on ahead of Sarah, and Tobias went in to his father and, as Raphael had instructed him, placed in his father's eyes the gall of the fish he had caught in the Tigris, at which Tobit regained his sight and was able to go out to meet Sarah at the city gate in time to welcome her to her new home. The marriage of Sarah and Tobias was celebrated for seven days. (9:1–11:19) Azarias then revealed himself to be the angel Raphael, and he explained that when God had heard the prayers of Sarah and Tobit, he had sent him to heal them. (12:11–15) Some years later Sarah returned with her husband and sons to Ecbatana, her parents' home, where the family spent their remaining years. (14:12–14)

Anna and Sarah in art

Images from the popular story of Tobias and the angel are fairly widespread, and include scenes with Anna and Sarah. A painting by Rembrandt in the Rijksmuseum in Amsterdam showing Anna with her blind husband has the elderly Anna holding the kid given her by her employer. Anna is also sometimes present in scenes of Tobit regaining his sight. Scenes of the marriage of Sarah and Tobias sometimes include Edna, Sarah's mother, while Rembrandt's *Sarah Waiting for Tobias*, in the National Gallery of Scotland, Edinburgh, depicts Sarah on her own, in bed on her wedding night, awaiting her husband.

EDNA

MEANING: PLEASURE OR DELIGHT

The mother of Sarah (see above).

† BIBLICAL REFERENCE: Tobit 7:2, 8; 16–18; 10:12

Edna was the wife of Raguel of Ecbatana. She met Tobias and Raphael when they stayed in her house, and wept when she learned that Tobias's father (her husband's cousin Tobit) had lost his sight. (7:2, 8) She prepared the bridal chamber for Sarah's wedding with Tobias, and comforted her daughter on her wedding night. (7:16–18) When Sarah and Tobias were preparing to return to Thisbe, Edna asked her son-in-law to come back with her grandchildren so that she might rejoice in them. (10:12)

JUDITH

MEANING: PRAISED

The beautiful woman who cut off a general's head and saved her people from certain death.

† BIBLICAL REFERENCE: Judith 8:1–15:25

The Book of Judith is one of only four books in the Bible to bear a woman's name, each of which portrays its central character – Judith, Ruth, Esther or Susanna – as a model of devotion and piety. Moreover, in spite of the patriarchal nature of contemporary Jewish religion and society, Judith and Esther are presented as heroines who save their people from extinction at the hands of their enemies. It is widely acknowledged, however, that the stories of both these women are works of fiction intended to inspire the Jewish people to re-dedicate themselves to God. Written in the latter part of the second century BC, the story of Judith contains enough historical and geographical anomalies to suggest the author included them deliberately. This literary device was, and still is, often employed to emphasize the fictitious nature of a story and thus direct the audience to its underlying allegorical meaning. In addition, the story's subtle intricacies and the drama of its skilfully constructed plot define it as a masterpiece of ancient Jewish narrative art. The story itself is not without irony, for Judith (a name that is also the feminine form of the Hebrew word for 'Jewish') challenges the worldly authority of the male (represented in her story by Holofernes and Uzziah) before putting to rout the vast army of King Nebuchadnezzar. She thus single-handedly saves the Jewish people and their religion. At an allegorical level, the story can be interpreted as the triumph of Divine Will over the human will.

The book's opening chapters tell how Nebuchadnezzar, king of the Assyrians and 'lord of the whole earth', set about conquering an area that extended from Egypt and Ethiopia in the west to the eastern borders of Persia. His military campaign was led by Holofernes, his chief general, who was second only to Nebuchadnezzar himself. On hearing of the Assyrians' conquests, the people of Israel, who had only recently returned from exile, prepared for war by fortifying the hilltop villages. Joakim, the high priest, also ordered the people of Bethulia to seize control of the narrow passes by which an advancing army would enter Judea. (4:1–7) Rather than launching a direct attack upon the mountain-top town of Bethulia, Holofernes' generals advised him to cut off their water supply and lay siege to the Israelites' stronghold. (7:1–18) After thirty-four days the Israelites ran out of water and the people demanded that their rulers save them by surrendering to Holofernes. However, Uzziah (one of the rulers of Bethulia) convinced the assembly to hold out for a further five days in the hope that God would intervene on their behalf. If help had not arrived by then, he would do as they suggested and surrender to the enemy. (7:19–31)

These things came to the attention of Judith, a beautiful widow of independent means who had lived a devout and celibate life since the death of her husband. On learning that the inhabitants of Bethulia were prepared to surrender to the Assyrians, Judith addressed the town's rulers, telling them that God was putting them to the test – a test that is also represented symbolically in the people's proposal to surrender on the *fortieth* day after the beginning of the siege by Holofernes. She also told them she had devised a plan to save Bethulia and its inhabitants, which she would only reveal to them when it had succeeded. (8:1–34)

Judith spent the next day in prayer, dressed in sackcloth. When she had finished praying, she took off the sackcloth, dressed herself in her most seductive clothes, and made herself so beautiful that no man would be able to resist her. She then gave her maid a bottle of wine and a flask of oil, and filled a bag with grain, a cake and bread. The two women then left the town and headed for the Assyrian encampment down on the plain. When they encountered an Assyrian patrol, Judith asked them to take her to Holofernes because she wished to tell him how he could defeat the Israelites without losing any of his men. As she entered the encampment with the patrol, all the soldiers marvelled at her great beauty. Holofernes was likewise captivated by her beauty. Having told Holofernes how he could defeat the Israelites, Judith obtained his permission to leave the camp with her maid during the night so that she could go out and pray. (9:1–12:7) Over the next three days Judith and her maid left the camp every night at midnight, carrying with them the bag of food. On the fourth night, Holofernes invited Judith to an intimate banquet in his tent with a view to seducing her. When they had finished eating, the servants withdrew and left them alone together. Holofernes, who had drunk a vast quantity of wine, lay down on his bed. Judith took down Holofernes' sword, which hung at the head of the bed, and cut off his head. (The humiliation incurred by a soldier when he was killed by a woman

 ABOVE
Saviour of her people: Judith decapitated the enemy general Holofernes, then
placed his head in a food bag and smuggled it out of the Assyrians' camp

has already been mentioned (*see above*, Jael, page 63, *and* The Woman of Thebez, page 65). She then picked up the severed head and placed it in her food bag, and at midnight she left the camp with her maid and returned to Bethulia. Judith told the rulers to hang the Assyrian general's head from the town's parapet, and when the sun rose the male inhabitants were to arm themselves and make as though they were going down to the enemy encampment on the plain. (12:8–14:4)

The next morning at dawn, the Assyrians saw the Israelites coming down towards them and went to waken Holofernes so that he could lead them into battle. But when they discovered his headless corpse lying on his bed, the Assyrians fled from the plain in a chaotic retreat. News of Holofernes' defeat was sent to Jerusalem and to the frontiers of Israel, and throughout the land the Israelites rose up and fell upon the Assyrians. (14:11–15:7) Judith was loudly praised by her people for having saved them from their enemy. Surrounded by the Israelite women, she made her way to Jerusalem, where the people made offerings to God and feasted for three months in celebration of their salvation. (15:12–16:20) At the end of that time, Judith returned to Bethulia. Although many men sought to marry her, she remained a widow for the remainder of her life. When she died aged 105, she was buried beside her husband Manasseh, and Israel mourned her for seven days. (16:21–24)

Judith in art

Judith exemplified virtue triumphing over vice for artists and patrons of the Middle Ages, Renaissance and post-Renaissance periods, and images of her were fairly popular – especially those depicting her decapitation of Holofernes. Examples of the latter include works by the painters Mantegna and Botticelli, and the sculptor Donatello. Judith is usually depicted with her maid in Holofernes' tent, either in the act of cutting off his head or holding up his freshly severed head by its hair. Works by Caravaggio and his seventeenth-century followers give her beheading of Holofernes added realism and visual impact through their dramatic composition and the artists' use of strong contrasts of light and shade.

WISDOM

The personification of what is most desirable.

† BIBLICAL REFERENCE: Wisdom of Solomon 6:12–23; 7:21–11:1; Ecclesiasticus (Sirach) 1:4–20; 4:11–19; 24:1–22

The traditional personification of Wisdom as a woman, which we encountered earlier in the Book

of Proverbs, is perpetuated in the above two books that were written between the second and first centuries BC. The following brief extracts give a taste of the books' style and content.

> Wisdom is radiant and
>   unfading.
> She is easily perceived by those
>   who love her,
> and readily found by those who
>   seek her.
> She willingly makes herself
>   known to those who desire
>   her.
>
>   (WISDOM 6:12–13)

> Wisdom raises up her own
>   children
> and assists those who seek her.
> Whoever loves her loves life,
> and those who seek her early
>   will be filled with joy …
> Those who serve her minister
>   to the Holy One,
> and the Lord loves those who
>   love her.
>
>   (ECCLESIASTICUS 4:11–12, 14)

THE GOOD WIFE

A man's gift from God.

† BIBLICAL REFERENCE: Ecclesiasticus 26:1–18; 36:22–4

Jesus, son of Sirach, the author of Ecclesiasticus, declares that a good wife is a great blessing to a man, for whether he be rich or poor she brings him happiness and a long life. She is 'like the sun rising in the heights of the

Lord,' and her beauty is 'like the shining lamp on the holy lamp-stand.' (26:16, 17) By contrast, a bad wife is 'like a chafing yoke' or 'like grasping a scorpion'. (26:7)

SUSANNA

MEANING: LILY

The brave and beautiful young woman who resisted the advances of two lecherous old men and challenged their libellous accusations against her.

† BIBLICAL REFERENCE: Susanna

The story of Susanna, which is set in Babylon during the exile, comprises a single chapter and was one of the additions made to the book of Daniel when it was translated into Greek some time around the second or first century BC. The beautiful Susanna was the devout wife of Joakim, one of the most wealthy and respected members of the Jewish community in Babylon. Two elders of the community, who had been appointed as judges, were frequent visitors to Joakim's house, where they heard the law-suits brought to them by the people. During their visits the two elders often caught sight of Susanna, whose beauty was so great that the two men developed a passionate desire for her that drove thoughts of God and matters of religious law from their minds. However, both men were ashamed of what the other might

think and so they kept their lecherous thoughts to themselves. Feasting their eyes on her day after day, they noticed that in the afternoons, when all the visitors had left, Susanna was in the habit of walking in the large garden attached to the house. One day when the morning's business was over, the two elders went their separate ways, telling each other that they were going home for lunch. But instead of returning home they both hurried back to Joakim's house where they met again, and on questioning each other about the reason for their presence there they both admitted to their lecherous motives. They decided to join forces and devise a plan as to how they might find Susanna on her own.

One very hot day, while the two men were hiding in the garden, Susanna came in with two maids. Wishing to bathe because of the heat, she instructed the maids to bring her oils and ointments and then close the garden doors so that she could be alone. When the maids had done as they were told, they left the garden by a side door. The two lechers now

ABOVE
Private moment: the beautiful Susanna bathes in her garden, unaware that she is being spied on by two lecherous elders

emerged from their hiding place and, confessing their love for her, demanded that Susanna allow them to make love to her. 'If you don't, we will bear witness against you and testify that you sent your maids away so that you could be alone with your lover.' Susanna sighed deeply, knowing that adultery was punishable by death, and said, 'Whatever I do, I am trapped. If I do agree to your demands, it is death for me; if I resist, I won't escape from your clutches. But I would rather refuse you and play into your hands than sin before God.' Susanna then called out at the top of her voice, at which the two elders began to shout accusations at her. Hearing the tumult in the garden, the servants rushed to see what had happened to their mistress, but when the elders had told them their fabricated tale they were taken aback because nothing of the kind had ever been said about Susanna before.

The next morning, as the people gathered as usual at Joakim's house, the two judges arrived with their plan to have Susanna put to death. When they summoned her to appear before them, she came with her parents, her children and her all relatives. Since her beauty was hidden by the veil she was wearing, the two lechers ordered Susanna to remove it so that they could feast their eyes on her. As they placed

their hands on her head to bear witness against her, she raised her eyes heavenwards and placed her fate in the hands of God. The men then gave their evidence, saying, 'We were walking in the garden when this woman came in with two maids, shut the garden doors, and dismissed the maids. Then a young man who had been hiding appeared, and lay down with her. We were at the end of the garden, and when we saw the crime they were committing we rushed up to them. Though we saw them embracing, we were unable to retain the young man for he was too strong for us; he opened the garden door and ran off. However, we were able to catch this woman and ask her who the young man was, but she refused to tell us. That is our account of what we witnessed.' Since the men were elders and judges, the people believed their story, and Susanna was condemned to death. When the sentence was pronounced, Susanna cried out to God in a loud voice, 'Eternal Lord, who knows all secrets and every thing before it comes to pass, you know that these men have given false evidence against me. And now I am to die, even though I am innocent of the malicious charges they have invented against me.' God heard her cry. And as she was being led away to be stoned to death, God inspired a young boy named Daniel to

shout out, 'I am innocent of this woman's death!' The people turned to him, and said, 'What do you mean?' Standing in the midst of the crowd, he said, 'O sons of Israel, are you so foolish that you would condemn a daughter of Israel without hearing her and without examining the facts? Let us return to the place of judgement, for these men

RIGHT

RIGHT
Trapped: the two elders emerged from their hiding place and offered Susanna a choice: let them make love to her or stand accused of having a secret lover

have borne false witness against her.' The people hurried back, and the community's elders invited Daniel to sit with them and explain himself. He told them to separate the two elders so that he could examine them individually. When they had been separated, he had one of them brought before him, and said, 'The sins you committed in the past have now caught up with you, you with your unjust judgements, condemning the innocent and letting the guilty go free, even though the Lord has said, "You must not put to death an innocent and upright person." Now, since you are so sure you saw her, tell me what sort of tree they were lying under?' The elder replied, 'An acacia tree.' And Daniel said, 'You have condemned yourself with your lies, for the angel of God has received your sentence and will cut you down.' Having sent the man away, Daniel had the other brought in to him, and said, 'Lust has got the better of you and perverted your heart. This is how you have been dealing with the daughters of Israel, and they were too

frightened to resist your advances. But here was a daughter of Judah who would not give in to your wicked ways. Now tell me, what sort of tree did you see them embracing under?' The elder answered, 'An evergreen oak.' And Daniel said, 'You, too, have condemned yourself with your lies. The angel of God is waiting with a sword to saw you in half, and thus destroy the pair of you.' Then all the people shouted aloud, praising God who saves those who place their trust in him, and they turned on the two judges, whom Daniel had convicted of giving false evidence through the testimony of their own words.

 ABOVE
A life spared: as Susanna was being led away to be stoned to death, the young prophet Daniel intervened and exposed the false evidence of the two elders

In accordance with the Law of Moses, the two men were subjected to the same punishment that they had intended for Susanna, and thus an innocent life was spared that day.

Susanna in art

The story of Susanna and the elders became a popular subject in the post-Renaissance period, with artists depicting Susanna bathing while the two elders are either looking on from their hiding place or in the act of propositioning her. Its popularity possibly lay in the opportunity it offered both artists and patrons to create a religious painting that illustrated the triumph of chastity over lust and yet which incorporated a sensual female nude. For example, the version of *Susanna and the Elders* by Tintoretto in the Kunsthistorisches Museum, Vienna, is dominated by the naked figure of Susanna. However, other examples are more discreet. In the version by Altdorfer in the Alte Pinakothek in Munich, Susanna is not only more or less fully clothed – her skirt is drawn up to her knees, thereby exposing her legs – she is a diminutive figure in relation to the elaborate house of Joakim which dominates the picture.

WOMEN MARTYRS

Three mothers who were martyred for practising their religion.

† BIBLICAL REFERENCE: 2 Maccabees 6:10; 7:1, 20–41; 4 Maccabees 8:4; 15:1–17:10; 18:6–2

When the Seleucid ruler Antiochus IV attacked Jerusalem in the second century BC, he pillaged the temple and opened it to all worshippers, thus removing its Jewish exclusivity. His Hellenization of Judah led to the suppression of Judaism and to Jews being forced to celebrate the feast of the Greek god Dionysus and offer sacrifices to him. The fate of those who refused to accept the Greek customs was death. (6:7–9) Among those who were slain were two women accused of having circumcised their children: the women were paraded through the streets of the city with their babies hung at their breasts, and then thrown down from the city wall. (6:10) Among others who were martyred were a mother and her seven sons. Antiochus attempted to force them to eat pork, which was against the laws of their religion. They refused to do so, even under torture, and so he began to kill the seven sons one by one in front of their mother. When only the youngest son was left, Antiochus urged the mother to persuade her son to renounce his religion, but she only encouraged him to face his death all the more bravely. The young man's defiance enraged Antiochus, who treated both mother and son with greater brutality than the others and then slaughtered them (7:20–41): 4 Maccabees provides an extended account of the torture and death of the mother and her seven sons.

Part 2
The New Testament

The books of the Old
Testament were written over
many centuries and cover an
historical period that extends over
several millennia. Those of the
New Testament were written over
a period of less than one hundred
years and relate events that occurred
over a handful of decades. The
difference in these timescales reflects
the subjects they address: whereas the
Old Testament records the history,
religious beliefs and laws of a people
or nation, the New Testament
Gospels focus on the life and
teachings of a single person: Jesus.
Its other books – the Acts of the
Apostles and the Epistles – describe
the dissemination of his teachings
by his earliest followers and the
establishment of the first Christian
communities. In spite of these overt
differences, the binding relationship
between the two Testaments led to
them being combined into one book:
the Christian Bible (from the Greek
biblia, meaning 'books'). The final
book of the New Testament, the
apocalyptic Book of Revelation,
echoes the apocalyptic visions of the
Old Testament prophets. As the final
book of the Bible, it could also be
said to complete the cycle of revelation that began with the opening
chapters of Genesis, for it culminates
in a vision of the Heavenly City and
thus brings to an end the separation
from God that began with the
Expulsion from Eden.

4 The Gospels

The first three Gospels – Matthew, Mark and Luke – are frequently referred to as the 'Synoptic Gospels' because they offer a common view (Greek *sunoptikos*) of the life of Jesus. The Gospel of John stands apart from the other three in that it contains a number of lengthy discourses, notably the discourse delivered by Jesus to his disciples at the Last Supper which extends over three chapters. Sometimes all four Gospels differ in their detail when describing a particular event or person, and this has been borne in mind when writing about the women who people their pages. We also need to bear in mind that, like the books of the Old Testament, the books of the New were written by men. At first glance, their male-oriented view of the world may give the impression that women were regarded as subordinate or inferior to men. Yet Jesus judged people according to the depth of their faith, not their gender. As we learn from the Gospels, it was the women in his closest circle who served Jesus and looked after him during his ministry in Galilee, and who provided for him and his disciples out of their private resources. Women were also the first to see and speak with the risen Jesus; but when they told the disciples what had transpired, the men accused them of talking nonsense and refused to believe them.

ELIZABETH

MEANING: OATH OF GOD

The barren woman who in her old age gave birth to John the Baptist.

† BIBLICAL REFERENCE: Luke 1:5–25; 39–66

Elizabeth, a descendant of Moses' brother Aaron, was the wife of Zechariah ('Remembered by God'), a priest in a town in the hill country of Judah. They were a devout elderly couple, who adhered strictly to the Law, but they were childless because Elizabeth was barren. One day, the angel Gabriel appeared to Zechariah while he was burning incense in the sanctuary. Having told Zechariah that his prayers had been answered, the angel said, 'Your wife Elizabeth will bear you a son, and you shall call him John.' Zechariah asked the angel how this could happen, since he was an old man and his wife was also well advanced in years. Gabriel replied, 'Look! I have been sent to bring you good news, but since you don't believe my words, you will be silenced and unable to speak until this has happened.' When Zechariah came out of the sanctuary he was unable to speak to the people; he could only gesticulate. At the end of the service, he went home. It was after this that Elizabeth conceived. She kept it to herself for five months, saying, 'This is what the Lord has done for me, to take away the shame I experienced in public.' In the sixth month Elizabeth received a visit from her cousin Mary, who had travelled from Galilee to the hill country of Judah to see her. (Mary had learnt of her elderly relative's pregnancy from the angel Gabriel. *See below,* Mary, Mother of Jesus.) When Mary entered the house and greeted her, Elizabeth felt the unborn baby jump in her womb. And she was inspired by the Holy Spirit to say to Mary, 'Blessed are you among women, and blessed is the fruit of your womb! How is it that the mother of my Lord honours me with a visit? For the moment your greeting touched my ears, the unborn child in my

ABOVE

The holy family: Mary and the infant Jesus are in the centre of the painting with
Joseph behind them. Mary's cousin Elizabeth holds a young John the Baptist

womb jumped for joy. Blessed indeed is she who has believed in the fulfilment of the Lord's promise.' And she said,

> My soul magnifies the Lord,
> My spirit rejoices in God my
>   saviour,
> For he has marked his servant's
>   disgrace.
> All ages will call me happy
>   henceforward;
> For the Mighty One has
>   wrought marvels for me,
> And holy is his name …
>
> (1:46–9, ONT)

(Although these words are normally attributed to Mary, Hugh Schonfield, the Jewish scholar and writer on Christian origins, whose translation is given above, asserts that 'the poem was subsequently transferred to Mary by simply adding her name, though the text makes it clear that the singer is Elizabeth.' ONT, 132) Mary stayed with her cousin for about three months and then returned home. When the time came for Elizabeth to deliver her child, she gave birth to a son. And when her neighbours and relations heard of the compassion shown her by the Lord, they rejoiced with her. On the eighth day the child was circumcised, and he would have been named Zechariah after his father, but his mother intervened, saying, 'No, he is to be called John ['The Lord is compassionate'].' And they said to her, 'But none of your

family bears that name.' They made signs to Zechariah to find out what name he wished for the child. He motioned for a writing-tablet, and wrote, 'His name is John.' The people were astonished. At that same moment Zechariah's power of speech returned, and he spoke and praised God. The couple's neighbours were filled with fear, and the events were widely talked about throughout the highlands of Judea. The events surrounding John's birth conclude with the Holy Spirit inspiring Zechariah to make a prophecy which begins with the words 'Blessed be the Lord God of Israel …' – incorporated into Christian liturgy as the *Benedictus*, after the Latin translation of the first word.

MARY, MOTHER OF JESUS

MEANING: BITTERNESS, OR POSSIBLY BELOVED (FROM EGYPTIAN MARYÏ; SEE MIRIAM, PAGE 54)

The young woman who gave birth to the Messiah.

✝ BIBLICAL REFERENCE: Matthew: 1:18–25; 2:1–23; 12:46–50; 13:55; Mark 3:31–5; 6:3; Luke: 1:26–56; 2:4–7, 16–19; 27–39; 41–51; 8:19–21; 11:27–8; John 2:1–5; 19:25–7; Acts 1:14

Most readers are probably already familiar with the story of Mary and the miraculous conception of Jesus, his birth and his presentation in the temple. Apart from these events, Mary's appearances in

 ABOVE
The Annunciation: the angel Gabriel was sent to Nazareth to give Mary news of the son she was to bear

ABOVE

The Nativity: Mary and Joseph kneel in adoration of the infant Jesus, while
the crucifix on the left serves as a reminder of their child's destiny

the narrative gospels are relatively brief: her discovery of Jesus in the temple when he was twelve, her presence at the wedding at Cana and at the foot of the cross on which Jesus was crucified. These events, which are retold below, are followed by some of the events recounted about Mary's life in extra-biblical sources.

The Gospel of Matthew relates that Mary was betrothed to Joseph, but before their marriage had been consummated she was found to be pregnant. Wishing to spare her from disgrace, Joseph had resolved to divorce her quietly when an angel appeared to him in a dream, and said, 'Joseph, son of David, do not be afraid to take Mary as your wife, for she has conceived by the Holy Spirit. She will give birth to a son, and you will call him Jesus ['He who saves' or 'Saviour'], because he is the one who will save his people from their sins.' This was to fulfil the prophecy given by Isaiah that 'a virgin will conceive and give birth to a son, and he will be called Immanuel ['God is with us']' (*see above*, 'The young woman who will give birth to a son', page 144). When Joseph awoke he did as the angel had told him, but he did not have intercourse with Mary until she gave birth to a son, to whom he gave the name Jesus. (1:18–25) Shortly after Jesus had been born, Mary was visited by some wise men from the East who had come to pay homage to the child who was destined to be king of the Jews. The star they had been following came to rest above Mary's house, and they entered and saw the child with his mother. Prostrating themselves before him, they offered him gifts of gold, frankincense and myrrh. After the wise men had left, an angel appeared to Joseph in a dream and told him to take the child and his mother to Egypt, and to remain there until the angel came to them again, because Herod intended to search out the child and kill him. That same night Joseph left for Egypt with Mary and the child, and they remained there until the angel appeared again and told him it was safe to take the child and his mother back to Israel. On arriving in Israel, however, he learned that Herod's son Archelaus was now reigning, and so the family settled in Galilee, in the town of Nazareth. (2:1–2, 9–11, 13–15, 19–23)

The Gospel of Luke begins with the story of Zechariah and Elizabeth, Mary's cousin (*see above*, Elizabeth). In the sixth month of Elizabeth's pregnancy, the angel Gabriel was sent to Mary in Nazareth. He greeted her, saying, 'Greetings, you who are highly favoured! The Lord is with you.' She found the angel's greeting deeply disturbing, and asked herself what it could mean. But the angel said, 'Do not be afraid, Mary; you have found favour with God. You are to conceive and give birth to a son, and you must call him Jesus. He will be great, and will be called the Son of the Most High. The Lord God will give him the throne of his father David, and he will reign over the house of Jacob for ever, and of his kingdom there will be no end.' Mary said to the angel, 'How can this come about, since I am not married?' And the angel said to her, 'The Holy Spirit will come upon you, and the power of the Most High will overshadow you. And so the child that is to be born will be holy, and will be called Son of God.' Gabriel then told Mary that her cousin Elizabeth, who had been barren, had conceived and was now in her sixth month, and he said, 'Nothing is impossible with God.' And Mary said, 'I am the servant of the Lord. Let it be to me as you have said.' And the angel left her. (1:26–38) Mary then set out to visit her cousin Elizabeth, and stayed with her three months (*see above*, Elizabeth). At about the time Mary's pregnancy reached full term, she and Joseph travelled to Bethlehem to be registered in the census ordered by the Roman governor. She gave birth to her son while they were in Bethlehem, and she wrapped him in swaddling clothes and laid him in a manger because there was no room for them in the inn. That night Mary and Joseph were visited by some shepherds who had been told of the birth of their child by angels. When the shepherds found them, they repeated to everyone what the angels had told them about the child. And Mary noted all these things, and pondered them in her heart. (2:1–7, 16–19) When the period of forty days for her purification after the birth was over, Mary and Joseph took Jesus to the temple to present him to the Lord and to offer a sacrifice, which they were required to do by religious law. As they entered the temple, they were approached by Simeon, an inhabitant of Jerusalem, who had himself been prompted by the Holy Spirit to enter the temple at that moment. Simeon took their child in his arms, and praised God for allowing him to see the salvation that had been promised to all nations. Mary and Joseph were amazed by what he said about their son. Then Simeon turned to the child's parents and blessed them, and said to Mary, 'This child is destined to bring about the fall and rising again of many in Israel, and to be a sign that will be opposed – and a sword will pierce your soul with uncertainty too – so that the secret thoughts of many will be revealed.' While they were in the temple they also met the prophetess Anna, who spent all her time there praying (*see below*, Anna). When Mary and Joseph had fulfilled what the Law

required them to do, they returned to Nazareth. (2:22–39) Every year Joseph and Mary went to Jerusalem for the feast of the Passover. When Jesus was twelve years old, they went to Jerusalem as usual, but unbeknown to them he stayed behind when they set off on the journey home to Nazareth. Assuming that he was somewhere in their party, they travelled on for a day before they began to look for him among their relatives and friends. When they did not find him they went back to Jerusalem to look for him there. After three days of searching everywhere for their son, they found him in the temple, sitting among the teachers, listening to them and asking them questions. All who heard him were amazed at his understanding and his answers. His parents were astonished when they saw him, and Mary said to him, 'Son, why have you treated us like this? Your father and I were worried, and have been looking for you.' He replied, 'Why were you looking for me? Did you not know that I must be in my Father's house?' But they could not understand what he was saying to them. He returned with them to Nazareth, and was obedient to them. But Mary stored up all these things in her heart. (2:41–51)

Some years later, Mary attended a wedding in the town of Cana in Galilee. Jesus (who by now was aged about thirty) and

his disciples were present there too, and according to the Gospel of John it was here that Jesus performed the first of his miracles by transforming water into wine. When the wine at the wedding had run out, Mary said to Jesus, 'They have no more wine.' He replied, 'Woman, what have you to do with me? My hour is not yet come.' And she turned to the servants and said, 'Do whatever he tells you.' (John 2:1–5) (Some authorities suggest that Jesus' response to his mother is spoken in his capacity as the Messiah: the timing of his self-disclosure was determined by God, not by his mother.) One day, after Jesus had performed further miracles, he was speaking in the synagogue in his home town of Nazareth. Many of the local people present were so astonished at what he said that they wondered how he had acquired his wisdom and healing powers, and said, 'Isn't this Mary's son, the brother of James, Joseph, Judas and Simon, and aren't his sisters here too?' And because of this they refused to accept him as a prophet, teacher or healer. (Matthew 13:53–7; Mark 6:2–6) On another occasion, Mary went to the synagogue to speak with Jesus, who was speaking to the people. She sent a message in to him and waited outside with his brothers. But Jesus said to the messenger, 'Who is my mother, and who are my brothers?'

Turning to indicate the people seated around him, he said, 'Here are my mother and brothers. Whoever undertakes to do the will of God is my brother, my sister and my mother.' (Matthew 12:46–50; Mark 3:31–5; Luke 8:19–21) Jesus made a similar comment when a woman in the crowd called out to him and praised his mother, 'Blessed is the womb that bore you and the breasts you sucked!' But Jesus replied, 'More blessed are those who hear the word of God and obey it!' (Luke 11:27–8) We do not hear of Mary again until the time of the crucifixion of Jesus. She was standing by the cross with Mary Clopas and Mary Magdalene. The disciple whom Jesus loved was standing near Mary, Jesus' mother, and he said to her, 'Woman, here is your son!' He then said to the disciple, 'Here is your mother.' And from that moment the disciple took Mary into his own home. (John 19:25–7) After the ascension of Jesus some forty days later, Mary joined the eleven remaining disciples in their ceaseless prayers in the upper room where they were staying. (Acts 1:12–14)

Mary, mother of Jesus, outside the Bible

The depth of Christian devotion to Mary is reflected in the vast corpus of extra-biblical material written about her. That which concerns us here relates to the

three periods of her life not found in the Bible: her birth and child-hood, her betrothal to Joseph, and the latter years of her life after the ascension of her son. The story of Mary's birth, child-hood and betrothal to Joseph is recounted in the apocryphal *Book of James* (also known as the *Protevangelium*) and in *The Golden Legend* (a collection of the lives of the saints) compiled by Jacobus de Voragine in the thirteenth century. According to these sources, Mary's parents – Anna and Joachim – were an elderly childless couple, who vowed that if God granted them a child they would dedicate it to the service of the Lord. One year when the wealthy Joachim went up to the temple in Jerusalem to make a sacrificial offering at the feast of Dedication, he was turned away by the priests because he had failed in his duty to have children.

Filled with shame, he withdrew to the wilderness and sought the company of his shepherds. While he was away an angel appeared to Anna and told her that she would bear a child who would become renowned throughout the whole world. Joachim received a similar visitation from an angel, who told him that he was to name his child Mary. Joachim returned to Jerusalem, where he met Anna at the Golden Gate. Mary was born nine months later. When she was three years old her parents took her to the temple and left her there to be raised by the temple virgins and priests, and when she was fourteen the high priest announced that all the virgins who had been raised in the temple were to return to their families so that they could be married. All the girls returned to their homes, except for Mary who told the high priest that her

ABOVE
The lamentation: the artist has added the figures of Saints Paul and Catherine of Alexandria to Mary Magdalene and the apostles Peter and Paul

parents had dedicated her to the service of the Lord. Moreover, she herself had vowed her virginity to God. Not knowing what to do with her since such a vow went against the religious obligation to have children, the priests and elders prayed to God for guidance. God answered their prayers, and told them that they were to assemble all the eligible, unmarried men belonging to the house of David. Each man was to bring with him a branch, which he would lay upon the altar. One of the branches would burst into blossom, and the Holy Spirit in the form of a dove would descend upon it to indicate that the owner of this branch was the man who was to take Mary as his wife. A certain Joseph was among the men who came to the temple. Because it seemed to him inappropriate that an elderly man like himself should marry such a young girl, he did not join the others in placing a branch on the altar. When none of the branches burst into flower, the high priest prayed to the Lord again, and God told him that the man who was destined to become Mary's husband was alone in not placing a branch on the altar. Having been discovered, Joseph placed a branch on the altar and it immediately burst into blossom, and a dove settled upon it. Joseph prepared his home to receive his new wife, but Mary went to her parents' house in Nazareth, and it

was while she was there that the angel Gabriel came to her and announced that she would bear a child. (de Voragine, 522–4) *The Golden Legend* also gives the following account – taken from an apocryphal book attributed to John the Evangelist – of Mary's death and assumption. After the ascension of her son, and the apostles had gone out into the world to preach, Mary spent a life of prayer and devotion in a house close to Mount Sion. One day an angel bearing a branch of the palm of Paradise came to her. The angel told her that Jesus awaited her, and in three days time she would leave her earthly body. The branch was to be carried ahead of her bier. Mary asked the angel to gather the apostles so that she might see them a last time before she died, and that they might bury her after her death. The angel replied that the apostles would gather around her that very day, and then he departed. Wherever in the world they happened to be preaching, the apostles were plucked up by clouds and carried to Mary's house. That same night, at about the third hour, Mary was sitting among the apostles when Jesus descended with a host of angels, and her soul left her body and flew to the arms of her son. Jesus told the apostles to take Mary's body to the valley of Josaphat, where a new tomb had been prepared for her. They were

then to wait three days for him to return. On the third day Jesus returned with a host of angels. He asked the apostles what honour he should confer on his mother, and they replied that her body should be taken up and placed at his right hand for all eternity. When Jesus nodded his approval, the archangel Michael immediately appeared carrying Mary's soul. Her soul entered her body, and when she emerged from the tomb she was assumed into heaven. Thomas, who had been absent when this happened, refused to believe what the other apostles told him. At that moment Mary's sash fell into his hands, the knot still tied so that he would know she had been assumed in her entirety. (de Voragine, 449–54) Jacobus adds, 'It is said that the Virgin's garments were left behind in the tomb for the consolation of the faithful' (*ibid.*, 454–5). The Virgin's tunic subsequently became the most treasured relic of the cathedral of Notre Dame in Chartres, France.

Mary, mother of Jesus, in art
The first images of Mary appeared in the Roman catacombs before the end of the second century, but since then Christian devotion to Mary has ensured the extensive proliferation of her image in every conceivable field of the visual, decorative and performing arts. Where the visual arts are concerned, the

cycle of images depicting the life of Mary was firmly established by the Middle Ages and included events from both Biblical and non-Biblical sources: the Nativity of Mary; the Betrothal of Mary to Joseph; the Annunciation; the Visitation; the Nativity; the Adoration (the shepherds and Magi); the Presentation in the Temple; the Flight into Egypt; the Finding of Jesus in the Temple; the Wedding at Cana; the Crucifixion; the Entombment (or Lamentation); the Empty Tomb; the Descent of the Spirit at Pentecost; the Dormition (her 'falling asleep' or 'death'); the Assumption ('into heaven'); and her Coronation as Queen of Heaven. These scenes were widely represented in the sculpture, stained glass and frescoes that decorated both the exterior and interior of medieval churches and cathedrals. Many of the great Gothic cathedrals were themselves dedicated to Mary and consequently bear the name 'Notre Dame' or 'Our Lady'. Mary also became the subject of devotional works in which she was depicted on her own. The Renaissance saw the widespread dissemination of works entitled *Madonna and Child*, which depicted Mary with her infant son, either in images that captured the intimate relationship of a mother and her child or in more formal works in which Mary is seated on a raised throne with the infant Jesus on her lap. Other types of image that became popular during the Renaissance were the large-scale *Sacra conversazione* (Holy Conversation), in which Mary and her son are surrounded by saints and other holy figures, and the *Madonna della Misericordia* (Our Lady of Mercy), which depicted Mary sheltering the faithful under her outspread cloak. As a sign of their personal devotion to Mary, the patrons of many of these Renaissance works stipulated that her blue robe was painted with the finest quality pigment made from the gemstone lapis lazuli.

ANNA

MEANING: GRACE

The prophetess who recognized Jesus as the salvation of Israel.

† BIBLICAL REFERENCE: Luke 2:36–9

Anna was an elderly prophetess who never left the temple, spending her days and nights there fasting and praying. It was there that she saw the infant Jesus when Mary and Joseph came to the temple, as required by religious law, to dedicate their first-born son to God. Afterwards Anna spoke about him 'to all who were looking for the salvation of Jerusalem'. We are told that Anna had lived with her husband for seven years before being widowed, and she was now eighty-four. In number symbolism, seven signifies completeness and perfection, as exemplified in the seven days in which God completed the creation of the world. The number seven derives its symbolic importance from the fact that it is the sum of the numbers three and four, which symbolize respectively heaven and earth, or the spiritual and physical realms. The number seven could thus be said to represent the *union* of the spiritual and material worlds. We encounter the number seven again, this time combined with the number twelve, to produce Anna's age which is given as eighty-four ($84 = 12 \times 7$). Like seven, the symbolic importance of the number twelve is derived from the numbers three and four since it is obtained by their multiplication. The number twelve could thus be said to signify the *fusion* of the spiritual and material worlds. In Anna's case, the numbers are possibly introduced to corroborate the importance of two simultaneous events: Jesus entering the temple for the first time, and his recognition as the salvation of Israel – the Messiah.

Anna in art

Anna is frequently depicted in images of the Presentation in the Temple, sometimes holding a scroll on which is written a relevant prophecy from the Old Testament.

Women who were close to Jesus

MARY MAGDALENE

MEANING: MARY, BITTERNESS, OR POSSIBLY BELOVED (see above, Mary, mother of Jesus);

MAGDALENE, FROM (THE TOWN OF) MAGDALA OR OF THE TOWER

The woman who was the first to see and speak with the resurrected Jesus.

† BIBLICAL REFERENCE: Matthew 27:55–61; 28:1–10; Mark 15:40, 47; 16:1–11; Luke 8:2–3; 24:10; John 19:25; 20:1–18

Over the centuries the popular image of Mary Magdalene has become embellished to such an extent that the person presented in the Gospels is barely recognizable: at one extreme she has become the 'penitent prostitute'; at the other, the lover or wife of Jesus and the mother of his children. (The first of these is explored below in 'Mary Magdalene in art' and 'The woman who anointed Jesus'; the second, in 'Mary Magdalene outside the Bible'.) Where the authors of the Gospels are concerned, Mary Magdalene was one of a group of women who had been healed by Jesus and who provided for him and the disciples out of their personal resources. In Mary's case, she had been healed of 'seven demons'. (Luke 8:2–3) Mary Magdalene is next mentioned at the time of the crucifixion, when she stood near the cross with Mary, the mother of Jesus, and Mary Clopas (John 19:25); although Mark says that she was among the group of women who looked on 'from afar'. (Mark 15:40) After Joseph of Arimathea had placed Jesus' body in the tomb, Mary Magdalene sat and watched over the tomb with Mary Clopas. When the two women went to the tomb the next morning, there was an earthquake, and an angel rolled away the stone from the entrance and sat on it. The angel told them that Jesus had risen from the dead and, having showed them the empty tomb, he told them to go and tell the disciples. According to Matthew, they left the tomb with mixed emotions of fear and joy. They sped off to tell the disciples the news and met Jesus on the way. He greeted them, and they fell at his feet and worshipped him. (Matthew 28:1–10. *See below,* Salome, for Mark's version.) When the women told the disciples about all this, the men thought their story was nonsense and did not believe them. (Luke 24:10–11) According to Mark, the risen Jesus first appeared to Mary Magdalene on her own. When she told the disciples that she had seen him alive, they did not believe her. (Mark 16:9–11) The lengthiest account of Mary Magdalene's meeting with the risen Jesus is in John, in which we are told that Mary went to the tomb early in the morning while it was still dark. When she saw that the stone had been rolled away from the entrance, she ran to tell Peter and 'the disciple whom Jesus loved'. The two men ran to the tomb. They went in, found the empty burial cloths lying on the tomb, and returned to their homes. Mary had remained outside, weeping, but after the men had left she looked into the tomb and saw two angels sitting where Jesus' body had been. They asked her why she was weeping, and she replied, 'Because they have taken away my Lord, and I do not know where they have put him.' As she said this, she turned around and saw Jesus standing nearby, and he also asked her why she was weeping. Because she did not recognize him, she

thought at first that he was the gardener; but when he addressed her by name, she exclaimed, 'Teacher!' Jesus said to her, 'Do not cling to me, for I have not yet ascended to the Father. Go to the brothers and tell them, I am ascending to my Father and your Father, to my God and your God.' And Mary went and told the disciples what she had seen, and what Jesus had said to her. (John 20:1–18)

Mary Magdalene outside the Bible

The legends and traditions that have grown up around Mary Magdalene are numerous, many having arisen through the confla- tion of three women mentioned in the Gospels: Mary of Magdala (Mary Magdalene), Mary of Bethany (sister of Martha and Lazarus), and the unnamed woman (a sinner) who anointed Jesus. Since the third of these women was absolved of her sins by Jesus, Mary Magdalene has become the archetypal repentant

sinner. She is also said to have been the bride at the wedding at Cana, at which she married John, one of the sons of Zebedee. According to a ninth-century Provençal legend (recorded in *The Golden Legend*, 357-60; *see* page 169), she was cast adrift in a boat with Mary, Martha and Lazarus, and came ashore at Marseilles. (Metford, 169–170) Several churches claim to house her relics; but claims to own the relics of saints proliferated during the Middle Ages when the possession of such relics was a guarantee that pilgrims would come to venerate them, and a guaranteed source of income for the religious establishments that housed them. The importance attached to relics was also enhanced by the legends concerning the saints that became

increasingly common at this time.

In recent years it has been proposed that Mary Magdalene was either the lover or the wife of Jesus, and that she was the mother of their children whose bloodline continues down to our own time. A discussion of the truth of this proposition is beyond the remit of this book, but it is worth quoting here some passages from two of the Gospels that were circulating in the early years of Christianity, and which were subsequently deemed heretical by the Church. According to the *Gospel of Philip*, discovered at Nag Hammadi in Egypt in 1945, Jesus 'loved her [Mary Magdalene] more than all the disciples and used to kiss her often', and the apostles asked him, 'Why do you love her more than all of us?'

(*Nag Hammadi Library*, 148) The jealousy of the apostles regarding Mary Magdalene's status – both personal and spiritual – among the followers of Jesus is referred to again in the *Gospel of Mary Magdalene*, discovered in Egypt in 1896. Mary was apparently the beneficiary of a teaching that Jesus chose not to give to other apostles. When she had finished explaining it to them, an argument erupted in the course of which Andrew's brother Peter said, 'Did he really speak with a woman without our knowledge, and not openly? Are we supposed to listen to *her*? Did he love her more than us?' Levi responded to Peter's attack on Mary, and said, 'Peter, you have always been hot-tempered. Now I see you contending against the woman as our enemies do. But if the Saviour made her worthy, who are you indeed, to reject her? Surely the Saviour knows her very well. That is why he loved her more than us. Rather, let us be ashamed, and ... preach the gospel.' (Pagels, 103–5)

Mary Magdalene in art

Mary Magdalene's representation in art as a penitent sinner, naked except for her long hair, arises from her conflation with Mary of Egypt, a fourth-century saint and reformed prostitute. The emaciated *Mary Magdalene* in Florence by the sculptor Donatello is one such example of Mary as the

ABOVE
Banquet in the house of Simon: the unnamed woman who annointed Jesus' feet is often identified as Mary Magdalene

penitent sinner. Mary Magdalene is frequently depicted in scenes of the crucifixion in which she is readily identified by her scarlet robe. She is also present in scenes of the entombment of Jesus. In these she can be identified by her alabaster jar (her legendary attribute) and her richly embroidered clothing (a reminder that she was one of the women who gave financial support to Jesus and his disciples).

MARTHA AND MARY

MEANING: MARY, BITTERNESS, OR POSSIBLY BELOVED (*see above*, MARY, MOTHER OF JESUS); MARTHA, (ARAMAIC) LADY OR MISTRESS

The sisters whose brother was raised from the dead.

† BIBLICAL REFERENCE: Luke 10:38–42; John 11:1–3, 5, 19–40; 12:2–8

Martha and Mary were two sisters from Bethany. Martha invited Jesus into their house when he visited their village, and busied herself with serving while her sister Mary sat at his feet and listened to his teaching. Martha complained to Jesus that Mary had left her to do all the serving on her own, and asked him to tell her sister to help her. In reply, Jesus told Martha that she worried about too many things while ignoring the one thing that was needed. Mary, on the other hand, had made the better choice and she was not to be distracted from it. (10:38–42) This passage led to Martha and Mary being seen by Christians as exemplars of the active and contemplative lives: the one actively serving in the world, the other contemplating the teachings of Jesus.

John introduces the two sisters from Bethany at the beginning of his account of the raising of Lazarus, their brother, and adds that it was Mary who anointed Jesus (*see below*, The woman who anointed Jesus). The sisters sent for Jesus when their brother was taken ill, but when Jesus received their message 'he said, "This illness is not fatal, but for the glory of God, that the Son of God may be glorified by it."' (11:6, ONT) When Jesus eventually arrived in Bethany, he found that Lazarus had already been in the tomb for four days. Mary remained in the house, but Martha went to meet Jesus. Martha told him that if he had been there, Lazarus would not have died. When Jesus replied

☦ ABOVE
In the house at Bethany: while Mary was listening to Jesus' teachings, her sister Martha complained she had been left to do all the serving on her own

 ABOVE
The one thing that is needed: Mary reprimands her sister Martha for busying
herself with everyday matters and neglecting what really matters – the spiritual life

that her brother would rise again, Martha said, 'I know that he will rise again at the resurrection on the last day.' It is at this point that Jesus delivers one of his most quoted sayings, 'I am the resurrection and the life. He who believes in me will live, even though he dies; and whoever lives and believes in me will never die. Do you believe this?' (11:25, NIV) Martha replied that she believed that Jesus was the Christ, the Son of God, and then went back to the village and told her sister that the Teacher was asking for her. Mary got up quickly and left, followed by the Jews who had been in the house comforting her. When she saw Jesus, she threw herself at his feet and repeated the words Martha had said when she had seen him: if he had been there, her brother would not have died. Jesus was deeply moved at the sight of Mary and the others weeping, and asked her where they had laid her brother. She took him to his tomb, the entrance of which was covered with a stone. Jesus told them to roll the stone away, but Martha remarked that Lazarus had been in the tomb for four days, and his body would smell. Jesus reminded her of what he had said earlier: if she believed, she would see the glory of God. When the stone had been rolled away, Jesus called out, 'Lazarus, come out!' Lazarus emerged, bound with bandages, and with a cloth over his face. Jesus told them to unbind him and let him go. (11:1–44)

Martha and Mary in art

Jesus in the house of Martha and Mary became a popular subject during the sixteenth and seventeenth centuries, and was given a wide range of treatments. Some images capture the intimacy of the interior setting, with Mary seated at Jesus' feet while Martha serves him with food. In other, more expansive works, the artists have combined interior and exterior settings, placing the figures outdoors in front of a receding landscape while using the kitchen and table spread with food as an opportunity to paint a lavish still life. The subject of the raising of Lazarus was an even more popular subject; but although Jesus and Lazarus are the focus of attention, Martha and Mary are usually present, sometimes with one or both kneeling at the feet of Jesus.

SALOME

MEANING: TRANQUIL

The mother of James and John, the sons of Zebedee.

✝ BIBLICAL REFERENCE: Matthew 20:20–4; 27:56 28:1; Mark 15:40, 16:1–8

Salome, also referred to as the 'mother of the sons of Zebedee', was not only the mother of two of the disciples – James and John

– but also one of Jesus' close followers, and while he was in Galilee she was one of the small group of women who looked after him. (Mark 15:40) While Jesus was going up to Jerusalem for the last time, he told the disciples about the fate that awaited him there. It was then that Salome approached Jesus and asked that her two sons might sit beside him in his kingdom – one at his right hand, the other at his left. Jesus told her sons that the seats at his right and left hand were not for him to give; they belonged to those for whom they had been prepared by God. (Matthew 20:20–4) Salome was among the women who looked on 'from afar' at the crucifixion. She was also with the women who took spices to the tomb of Jesus early in the morning and

found that the stone covering the entrance had been rolled away. On entering the tomb they saw a young man in a white robe, who told them that Jesus had risen and was not there. According to Mark, when they ran away they were scared witless and didn't say a word to anyone. (Mark 16:1–9)

MARY (THE WIFE OF) CLOPAS

MEANING: BITTERNESS, OR POSSIBLY BELOVED (*see above*, MARY, MOTHER OF JESUS)

The mother of James and Joses.

✝ BIBLICAL REFERENCE: Matthew 27:55–61; 28:1–10; Mark 15:40, 47; 16:1–8; Luke 24:10; John 19:25

Like Salome, Mary Clopas was the mother of two disciples – James the younger and Joses –

ABOVE
Witness to momentous events: Mary the mother of Jesus (centre), Mary Magdalene (left) and Mary Clopas share in their grief at the foot of the cross

and a close follower of Jesus, serving him while he was in Galilee. She was also one of the group of women who watched the crucifixion 'from afar'. (According to John 19:25, she stood near the cross with Mary, the mother of Jesus.) After Joseph of Arimathea had placed Jesus' body in the tomb, she sat with Mary Magdalene opposite the sepulchre. When the two women went to the tomb the next morning, there was an earthquake, and an angel rolled away the stone from the entrance and sat on it. He told them that Jesus had risen from the dead and, having showed them the empty tomb, told them to go and tell the disciples. According to Matthew, they left the tomb with mixed emotions of fear and joy. They sped off to tell the disciples the news and met Jesus on the way. He greeted them, and they fell at his feet and worshipped him. (Matthew 28:1–10. *See above*, Salome, for Mark's version.) When the women told the disciples, the men thought their story was a lot of nonsense and didn't believe them. (Luke 24:10–11)

JOANNA

MEANING: GIFT FROM GOD

One of the women who provided for Jesus.

† BIBLICAL REFERENCE: Luke 8:3; 24:10

Joanna was the wife of Chuza, Herod's steward. She had been healed by Jesus, and was one of the women who provided for Jesus out of their personal resources. (8:3) She was also among the women who were not believed when they told the disciples that Jesus had risen from the dead. (Luke 24:10–11)

SUSANNA

MEANING: LILY

One of the women who provided for Jesus.

† BIBLICAL REFERENCE: Luke 8:3

Like Joanna, Susanna was one of the women who, having been healed by Jesus, provided for him out of their personal resources.

THE WOMAN WHO ANOINTED JESUS

The enigmatic woman with a jar of expensive ointment.

† BIBLICAL REFERENCE: Matthew 26:6–13; Mark 14:3–9; Luke 7:36–50; John 12:1–7

Although the woman who anointed Jesus is mentioned in all four Gospels, the individual accounts differ in their detail. In Matthew and Mark, whose accounts are very similar, the unnamed woman anointed Jesus in the house of Simon the leper at Bethany, two days before the Passover at which he was to be crucified. In Luke, the woman is described as 'a sinner', the setting is the house of a Pharisee named Simon who had invited Jesus to eat with him, and the incident is placed early in Jesus' mission, shortly after he had received a visit from some disciples of John the Baptist. In John, the woman is named as Mary, sister of Martha and Lazarus, and the anointing is set in their house at Bethany six days before the Passover. All four Gospels relate that the woman anointed Jesus while he was seated at table. In Matthew and Mark, she anointed his head. In Luke and John, she anointed his feet and wiped them with her hair. According to all four accounts, the woman's action caused dissent. For Matthew, Mark and John, the disciples protested over what they considered to be a waste of expensive ointment, which could have been sold and the money given to the poor. For John, it was Judas alone who protested, but this was because he was in charge of the common fund from which he stole money for himself. In Luke's account, it was initially Simon the Pharisee who dissented quietly to himself because Jesus had allowed the woman who was a sinner to touch him, and so in Simon's mind Jesus could not be a prophet. The others at table with them objected when Jesus said to the woman, 'Your sins are forgiven,' and they talked among themselves, saying, 'Who is this man, who even forgives sins?' In all four accounts, Jesus reprimanded the protesters. In

Matthew, Mark and John, he said to his disciples, 'Leave the woman alone. For you will always have the poor with you, but you will not always have me.' In Matthew and Mark, he added, 'She has done a beautiful thing to me. She has anointed me in preparation for my burial. Wherever the gospel is proclaimed in the world, what she has done will also be told in memory of her.' John uses a slightly different formula, for he records Jesus as saying, 'Let her keep it for the day of my burial.' In Luke's account of the anointing, Jesus responded to Simon's unspoken criticism by telling him a parable about a creditor and two debtors. He then told Simon that, as his host, he had failed to receive him properly for he had not offered him water, nor had he anointed his head with oil. But the woman had washed his feet with the water of her tears, anointed them with oil, and had not ceased kissing them. For this reason, her sins were forgiven, and turning to the woman he said, 'Your sins are forgiven. Your faith has saved you. Go in peace.' None of these accounts names the woman as Mary Magdalene.

THE WOMAN OF SAMARIA

The woman to whom Jesus revealed himself to be the Messiah.

† BIBLICAL REFERENCE: John 4:7–42

While Jesus was travelling through Samaria on his way from Judea to Galilee, he encountered this unnamed Samaritan woman as he was resting beside a well outside the village of Sychar. The disciples with whom he was travelling had gone to the village to buy food, and when the woman approached the well – known as Jacob's well – to draw water, Jesus asked her to give him a drink. Because of the religious differences between the Samaritans and the Jews of Jerusalem, the woman expressed her surprise that a Jewish rabbi should ask her such a question. In their ensuing conversation, Jesus revealed to the woman that he was the Messiah, upon which she returned to Sychar and told the people there about the man she had met, asking them, 'Can this man be the Messiah?' Many of the villagers believed the woman, while others believed once they had met Jesus for themselves. The woman of Samaria was thus one of the first people to whom Jesus revealed his true nature, and one of the first outside Jesus' immediate circle to spread the news of his coming. And this at a time when the diminished position accorded women in society is evidenced by John's comment that when the disciples returned 'they marvelled that he was talking with a woman.' Perhaps they were aware that Jesus disapproved of

gender discrimination, for we are told that they kept their thoughts to themselves

One particular element in the conversation between Jesus and the woman of Samaria has led some commentators to assume that she was a prostitute. (Metford, 266) This assumption is based on the exchange that followed Jesus telling the woman to fetch her husband. The woman replied that she had no husband, at which Jesus said, 'You are right when you say, "I have no husband," for you have had five husbands, and the one with whom you are now is not your husband.' The potential significance of this exchange is revealed by what Jesus said next; but first we need to remind ourselves that the term 'husband' was often used as a synonym for God. Jesus said to the woman, 'Believe me, the time will come when you will worship the Father neither on this mountain nor in Jerusalem. You worship what you do not know …. But the time will come, is indeed already here, when true worshippers will worship the Father in spirit and in truth. For God is spirit, and those who worship him must worship in spirit and truth.' In this context, the words spoken by the Samaritan woman ('I have no husband') and Jesus ('the one with whom you are now is not your husband') suggest that, rather than being a prostitute, the woman had merely

 ABOVE
The chosen one: Jesus revealed to the Samarian woman
that he was the Messiah

not yet learnt to worship God 'in spirit and truth'.

THE POOR WIDOW

✝ BIBLICAL REFERENCE: Luke 21:2–4

One day when Jesus was teaching in the temple he saw the rich people putting their offerings into the treasury, and an impoverished widow who put in two very small copper coins. Jesus remarked that the poor widow had put in more than anyone. Others had put in what they could spare from their wealth, but the poverty-stricken widow had put in all she had to live on.

THE ADULTEROUS WOMAN

✝ BIBLICAL REFERENCE: John 8:3–11

This unnamed woman, who had been caught in the act of committing adultery, was brought before Jesus by the scribes and Pharisees so that they could test him. Having told him what she had done, they said that according to the Law of Moses her punishment was to be stoned. They then asked Jesus what he had to say, hoping that his reply would leave him open to a charge of breaking the Law. Jesus stooped down and began to write on the ground

with his finger, but when they persisted with their question he stood up, and said, 'Let the one among you who is free from sin be the first to throw a stone at her.' Then he bent down again and continued writing on the ground. When they heard his reply, they began to leave one by one, starting with the eldest, until they had all gone and Jesus was left alone with the woman. He stood up again, and asked her, 'Where are they? Has no one condemned you?' When she replied, 'No one,' Jesus said, 'Neither do I condemn you. Now go away, and do not sin any more.'

Women who were healed by Jesus

THE WOMEN WHO WERE FOLLOWERS OF JESUS

✝ BIBLICAL REFERENCE: Luke 8:2–3

Some of the women who became closely associated with Jesus were among the 'certain women who had been cured of evil spirits and ailments.' (8:2, RSV) (*See above,* Mary Magdalene, Joanna *and* Susanna.)

THE MOTHER-IN-LAW OF SIMON PETER

The woman who was in bed with a fever.

✝ BIBLICAL REFERENCE: Matthew 8:14; Mark 1:30; Luke 4:38

When Jesus went to the house of Simon Peter and Andrew, they asked him to ease the suffering of Simon's mother-in-law who was in bed with a high fever. Jesus took her hand to help her up. As soon as he touched her hand, the fever left her, and she immediately got up and began to serve them.

JAIRUS'S DAUGHTER

The twelve-year-old girl who was raised from the dead.

✝ BIBLICAL REFERENCE: Matthew

9:18–19, 23–5; Mark 5:22–4, 35–43; Luke 8:41–2, 49–56

One day while Jesus was surrounded by a crowd of people, he was approached by Jairus, the president of a synagogue, who prostrated himself at Jesus' feet, saying, 'My twelve-year-old daughter is dying, but if you come and lay your hands on her she will live.' Jesus got up, and accompanied by his disciples went with Jairus. While they were on their way to Jairus's house, they received word that his daughter had died. Jesus turned to Jairus, and said, 'Don't be afraid, just have faith and she will be saved.' When they reached the president's house, they were confronted with a crowd of mourners weeping and wailing. Jesus told them to leave, saying, 'Why are you making such a noise? The girl is not dead, only sleeping.' But the crowd jeered at him, for they knew she was dead. Telling everyone else to wait outside, Jesus entered the house with Peter and James, and James's brother John, and the girl's parents. Once inside the girl's room, Jesus took her by the hand, and said, '*Talitha, koum*!' which means, 'Little girl, wake up!' And the girl's spirit returned, and she immediately got up and walked about. Her parents were overcome with emotion, but he gave them strict instructions not to tell anyone what had taken place, and told them to give their daughter something to eat.

 ABOVE
Jairus's daughter: Jesus brought the twelve-year-old girl back to life.
He told her father she was 'only sleeping'

THE WOMAN WITH A HAEMORRHAGE

The woman who was healed by touching Jesus' robe.

† BIBLICAL REFERENCE: Matthew 9:20–2; Mark 5:25–34; Luke 8:43–8

A certain woman had been suffering from a haemorrhage for twelve years. She had been subjected to a variety of treatments by many different doctors, and had spent everything she had in the process, but none had been able to cure her. If anything, her condition had worsened. Having heard about Jesus, she came up behind him while he was on his way to Jairus's house (*see above*), saying to herself, 'If I can just touch his robe, I shall be healed.' When she touched his robe, the haemorrhage stopped immediately, and she knew in her body that she had been cured. And Jesus knew at once that power had been drawn from him. Turning to the crowd, he asked, 'Who touched my robe?' When no one answered, Peter said, 'Master, you can see the crowd pressing around you, and yet you ask, "Who touched me?"' But Jesus said, 'Somebody touched me. I felt the power drawn out of me.' And he continued looking around to find who had touched him. Aware of what had just happened to her, the woman came forward trembling with fear, prostrated herself at Jesus'

feet, and explained why she had touched him and how she had immediately been healed. 'Daughter,' Jesus said to her, 'your faith has made you whole. Go in peace, and be free of your complaint.'

THE SYRO-PHOENICIAN WOMAN AND HER DAUGHTER

The non-Jew who asked Jesus to heal her daughter.

† BIBLICAL REFERENCE: Matthew 15:22–28; Mark 7:24–30

This woman – a Canaanite according to Matthew; Syro-Phoenician according to Mark – approached Jesus while he was in the region of Tyre and asked him to heal her daughter who was possessed by an unclean spirit. Although a non-Jew, she addressed him as 'Lord, Son of David' (i.e. the Jewish Messiah). Jesus ignored her, but his disciples begged him to send her away because she kept shouting at them. He replied that he had been sent only to minister to the lost sheep of Israel. But the woman was persistent and knelt at his feet, pleading with him to help her. When Jesus said to her, 'It is not fair to throw the children's food to dogs,' she retorted, 'Yes, but even the dogs under the table eat the crumbs from the children.' Because her answer revealed the extent of her faith, Jesus told her

that she could be happy in the knowledge that her daughter had been healed. When the woman got home she found her child lying on the bed, and the unclean spirit had left her.

THE WOMAN WITH AN INFIRMITY

The woman who was healed on the Sabbath.

† BIBLICAL REFERENCE: Luke 13:10–13, 16

This unnamed woman had been possessed by a spirit for eighteen years. It had crippled her, bending her double so that she was unable to stand upright. Seeing her in a synagogue where he was teaching one Sabbath day, Jesus called her over to him, laid his hands on her, and healed her. This incensed the president of the synagogue, who said that if people wished to be healed they should come during the six days when it was permitted to work, but not on the Sabbath. Jesus replied, 'You hypocrites! Is there one of you who does not untie his ox or ass from its manger and take it to water on the Sabbath? And was it wrong for this daughter of Abraham, who has been bound by Satan for eighteen years, to have her bonds untied on the Sabbath?' His reply put his opponents to shame, but the people rejoiced at the wonders he performed. (13:10–17)

Women in the parables

THE WOMAN AND THE LOST COIN

† BIBLICAL REFERENCE: Luke 15:8–9

When Jesus was criticized by the Pharisees and scribes for receiving sinners and eating with them, he told them this parable to illustrate the joy in heaven when a sinner repents. 'What woman, having ten silver coins, if she loses one coin, does not light a lamp and sweep the house and seek diligently until she finds it? And when she has found it, she calls her friends and neighbours, saying, "Rejoice with me, for I have found the coin which I had lost." Just so, I tell you, there is joy before the angels of God over one sinner who repents.' (15:8–9, RSV)

THE WOMAN AND THE YEAST

† BIBLICAL REFERENCE: Matthew 13:33; Luke 13:20

Jesus likened the kingdom of God to a woman adding some yeast to three measures of flour and then mixing the two thoroughly until the entire lump of dough was leavened.

THE WISE AND FOOLISH MAIDENS

† BIBLICAL REFERENCE: Matthew 25:1–13

The parable of the wise and foolish maidens draws on the Palestinian custom that the bride-groom brought his bride from her parents' house to his own (NOAB, 1205), and was told by Jesus as part of his lengthy response to a question posed by his disciples. While in the temple with his disciples, Jesus had predicted its destruction, and afterwards he withdrew to the Mount of Olives where his disciples came to him in private and asked him to tell them about the signs that would foretell his second coming and the close of the age. Having told his disciples that the hour of his coming will be totally unexpected, he proceeded to tell them the parable in which he likened the kingdom of heaven to ten maidens who took their lamps and went to meet the bridegroom. Five of the maidens were foolish and five were wise. The foolish maidens took their lamps, but no oil, whereas the wise maidens took containers of oil with their lamps. When the bridegroom's arrival was delayed, the maidens began to doze and soon fell asleep. In the middle of the night they were awoken by shouting, 'The bridegroom is coming! Go out and meet him!' The maidens arose from their sleep and trimmed their lamps,

and the foolish maidens said to the wise, 'Give us some of your oil, for our lamps are going out.' But the wise maidens replied, 'We cannot, for there might not be enough for both of us. It would be better if you went to the merchant and bought your own oil.' While the foolish maidens were away buying their oil, the bridegroom arrived. Those who were ready went in with him to the marriage feast, and the doors were closed behind them. After a while the foolish maidens arrived, and said, 'Lord, lord, let us in!' But he replied, 'I tell you truly, I do not know you.' Jesus concluded the parable with a cautionary word to his disciples about the coming of the kingdom of heaven, 'So stay awake, for you know neither the day nor the hour'. (25:1–13)

In his analysis of the parable, the Italian author Stefano Zuffi states that 'as often occurs in Gospel parables, a deeper reading raises questions: the strangeness of a bridegroom arriving at midnight, the selfishness of the 'wise' virgins, and so on'. (Zuffi, 232) However, such questions do not take into account the allegorical language that is an essential feature of many of the parables and is a key to their deeper meaning – a language whose roots are

ABOVE
The parable of the ten maidens: 'So stay awake, for you know
neither the day nor the hour'

frequently to be found in the Old Testament. For example, the maidens in the parable have their forerunners in the women who personify Wisdom and Folly in the Book of Proverbs (*see* page 140). The Old Testament frequently equates the relationship between God and the Israelites with that of husband and wife, but by the time the Gospels came to be written the Israelite's failure to behave like a faithful wife had led to a change in terminology. To convey the idea that the relationship between God and his people remained unconsummated, so to speak, the word 'husband' was dropped in favour of 'bridegroom' – a synonym for the Spirit of God, which was embodied in the person of Jesus. The supposed strangeness of the bridegroom's arrival at midnight is accounted for in the prelude to the parable, when Jesus tells his disciples that the hour of his coming will be totally unexpected. The fact that the maidens are all asleep when he arrives represents our own state of spiritual 'sleep'. When we eventually experience a spiritual awakening, we can either respond to it like the wise maidens, who have prepared themselves for this moment, or like the foolish maidens, who have not. As the parable reveals, the opportunity for spiritual awakening is but a fleeting moment. Unless we remain alert and watchful, we will emulate the foolish maidens and miss it.

The wise and foolish maidens in art

Considering the 'closed door' at the end of the parable, it seems appropriate that the wise and foolish maidens are often found carved on or around the doorways of medieval cathedrals and churches – e.g. Strasbourg, Chartres, Notre-Dame (Paris). Generally , the wise maidens are to one side of the entrance, the foolish maidens to the other. The wise maidens' cup-shaped lamps have small flames burning in them, but the foolish maidens' lamps posed a problem. How do you depict an unlit lamp in stone? The sculptors overcame this by carving the maidens holding their cup-shaped lamps upside-down. To the medieval mind the symbolism was obvious – an oil lamp will not burn if it is the wrong way up. Sometimes the sculptors have included small doors. At Notre-Dame in Paris, the door carved above the wise maidens is open; the one above the foolish maidens is closed.

Other women in the Gospels

HERODIAS AND SALOME

MEANING: HERODIAS (FROM HEROD), HEROIC; SALOME, TRANQUIL

The mother and daughter who brought about the death of John the Baptist.

† BIBLICAL REFERENCE: Matthew 14:1–11; Mark 6:17–28

Herodias was first married to Herod Philip and then to his half-brother, Herod Antipas (who was also her uncle), the tetrarch of Galilee, while Philip was still alive. Although her daughter remains unnamed in the Bible, it is known that her name was Salome. Herodias was denounced publicly by John the Baptist for what was regarded as an adulterous union with her second husband, and for this Herod Antipas put him into prison. According to Matthew's account, Herod wanted to have John killed but refrained from doing so because he was afraid of the unrest this might foment among the people, who believed that John was a prophet. (14:5) According to Mark, it was Herodias who wanted John killed, but Herod prevented this because he respected John and gave him his protection. (6:19–20) However, both sources agree on the events that unfolded at the feast held to mark Herod's birthday. It was at this feast that Herodias's daughter danced before Herod and his guests. Herod was so delighted by her that he said, 'Ask me for what-ever you wish, and I promise it will be yours. I will even give you half my kingdom.' The girl turned to her mother, who prompted her to ask for the head of John the Baptist on a platter. Her request filled Herod with remorse, but because he had made his promise in front of his guests, he felt obliged to grant her what she had asked for. He sent his guards to the prison, where they decapitated John and then put his head on a platter which they gave to Salome, and Salome gave it to her mother.

Herodias and Salome in art

Images of Herodias and Salome are fairly widespread in Christian art since Herod's banquet is one of a traditional cycle of scenes depicting the life and death of John the Baptist – a cycle that is sometimes found in baptisteries or on baptismal fonts. Herodias is generally seated beside Herod while Salome presents her with John the Baptist's head on a platter; the other guests are either leaning forward out of morbid curiosity or leaning away in horror at the sight. Sometimes the sequence of events that

unfolded at the banquet are depicted in one image, with Salome dancing before Herod, the beheading of the Baptist and the bringing of his head on a platter arranged in such a way that the image can be read like a story book.

THE MAIDS AT THE HIGH PRIEST'S HOUSE

The women who questioned Peter about Jesus.

† BIBLICAL REFERENCE: Matthew 26:69–71; Mark 14:66–9; Luke 22:56–9; John 18:16–7

After Jesus had been arrested at Gethsemane, he was taken to the house of the high priest to be tried. Peter followed him there

and joined the people sitting around a fire in the courtyard. Peter had previously boasted that he would never forsake Jesus, but Jesus had foretold that he would. When one of the high priest's maids saw him, she stared at him in the firelight, and said, 'You were also with Jesus.' But Peter denied it, told the woman that he did not know him, and went and stood in the porch. While he was standing there, another maid saw him, and said to the people nearby, 'This man was with Jesus.' He again denied it. When the bystanders pressed him, he denied for a third time that he knew Jesus. At that moment a cock crowed, reminding Peter that Jesus

had said he would deny him three times before the cock crowed, and he broke down and wept.

PILATE'S WIFE

The woman who warned her husband not to harm Jesus.

† BIBLICAL REFERENCE: Matthew 27:19

Pilate's wife dreamt about Jesus and sent word to her husband, governor of Judea, as he sat in judgement on Jesus, warning him to 'have nothing to do with that righteous man, for I was deeply disturbed by a dream I had about him today'. It was after this that Pilate washed his hands in front of the crowd, saying, 'I am innocent of this man's blood.' (27:24)

ABOVE

A gruesome dish: having decapitated John the Baptist, the executioner places John's head on Salome's platter

5 The Acts of the Apostles, the Epistles and the Book of Revelation

ABOVE
The death of Sapphira: the wife of Ananias sought to hang on to money
belonging to others and lost everything in the process

Originally written as a sequel to the Gospel of Luke, the Acts of the Apostles recounts the events that took place after Jesus had ascended to heaven. Foremost among these were the dissemination of the gospel across the Mediterranean world – from Palestine to Rome – by the apostles, and the establishment of the first churches or Christian communities. Although the stage is dominated by Peter and Paul, it is clear from the number of women mentioned in Acts (and in the Epistles) that they shared a similar function to men in the early years of the expanding Christian community. The evidence suggests some were active leaders too, hosting house-churches and prayer meetings in their homes. Yet it is also clear from the Epistles that some leaders in the Christian community advocated the subordination of women to men (*see below*, Women in the Epistles), thus setting a trend that was to continue through to the fourth century and has widely endured ever since in both the religious and social contexts.

SAPPHIRA

MEANING: SAPPHIRE OR BEAUTIFUL

The woman who lost her life because she wanted to keep her money.

✝ BIBLICAL REFERENCE: Acts 5:1–11

Sapphira was the wife of Ananias, a member of the early Christian community in Jerusalem. Members of the community, who are described as being united in heart and soul, had no personal possessions, since everything was held in common ownership. Those who owned land or houses sold them and gave the proceeds of the sale to the apostles to distribute among those who were in need. (4:32–35) Sapphira and her husband sold a plot of land, but conspired to withhold some of the money they had received. When Ananias brought only part of the proceeds to the apostles, he was confronted by Peter, who accused him of lying – not to the community, but to God. When Ananias heard this, he dropped down dead. Some three hours later, Sapphira came looking for her husband. Peter accused her of lying, and she too dropped down dead. She was buried beside her husband.

TABITHA/DORCAS

MEANING: TABITHA (ARAMAIC) AND DORCAS (GREEK) BOTH MEAN GAZELLE

The woman whom Peter raised from the dead.

✝ BIBLICAL REFERENCE: Acts 9:36–41

A devout Christian woman who lived in Joppa. When she died, her fellow Christians sent for Peter who was staying at the nearby town of Lydda. When Peter arrived, the women mourners showed him tunics and other clothes that Dorcas had made. Peter dismissed the weeping mourners, and knelt down and prayed. He then turned to the body of the deceased woman, and said, 'Tabitha, arise.' She opened her eyes, and sat up. Having helped her to her feet, Peter took her outside and showed the community that she was alive.

MARY, MOTHER OF JOHN MARK

MEANING: MARY, BITTERNESS, OR POSSIBLY BELOVED (*see above*, MARY, MOTHER OF JESUS)

The woman whose house in Jerusalem was used for meeting and prayer.

✝ BIBLICAL REFERENCE: Acts 12:12

The mother of 'John Mark' (NJB), 'John whose other name was Mark' (RSV), or 'John known as Mark' (ONT), owned a house in Jerusalem which served as a place of meeting and prayer – perhaps even an early house-church – for members of the early church. It was to Mary's house that Peter went after an

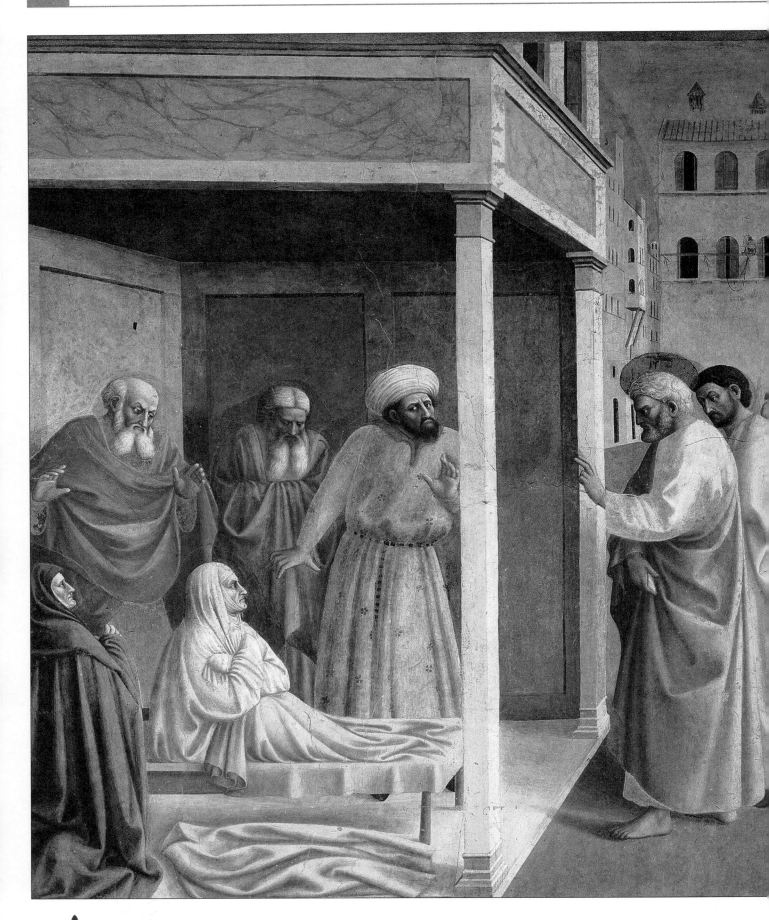

 ABOVE
Virtue rewarded: Peter told Tabitha to arise, upon which she
opened her eyes and sat up

angel had released him from prison the night before he was due to be tried by Herod Agrippa I, who had begun to persecute members of the church and had recently had James the brother of John beheaded. An early Christian tradition identifies her son as the evangelist Mark, while another tradition holds that an upper room in her house was where Jesus and his disciples had their last Passover supper together. (12:1–17)

RHODA

MEANING: ROSE

The servant girl who heard Peter knocking at the door, but didn't let him in.

† BIBLICAL REFERENCE: Acts 12:12–17

A servant in the house of John Mark's mother. The night Peter came to the house (*see above*), Rhoda heard someone knocking at the outer, street door and went to answer. When she recognized Peter's voice, she was so overcome with excitement that she didn't open the door to let him in. Instead, she ran into the house to tell the others that Peter was standing outside. 'You must be out of your mind,' was their response, and they added, 'It must be his angel.' Meanwhile Peter was still standing outside, knocking on the door.

EUNICE

MEANING: GOOD VICTORY

The woman who knew the scriptures.

† BIBLICAL REFERENCE: Acts 16:1; 2 Timothy 1:5; 3:14

A Jewish woman married to a Greek, Eunice was the devout mother of the disciple Timothy. (16:1) The Second Letter to Timothy refers to Timothy's 'sincere faith', a faith derived from his grandmother Lois and his mother Eunice (1:5), who instructed him in the scriptures while he was still a child. (3:14)

LYDIA

MEANING: TRAVAIL OR THE LYDIAN (I.E. A PERSON FROM THE ANCIENT KINGDOM OF LYDIA IN ASIA MINOR)

The business woman who was converted by Paul.

† BIBLICAL REFERENCE: Acts 16:13–15

A woman from Thyatira, near Ephesus, who traded in dyed cloth. She listened to Paul preaching by the river at Philippi during his missionary journey to Macedonia, and her heart was opened by what she heard. After Lydia and her family had been baptised, she insisted that Paul stayed at her house. It was possibly while Paul was lodging with Lydia that he encountered a young fortune-teller (*see below*).

THE FORTUNE-TELLER

The girl who annoyed Paul with her predictions.

† BIBLICAL REFERENCE: Acts 16:16–18

One day, Paul and Silas were on their way to prayers when they encountered a slave-girl who earned her owners a lot of money by foretelling the future. The girl followed Paul and those with him, shouting, 'These men are servants of the Most High God, come to tell you how you can be saved!' She did the same thing day after day, much to Paul's annoyance. He eventually turned on her and addressed the spirit that had possessed her, saying, 'In the name of Jesus Christ, I command you to leave this woman!' And immediately the spirit left her. When the girl's owners saw that their source of income had gone, they took hold of Paul and Silas and dragged them before the local magistrates who had the two men flogged and put into prison. (Acts 16:16–23)

PRISCA/PRISCILLA

MEANING: ANCIENT OR PRIMITIVE

The woman who taught Apollos about the Way.

† BIBLICAL REFERENCE: Acts 18:2–3; 18; 26; Romans 16:3; 1 Corinthians 16:19; 2 Timothy 4:19

Prisca was the wife of Aquila, a Jew who lived in Rome. When Claudius banished the Jews from Rome in AD 52, Prisca and her husband left for the city of Corinth where they worked as tentmakers. Paul visited them in Corinth, and when he found out that they practised the same trade as himself he lodged with them and joined them in their work. (18:2–3) Prisca and Aquila left Corinth and travelled with Paul to Ephesus, staying there when he journeyed on to Caesarea and Antioch. While Prisca and her husband were in Ephesus, an Alexandrian Jew named Apollos came to the town. Even though Apollos – who was well versed in the scriptures – taught about Jesus, 'he had experienced only the baptism of John'. When Prisca and Aquila heard him teaching in the synagogue, they took him under their wing and initiated him into a more accurate understanding of the way of God. (18:18–26) In his Letter to the Romans, Paul states that Prisca and Aquila had risked their own necks to save his life; for this, he and all the gentile

ABOVE
Goddess of Ephesus: the many-breasted Artemis/Diana was a fertility goddess and the protector of women in labour and newborn children

communities of believers gave thanks. (Romans 16:3) Other letters mention that the local Christian community met in the couple's house. (1 Corinthians 16:19; 2 Timothy 4:19)

Luke, the author of Acts, calls her Priscilla, the diminutive of Prisca.

ARTEMIS

The goddess whose Ephesian followers complained that Paul was bad for business.

† BIBLICAL REFERENCE: Acts 19:23–41

One of the Seven Wonders of the ancient world was the temple of the Greek goddess Artemis at Ephesus. Artemis (Diana to the Romans) was Apollo's twin sister and the daughter of Zeus and Leto. Artemis/Diana was the virginal goddess of hunting, usually depicted in a short tunic and armed with a bow and quiver of arrows, but at Ephesus she was represented as a many-breasted fertility goddess, protector of women in labour and newborn children. An Ephesian silversmith by the name of Demetrius, who made his living by making and selling silver shrines of Artemis, called a meeting of his fellow craftsmen at which he complained that Paul's missionary campaign was affecting their trade and threatening to deprive them of their source of income. A near-riot followed, but this was subdued by the town clerk who

told the crowd that Paul and his followers had committed no sacrilege or blasphemy against Artemis. They therefore had no just cause to protest.

THE DAUGHTERS OF PHILIP

† BIBLICAL REFERENCE: Acts 21:9

The evangelist Philip, appointed with six others to see to the day-to-day care of the needs of the growing Christian community, had four unmarried daughters 'who prophesied'. They lived in their father's house in Caesarea, where Paul stayed on his way from Ephesus to Jerusalem.

THE SISTER OF PAUL

† BIBLICAL REFERENCE: Acts 23:16

Paul's sister is mentioned briefly in connection with her son, who warned Paul about an ambush being laid for him by the Jews.

DRUSILLA

MEANING: WATERED BY THE DEW

The woman with two husbands.

† BIBLICAL REFERENCE: Acts 24:24

The Jewish wife of the Roman procurator of Judea, Antonius Felix, Drusilla was the second daughter of Herod Agrippa I, and sister to Bernice and Herod Agrippa II who ruled over part of Palestine. She was also the granddaughter of Herod the Great. Her marriage to Felix was

considered illegal because she had not divorced her first husband. Drusilla attended one of the hearings in Caesarea at which Felix questioned Paul regarding the charges laid against him of being a trouble-maker and profanity against the Temple. On this particular occasion, Felix questioned Paul about faith in Christ Jesus; but Paul must have pricked Felix's conscience when he began to talk about justice, self-control and the coming Judgement, for Felix sent him away. (24:24–25)

BERNICE

MEANING: VICTORIOUS

The woman who married her uncle, committed incest with her brother, and was the mistress of an emperor.

† BIBLICAL REFERENCE: Acts 25:13, 23, 30

Bernice was the oldest daughter of Herod Agrippa I, sister to Drusilla and Herod Agrippa II. Bernice caused a scandal when she married her uncle, Herod, king of Chalcis. After his death, she had an incestuous relationship with her brother, Herod Agrippa II, and it was with him that she attended Paul's trial in Caesarea before Porcius Festus, who had replaced Felix as procurator of Judea. Bernice later married the king of Cilicia, and later still became the mistress of Emperor Vespasian and then of his son Titus. (Lockyer, 37)

Women in the Epistles

References to named women and men in the Epistles are brief, usually appearing at the beginning or end of a letter as recipients of the sender's greetings. On the other hand, the Epistles contain much guidance and pastoral advice destined for the early churches.

Most of the Epistles were written by Paul, but there is general agreement that the so-called 'Pastoral Epistles' – 1 and 2 Timothy, and Titus – were probably not written by him, even though the author introduces himself as such, nor was the Letter to the Hebrews. The true authorship of the Letter to the Ephesians and the Letters of James, Peter, John and Jude has been similarly questioned. (The latter were addressed to the wider Christian church rather than any one specific community.) It was a common practice at the time for a little-known author to attribute his work to someone who was both known and respected in order to give it greater authority.

In view of the active role played by women in the early church, the patriarchal attitude towards women expressed by the authors of two of the Pastoral Epistles is of particular interest. The author of the First Letter to Timothy states, 'I permit no woman to have authority over men; she is to keep silent. For Adam was formed first, then Eve; and Adam was not deceived, but the woman was deceived and became the transgressor. Yet woman will be saved through bearing children, if she continues in faith and love and holiness, with modesty.' (2:12–15, RSV) In describing what is required of a bishop, the author of Titus assumes that only men will be elevated to this position. (1:7–9) By contrast, although the author of the First Letter of Peter tells women to be submissive to their husbands, he reminds men of the equality of the genders. He explains that Christian wives should be submissive to their husbands so that, even though their husbands might not be spiritually inclined, they might be converted by the example of their wives' spiritually-inspired behaviour. He also encourages women to develop their inner life – 'the hidden person of the heart' – rather than embellish their outer person, so that they may thereby attain that which is ultimately more precious. He then addresses Christian husbands, telling them to show consideration and respect towards their wives, even though they may regard them as the weaker sex, since the gift of life is bestowed equally on men and women. In this way, they will not hinder their own spiritual development. (1 Peter 3:1–7)

PHOEBE

MEANING: PURE

A deaconess of the church at Cenchreae.

† BIBLICAL REFERENCE: Romans 16:1–2

The concluding chapter of Paul's letter to the Christian community in Rome begins with him commending to the community 'our sister Phoebe, a deaconess of the church at Cenchreae' (a port near Corinth), and asks them to help her in whatever way she might require 'for she has helped many people' including Paul himself. (16:1–2) From the few details given here, it is possible to deduce that Phoebe was an active if not prominent member of the early church. She was also trusted by Paul, for according to many authorities it was Phoebe who made the journey to Rome to deliver Paul's letter.

WOMEN OF THE CHRISTIAN COMMUNITY IN ROME

The Roman women to whom Paul sent his personal greetings.

† BIBLICAL REFERENCE: Romans 16:3; 6; 12; 13; 15

Paul's letter to Rome ends with his personal greetings to a number of named members of the community. The women thus named are: Prisca and her husband Aquila, who 'risked their own necks to save my life' (16:3; *also see above*, Prisca/Priscilla); Mary, 'who has worked so hard for you' (16:6); Tryphaena and Tryphosa, who are described as 'workers in the Lord' (16:12); likewise 'the beloved Persis, who has worked hard in the Lord' (16:12); the mother of Rufus (16:13); Julia and the sister of Nereus. (16:15)

CHLOE

A member of the church at Corinth.

† BIBLICAL REFERENCE: 1 Corinthians 1:11

Although she is given only the briefest of mentions by Paul, the evidence suggests that it was Chloe, a member of the church at Corinth, who prompted him to write his first letter to the Corinthians. For Chloe – or, to be more precise, 'Chloe's people' – had informed Paul of the differences that were creating dissent among the members of the community at Corinth. (1:11) These differences were generated by the members' personal allegiance to individual religious teachers: some were saying, 'I belong to Paul', others 'I belong to Apollos', and yet others, 'I belong to Cephas [Peter]'. Paul counters this disunity with the question, 'Is Christ divided?'

EUODIA AND SYNTYCHE

Two women who were reprimanded by Paul for disagreeing with each other.

† BIBLICAL REFERENCE: Philippians 4:2

The opening chapter of Paul's first letter to the Corinthians indicates that agreement was not universal among the members of the early Christian community (*see above*, Chloe), and his letter to the church at Philippi reveals that dissent was not confined to Corinth. Euodia and Syntyche had been co-workers with Paul, Clement and the others in spreading the gospel, yet there was clearly something on which the two women disagreed, for Paul urges Syzygus (whose name means 'Yokefellow' or 'Partner') to be a true 'partner' to them and help them to overcome their differences.

CLAUDIA

MEANING: LAME

† BIBLICAL REFERENCE: 2 Timothy 4:21

Claudia was a member of the early Christian community whose greetings to Timothy were added at the end of this letter, together with those of Pudens and Linus. It has been suggested that she was the wife of Pudens, and the mother of Linus, who became a bishop of Rome. (Lockyer, 38)

APPHIA

MEANING: FRUITFUL OR INCREASING

† BIBLICAL REFERENCE: Philemon 2

Apphia was an active member of the Christian community at Colossae in Phrygia. It has been suggested that she was the wife of Philemon, to whom this letter was addressed.

THE 'ELECT LADY'

† BIBLICAL REFERENCE: 2 John 1

The 'elect lady' to whom the author of 2 John addresses his letter was probably one of the local churches in Asia Minor rather than an individual member of the Christian community.

Women in the Book of Revelation

The Book of Revelation was written toward the end of the first century, during the author's exile on the island of Patmos. The rich, visionary symbolism of its women is in striking contrast to the women encountered in the other books of the New Testament.

THE WOMAN CLOTHED WITH THE SUN

A vision in which a woman gives birth to a son and is persecuted by Satan.

† BIBLICAL REFERENCE: Revelation 12:1–6, 13–17

John, the author of the Book of Revelation, describes two portents that appear in heaven. The first is a woman 'clothed with the sun, with the moon under her feet, and a crown of twelve stars on her head.' She was pregnant and about to give birth, and she cried out in pain. The second portent was 'a great red dragon, with seven heads and ten horns, and seven crowns on his heads.' His tail was so great that it swept a third of the stars out of the heavens, hurling them down to the earth. And the dragon placed itself in front of the woman so that it could devour her child when it was born. She gave birth to a male child who would rule the nations of the world, but the child was taken up to God and his throne, and the woman escaped into the wilderness where God had prepared a place in which she would be provided for. (12:1–6) The dragon, whose name is Satan, was now attacked by Michael and his angels, who hurled him down to the earth from where he went in pursuit of the woman who had given birth to the male child. But the woman was given the wings of an eagle and fled from the serpent into the wilderness where she would be provided for. The serpent now poured a river of water after the woman to carry her away on its current. But the earth came to her rescue, opening its mouth and swallowing the river that poured from the dragon's mouth. Then the dragon grew angry with the woman, and went away to make war on the rest of her children, on those who obey the will of God and hold the testimony of Jesus. (12:7–17)

THE GREAT WHORE OF BABYLON

The antithesis of the heavenly city.

† BIBLICAL REFERENCE: Revelation 17:1–24

When an angel offered to show John the great whore with whom all the kings of the earth had

prostituted themselves, and on whose wine of adultery the people of the world had become drunk, he carried him away 'in the Spirit' to the wilderness. In his vision John saw a woman riding a scarlet beast with seven heads and ten horns. The woman was dressed in purple and scarlet, and covered in gold, jewels and pearls. In her hand she held a golden cup filled with the products of her prostitution, and on her forehead were written the words, 'Babylon the Great, mother of all prostitutes and all the obscene practices of the earth'. The woman was drunk with the blood of the saints and Christian martyrs. John was mystified by the vision, so the angel explained the significance of what he saw, and concluded his explanation with the words, 'The woman you saw is the great city which has authority over the rulers of the earth.' (17:1–18)

ABOVE
The Whore of Babylon: in a vision, an angel showed John a dissolute woman who was drunk with the blood of the saints and Christian martyrs

PLANCHE SPÉCIMEN

HORTUS DELICIARUM

XIIe Strasbourg

PLANCHE XLV

LA GRANDE BABYLONE APOCALYPTIQUE

ABOVE

Apocalyptic Babylon: worshipped by kings, the people and the clergy,
the whore rode a seven-headed beast

According to the traditional interpretation of this vision, the scarlet beast is Emperor Nero and the beast's seven heads represent the seven hills of Rome. In a more universal sense, the Great Whore represents the 'earthly city' (the antithesis of the heavenly city), which will be destroyed to make way for a new heaven and a new earth. (21:1)

THE BRIDE

A personification of the new Jerusalem.

† BIBLICAL REFERENCE: Revelation 19:7–9; 21:2, 9–10; 22:17

In his vision, John heard what seemed to him a great multitude rejoicing that the marriage was about to take place of the Lamb and his Bride, who would be dressed in fine, pure linen. And an angel told him to write down that those who are invited to the wedding feast are blessed. (19:7–9) John then saw a heavenly city, 'the new Jerusalem, coming down out of heaven from God, prepared as a bride beautifully dressed for her husband. And [John] heard a loud voice from the throne saying, "Now

ABOVE
Left: the Whore of Babylon and the seven-headed beast. Right: John's vision of the woman clothed with the sun and with a crown of stars

the dwelling of God is with men, and he will live with them. They will be his people, and God himself will be with them and be their God."' (21:2–3, NIV) After John had been shown the heavenly city and the water of life flowing from the throne of God, he heard the voice of Jesus telling him that entrance to the city was for those who followed the commandments of God; the others will stay outside. (22:14–15)

John's powerful vision of the birth of a new heaven and a new earth, of the Bride and the Heavenly City descending from heaven, and of the river of life flowing from the throne of God, brings the Bible to a fitting close, for it depicts 'the consummation toward which the whole Biblical message of redemption is focussed.' (NOAB, 1493)

Both the Spirit and the Bride say, 'Come!' Let the hearer too say, 'Come!' Let him who is thirsty come. Let whoever wishes take the Water of Life freely.

(22:17, ONT)

Bibliography

Holy Bible: New International Version, International Bible Society, Colorado Springs, 1984 (NIV)

The Holy Bible (King James Version), Oxford University Press, Oxford (KJ)

The New Jerusalem Bible (Reader's Edition), Darton, Longman & Todd, London, 1990 (NJB)

The New Oxford Annotated Bible with The Apocrypha (Revised Standard Version), Oxford University Press, New York, 1977 (RSV; Editors' notes: NOAB)

The Original New Testament (trans. Hugh J. Schonfield), Firehorn Press, London, 1985 (ONT)

Bauckham, Richard, *Gospel Women: Studies of the Named Women in the Gospels*, Wm. B. Eerdmans Publishing Co., Grand Rapids, Michigan, 2002

Dante, *The Divine Comedy* (trans. Dorothy L. Sayers), Penguin Books, Harmondsworth, 1949

de Capoa, Chiara, *Old Testament Figures in Art*, J. Paul Getty Museum, Los Angeles, 2003

Deen, Edith, *All of the Women of the Bible*, HarperCollins, New York, 1988

Hall, James, *Dictionary of Subjects and Symbols in Art*, John Murray, London, 1985

Ieron, Julie-Allyson, *Names of Women of the Bible*, Moody Press, Chicago, 1998

Knappert, Jan, *The Encyclopaedia of Middle Eastern Mythology and Religion*, Element Books, Shaftesbury, 1993

Literary Guide to the Bible, The, (ed. Robert Alter and Frank Kermode), Fontana Press, London, 1997

Lockyer, Herbert, *All the Women of the Bible*, Zondervan, Grand Rapids, Michigan, 1967

Metford, J. C. J., *Dictionary of Christian Lore and Legend*, Thames & Hudson, London, 1983

Nag Hammadi Library, The, (ed. James M. Robinson), HarperCollins, San Francisco, 1990

New Bible Dictionary, (ed. J. D. Douglas, N. Hillyer et al), Inter-Varsity Press, Leicester, (2nd Edition), 1982

New Larousse Encyclopedia of Mythology, (trans. Richard Aldington and Delano Ames; introduction by Robert Graves), Hamlyn Publishing Group, London, 1989

Oxford Companion to the Bible, The, (ed. Bruce Metzger and Michael D. Coogan), Oxford University Press, New York, 1993

Pagels, Elaine, *Beyond Belief: the Secret Gospel of Thomas*, Pan Books, London, 2005

Parales, Heidi, *Bright Hidden Voices: Christian Women and Our Christian Heritage*, Smith & Helwys Publishing, Macon, Georgia, 1998

Suarès, Carlo, *The Qabala Trilogy*, Shambhala, Boston, 1985

de Voragine, Jacobus, *The Golden Legend* (trans. Granger Ryan and Helmut Ripperger), Ayer Company, Salem, New Hampshire, 1989 (reprint edition)

Warner, Marina, *Alone of All Her Sex: The Myth and Cult of the Virgin Mary*, Pan Books, London, 1985

Zuffi, Stefano, *Gospel Figures in Art*, J. Paul Getty Museum, Los Angeles, 2002

Picture credits

Cover: 'Mary Magdalene' by Carlo Dolci (1616–1686) **corbis**; **back cover:** 'Judith with the head of Holofernes' by Cristofano Allori (1577–1621) **corbis**; 'Lot and his daughters flee from Sodom' by Paolo Veronese (1528–1588) **akg-images**; **page 11:** 'Adam and Eve driven out of Eden' by Gustave Dore **Dover** (1832-1883); **13:** 'The creation of Eve' by Michelangelo (1475–1564) **akg-images**; **14-15:** 'The wife of Cain' by Fernand Cormon (1854–1924) **Art Archive**; **16-17:** 'The wife and daughters-in-law of Noah' by Joaquim Ramirez

(c19th) **Art Archive**; **21:** 'Sarah' by Victor Orsel (1795–1850) **Art Archive**; **22:** 'The expulsion of Hagar' by Peter Paul Rubens (1577–1640) **akg-images**; **24-25:** 'The repudiation of Hagar' by Giovanni Francesco Barbieri (1591–1666) **akg-images**; **26:** 'Hagar and Ishmael in the wilderness' by Giovanni Battista Tiepolo (1696–1770) **akg-images**; **28-29:** 'Lot and his daughters flee from Sodom' by Paolo Veronese (1528–1588) **akg-images**; **30:** 'Lot and his daughters' by Jan Massys (1508–1575) **akg-images**; **31:** 'Rebecca at the well' by Giovanni

Battista Piazzetta (1682–1754) **akg-images**; **32–33** 'Esau hunting, Isaac blesses Jacob' by Matthaeus the Younger Merian (1593–1650) **akg-images**; **34:** 'The reconciliation of Jacob' by Johann Baumgartner (1712–1761) **akg-images**; **36–37:** 'Jacob meeting Rachel near her father's flocks' by Joseph Ritter von Fuehrich (1800–1876) **akg-images**; **38:** 'Jacob and Laban' by Jean Restout (1692–1768) **Bridgeman**; **41:** 'Rebecca sees Isaac' by Julius Schnorr von Carolsfeld (1794–1874) **akg-images**; **43:** 'The bloodbath of Schechem' by

Matthaeus the Elder Merian (1593–1650) **akg-images**; 45: 'Juda and Thamar' by Jacopo Bassano (c.1510–1592) **akg-images**; 46; 'Tamar' by Francesco Hayez (1791–1882) **Art Archive**; 47: 'Potiphar's wife shows her husband Joseph's garment' by Lucas van Leyden (c1510) **corbis**; 48–49: 'Joseph's chasteness and the deceit of Potiphar' by Julius Schnorr von Carolsfeld **akg-images**; 51: 'Moses abandoned by his mother' by Nicolas Poussin (1594–1665) **akg-images**; 52: 'The finding of Moses' by Nicola Poussin **Art Archive**; 53: 'Moses defending the seven daughters of Jethro' by Giovanni Rosso (1494–1541) **Art Archive**; 55: 'The song of Miriam the Prophetess' by William Gaele (1823–1909) **Bridgeman**; 60: 'Joshua spares Rahab' by Gustave Dore **Dover**; 62–63: 'Deborah' by Gustave Dore **Dover**; 64: 'Jael, Deborah and Barak' by Salomon Bray (1597–1664) **akg-images**; 65: 'Jael and Sisera' by Jacopo Amigoni (1682–1752) **akg-images**; 66: 'Jephthah's daughter' by Gustave Dore **Dover**; 67: 'Jepthath and his daughter' by Julius Schnorr von Carolsfeld **akg-images**; 68–69: 'Manoah's offering' by Rembrandt (1606–1669) **akg-images**; 72: 'Samson and Delilah' by Peter Paul Rubens **akg-images**; 74–75 'The Levite finding the corpse of the woman' by Gustave Dore **Dover**; 77: 'The Levite bearing away the body of the woman' by Gustave Dore **Dover**; 78–79: 'The children of Benjamin carrying off the virgins of Jabesh-Gilead' by Gustave Dore **Dover**; 80: 'Ruth and Naomi travel to Bethlehem' by Julius Schnorr von Carolsfeld **akg-images**; 82–83: 'Boaz and Ruth' by Gustave Dore **Dover**; 86: 'The escape of David through the window' by Gustave Dore **Dover**; 89: 'David calms Saul' by Silvestro Lega (1826–1895) **akg-images**; 90–91: 'David and Abigail' by Guido Reni (1575–1642) **akg-images**; 93: 'Saul and the witch of Endor' by Januarius Zick (1730–1797) **akg-images**; 95: 'Rizpah's kindness unto the dead' by Gustave Dore **Dover**; 96–97: 'David and

Bathsheba' by Jan Massys **akg-images**; 98: 'Bathsheba Bathing' by Pietro Liberi (1614–1687) **Bridgeman**; 99: 'David and Bathsheba's child' by Julius Schnorr von Carolsfeld **akg-images**; 100: 'Amnon's rape of Tamar' by Matthaeus the Elder Merian **akg-images**; 104: 'The judgement of Solomon' by Nikolai Nikolaievich Gay (1831–1894) **akg-images**; 105–106: 'The Queen of Sheba pays homage to Solomon' by Julius Schnorr von Carolsfeld **akg-images**; 109: 'Solomon's idolatry' by Jacopo Amigoni (1682–1752) **akg-images**; 110–111: 'The wife of Jerobeam with prophet Ahia' by Lodovico Venuti (the first half of the 19th century) **akg-images**; 113: 'The prophet Elijah and the widow of Sarepta' by Bernardo Strozzi (1581-1644) **akg-images**; 114: 'The awakening of the widow's son' by Julius Schnorr von Carolsfeld **akg-images**; 115: 'Jezebel and Ahab met at the entrance Elijah the Thisbite' by Frederic Leighton (1836–1896) **akg-images**; 116: 'Jehu lets Jezebel fall from the window' by Gustave Dore **Dover**; 120: 'Elisha raising the son of the Shunamite' by Frederic Leighton **Bridgeman**; 123: 'The captive Hebrew maid that waited on Naaman's wife' by Sigfried Bendixen (1786–1864) **Bridgeman**; 124-125: 'The death of Athalia' by Gustave Dore **Dover**; 130: 'Queen Vashti refuses to come to the king' by Gustave Dore **Dover**; 133: 'Esther fainting before Ahasueros' (18th century school) **akg-images**; 134: 'Esther ruins Haman' by Gustave Dore **Dover**; 137: 'The happy days of Job' by William Dobson (1817–1898) **Art Archive**; 138: 'Job entertained by music during feasting' by Bartolo di Fredi (1330-1410) **Art Archive**; 139: 'Job's children killed', illuminated manuscript, c.1500 **Bridgeman**; 140–141: 'The garden of opportunity' by Evelyn de Morgan (1855–1919) **akg-images**; 144: 'The beloved' by Dante Rossetti (1828–1882) **Art Archive**; 147: 'Tobias heals his blind father' by Annibale Carracci (1560–1609) **akg-images**; 149: 'Tobias and Sarah' by Julius Schnorr von Carolsfeld **akg-images**;

152: 'Judith and Holofernes' by Artemisia Gentileschi (1597–1651) **akg-images**; 155: 'Susannah and the elders' by Tintoretto (1518–1594) **akg-images**; 156–157: 'Susannah and the elders' by Domenichino (1581–1641) **akg-images**; 158–159: 'Daniel saves Susanna' by Julius Schnorr von Carolsfeld **akg-images**; 160: 'Crucifixion Triptych' by Rogier van der Weyden (1399–1464) **akg-images**; 163: 'The large Holy Family' by Raphael (1483–1520) **akg-images**; 164–165: 'The Annunciation' by Sandro Botticelli (1445-1510) **akg-images**; 166: 'The birth of Christ' by Lorenzo Lotto (c.1480–1556) **akg-images**; 169: 'The lamentation of Christ' by Andrea del Sarto (1486–1531) **akg-images**; 173: 'Christ appearing to Mary Magdalene' by Correggio (1489-1534) **akg-images**; 174: 'Banquet in the house of Simon' by Tintoretto (1538–1594) **akg-images**; 175: 'Christ in the house of Martha' by Diego Velasquez (1599–1660) **akg-images**; 176–177: 'Mary reprimands her vain sister Martha' by Simon Vouet (1590–1649) **akg-images**; 178: 'Mary swooning at the Crucifixion', Byzantine enamel **corbis**; 181: 'Jesus and the Samarian woman' by Gustave Dore **Dover**; 183: 'Jesus raising up the daughter of Jairus' by Gustave Dore **Dover**; 186-187: 'The five wise and the five foolish virgins' by Peter von Cornelius (1783–1867) **akg-images**; 189: 'Salome receiving the head of John the Baptist' by Giovanni Guercino (1591–1666) **Art Archive**; 190: 'The death of Sapphira' by Nicolas Poussin **akg-images**; 192: 'Saint Peter and the resurrection of Tabitha' by Masolino da Panicale (1383–1447) **Art Archive**; 194: 'Artemis Ephesia', Roman (2nd century BC) **akg-images**; 198–199: 'Babylonian Whore' from the Apocalypse Tapestry of Angers (c.1375–1380) **akg-images**; 200: 'Apocalyptic Babylon' detail from a 12th century manuscript **Art Archive**; 201: 'Revelation of St John: the Babylonian Whore and beast' by Albrecht Durer (1471–1528) **akg-images**; 201: 'The woman and the dragon scene from the Apocalypse' by Juan Gerson (16th century) **Art Archive**

Index